CONCENTRATE Q&A
CRIMINAL LAW

CONCENTRATE Q&A CRIMINAL LAW

Mischa Allen

Senior Lecturer in Law
London Metropolitan University

OXFORD
UNIVERSITY PRESS

OXFORD
UNIVERSITY PRESS

Great Clarendon Street, Oxford, OX2 6DP,
United Kingdom

Oxford University Press is a department of the University of Oxford.
It furthers the University's objective of excellence in research, scholarship,
and education by publishing worldwide. Oxford is a registered trade mark of
Oxford University Press in the UK and in certain other countries

Published in the United States of America by Oxford University Press
198 Madison Avenue, New York, NY 10016, United States of America

British Library Cataloguing in Publication Data
Data available

Library of Congress Control Number: 2016942521

ISBN 978–0–19–874520–4

Printed in Great Britain by
Bell & Bain Ltd., Glasgow

Contents

Editor's acknowledgements

The brand-new Concentrate Q&A series from Oxford University Press has been developed alongside hundreds of students and lecturers from a range of universities across the UK.

I'd like to take this opportunity to thank all those law students who've filled in questionnaires, completed in-depth reviews of sample materials, attended focus groups, and provided us with the insight and feedback we needed to shape a series relevant for today's law students.

Also to the lecturers the length and breadth of the UK who given so generously of their time by being heavily involved in our lengthy review process; their inside information gained from experience as teachers and examiners has been vital in the shaping of this new series.

You told us that you wanted a Q&A book that:

- gives you tips to help you understand exactly what the question is asking
- offers focused guidance on how to structure your answer and develop your arguments
- uses clear and simple diagrams to help you see how to structure your answers at a glance
- highlights key debates and extra points for you to add to your answers to get the highest marks
- flags common mistakes to avoid when answering questions
- offers detailed advice on coursework assignments as well as exams
- provides focused reading suggestions to help you develop in-depth knowledge for when you are looking for the highest marks
- is accompanied by a great range of online support

We listened and we have delivered.

We are confident that because they provide exactly what you told us you need the Concentrate Q&As offer you better support and a greater chance for succeeding than any competing series.

We wish you all the best throughout your law course and in your exams and hope that these guides give you the confidence to tackle any question that you encounter, and give you the skills you need to excel during your studies and beyond.

Good luck
Carol Barber, Senior Publishing Editor

This is what you said:

'Since I started using the OUP Q&A guides my grades have dramatically improved'

Glen Sylvester, law student, Bournemouth University

'A sure-fire way to get a 1st class result'

Naomi M, law student, Coventry University

'100% would recommend. Makes you feel like you will pass with flying colours'

Elysia Marie Vaughan, law student, University of Hertfordshire

'Excellent. Very detailed which makes a change from the brief answers in other Q&A books... fantastic'

Frances Easton, law student, University of Birmingham

'The content is exceptional; the best Q&A books that I've read'

Wendy Chinenye Akaigwe, law student, London Metropolitan University

This is what your lecturers said:

'Much more substantial and less superficial than competitor Q&As. Some guides are rather too simplistic but the OUP guides are much better than the norm'

Dr Tony Harvey, Principal law lecturer, Liverpool John Moores University

'Cleverly and carefully put together. Every bit as good as one would expect from OUP, you really have cornered the market in the revision guides sector. I am also a huge fan of the OUP Concentrate series and I think that these books sit neatly alongside this'

Alice Blythe, law lecturer, University of Bolton

'I think Q&A guides are crucial and advise my students to buy early on'

Loretta Trickett, law lecturer, Nottingham Trent University

'Students often lack experience in writing full answers but seeing suggested answers like this provides them with confidence and structure. I will be recommending this book to my students not just for revision purposes but for the duration of the unit'

Nick Longworth, law lecturer, Manchester Metropolitan University

Guide to the book

Every book in the Concentrate Q&A series contains the following features:

Are you ready to face the exam? This box at the start of each chapter identifies the key topics and cases that you need to have learned, revised, and understood before tackling the questions in each chapter.

Not sure where to begin? Clear diagram answer plans at the start of each question help you see how to structure your answer at a glance, and take you through each point step-by-step.

Demonstrating your knowledge of the crucial debates is a sure-fire way to impress examiners. These at-a-glance boxes help remind you of the key debates relevant to each topic, which you should discuss in your answers to get the highest marks.

What makes a great answer great? Our authors show you the thought process behind their own answers, and how you can do the same in your exam. Key sentences are highlighted and advice is given on how to structure your answer well and develop your arguments.

Each question represents a typical essay or problem question so that you know exactly what to expect in your exam.

Don't settle for a good answer—make it great! This feature gives you extra points to include in the exam if you want to gain more marks and make your answer stand out.

Don't fall into any traps! This feature points out common mistakes that students make, and which you need to avoid when answering each question.

TAKING THINGS FURTHER

Really push yourself and impress your examiner by going beyond what is expected. Focused further reading suggestions allow you to develop in-depth knowledge of the subject for when you are looking for the highest marks.

Guide to the Online Resource Centre

Every book in the Concentrate Q&A series is supported by additional online materials to aid your study and revision: www.oxfordtextbooks.co.uk/orc/qanda

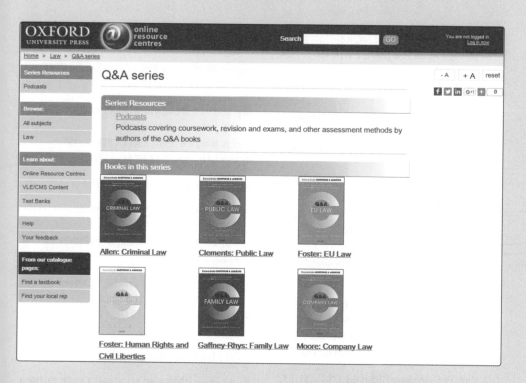

- Extra essay and problem questions.

- Bonus questions to help you practise and refine your technique. Questions are annotated, highlighting key terms and legal issues to help you plan your own answers. An indication of what your answers should cover is also provided.

- Online versions of the diagram answer plans.

- Video guidance on how to put an answer plan together.

- Flashcard glossaries of key terms.

- Audio advice on revision and exam technique from Nigel Foster.

- Audio advice on coursework technique.

- Audio advice on other assessment methods, for example MCQs, presentations, or mooting.

Table of cases

Table of statutes

Table of conventions

Exam Skills for Success in Criminal Law

1

The Challenges of Studying Criminal Law

Criminal law is usually attractive to students due to its media presence. However, this can give the impression that it is an easy subject because students will be familiar with it. In fact, it is conceptually difficult, and technical, so care must be taken over structure.

There is also more topic overlap in criminal law than you will find in other subjects. Whilst there are distinct crimes to study, all crimes will share common features such as *actus reus*, *mens rea*, and the defences.

The criminal law necessarily deals with issues of morality. It is political and policy-driven, which means that the cases sometimes contain contradictory decisions. One example of this is the way in which the courts apply subjective and objective tests for liability. Should a defendant be judged on the facts as he believed them to be, or according to the standards of a reasonable person? In *mens rea*, a subjective approach is used, but in the defences, an objective standard is becoming the norm. Finally, in order to understand current definitions, you will need to appreciate how the law has developed historically. For this, you'll need a keen understanding of statutory interpretation and the common law rules. Criminal law is a mixture of both. For example, in understanding the topic of recklessness (a form of *mens rea*), you will study how the House of Lords settled on an interpretation of this concept in the **Criminal Damage Act 1971**, then changed its mind ten years later. This affected the concept throughout the criminal law.

Your examiners want to see that you understand the law, that you can apply it with reason, and that you can criticise it, if asked to do so. This chapter will explore some techniques to help you achieve this to a high standard.

Achieving Success in Criminal Law Assessments

The best route to good examination skills is to *develop good study and revision skills* from the outset. You should pay attention to the reading lists provided by your lecturers, and obtain a good textbook, and a casebook. Alternatively, a 'cases and materials' book combines these. You are likely to need a book of statutory material as well, especially if your module is assessed by exam. Attendance at classes is key, especially at seminars, where you will be taught the fundamental skills for success in exams. These skills cannot be learned by downloading notes or even attending lectures, but by practising exam-style questions. In this way, you will start to think like a lawyer. Examiners are interested in your ability to say *how* the law works, not just what it is. In other words, you should avoid being too descriptive, and concentrate on analysis. When a question is set for discussion in lectures or seminars, you should treat it as a possible exam question. In this way you will acquire good habits, which may need only minor modification in the examination. Don't forget to take good notes in tutorials, as these will be invaluable later on. One method which works well is to make notes before the lecture on your set reading or before the seminar on the questions set, then add to your notes during or after the session. In this way you are *making* notes from your reading, and *taking* notes from your lecturer or tutor. These are both crucial skills.

Closer to the time of the exam, *consolidate your material* as much as possible. Prepare two separate lists for each topic. One list is a checklist of the main points to be considered when answering any question on that topic. The second is a list of the key cases and the legal principle the case contains. Once you have mastered the 'bare bones' of each topic, you can concentrate on refining your answers, and working on critical analysis.

Planning and time management are essential. During the exam, manage your time well. Make sure you answer all the questions set and read the instructions carefully. Stick strictly to your time plan, leaving one question and passing on to another when that time is up.

Relevance and structure are vital. If you are answering a question in which the defendant in charge of a level crossing has left the gate open, leaving an express train free to pass, killing a man who crosses, you should get straight to the point, which is that the case of *R v Pittwood* (1902) **19 TLR 37** establishes that a breach of contract leading to death imposes a duty of care on the defendant. You should not simply write everything you know about liability for omissions. Irrelevant material, however well researched or presented, will gain no marks. If the man is a volunteer, however, you will gain extra marks for distinguishing your facts from the facts of **Pittwood**.

A good structure will help you cope with overlap, and prevent your answer from being muddled. For example, if you are told that a defendant is under the influence of drugs or alcohol at the time of committing the offence, you need to consider the possibility that intoxication has negated *mens rea*, that a plea of automatism could be raised, or, in a murder case, that an abnormality of mental functioning arises for the purposes of diminished responsibility. The best thing to do is to consider the technical requirements of each 'defence' to enable you to make the correct decision. This difficulty also highlights the importance of planning your answer at the start of the exam. If you do not do this, you may find that you waste valuable time on an issue which you decide to eliminate later.

You may be allowed to bring *statutory material* into the examination with you. Usually, the rules are that the statutes can be highlighted, but not annotated. Make sure that you do not copy them out—you are not going to gain credit for this! A better technique is to write, say, a theft question: 'in taking the book from Jo's bag, Millie has assumed one of Jo's rights and has therefore appropriated the book (**s. 3** of the **Theft Act 1968**)'. In this way, you are demonstrating that you know the broad effect of the statute and can apply it.

Your lecturers may emphasise the importance of *critical analysis*. The ability to evaluate academic opinions on a topic is crucial. In essay questions, this means that you need to be able to assess the relative importance of academic views on a topic, and formulate your own view. These opinions can be in the form of legal judgments, or journal articles in which academics have expressed their opinions on a legal issue. Which of the arguments is the more convincing? In problem questions, critical analysis comes from application of the law to the facts. Students who write excellent answers will be able to use the judgments from the cases to answer the question, and will be able to distinguish cases by using minority judgments of their own analysis.

Problem questions: planning and writing your answer

The best method to adopt, and the one adopted throughout this book, is IRAC—identify the issues, explain the rule, apply the law to the facts and reach a conclusion.

Identify the legal issues and relevant facts. Deal with each defendant separately. Make a list of all possible offences. What is the *actus reus* and *mens rea* of these offences? Now apply each element to the facts in the scenario. You should then consider defences. Some defences should be dealt with at the end of your discussion on *actus reus* and *mens rea*. Loss of control and diminished responsibility are examples of this type of defence. Other 'defences' such as intoxication are not, strictly speaking, defences, but a negation of one element of the offence.

Working through the structure of *actus reus, mens rea*, and defences for each defendant, you should explain the *rule of law* (the *ratio* of a case or a statutory provision) and explain it. For example, in discussing the **Adomako** test, discuss all four guidelines to establish a finding of gross negligence manslaughter. Precision and detail are key.

Your points must be backed up with authority (relevant cases and statutory provisions), and be *applied* to the facts. In an examination, you are generally not expected to include dates, courts, or citations (although they are included in this book for ease of reference). Do not 'invent' facts. Sometimes the facts are deliberately ambiguous. Do not feel you have to reach a definite conclusion. In a criminal trial, there is no guarantee of a particular outcome. This does not matter as long as you can illustrate your argument by reference to authorities. Quite often you will need to argue in the alternative. For example, if the harm done to the victim amounts to a wound, then the answer is . . . on the other hand, if the harm is held not to amount to a wound the alternative lesser offences may be . . .

Now, consider your *conclusion*. Is the defendant guilty of murder or manslaughter? Do any defences work? What is the most likely outcome?

Essay Questions

Essay questions are quite different to problem questions. In problem questions, you are asked to give specific legal advice on a factual scenario. In essay questions, you are normally being asked to discuss or analyse a legal issue which is the subject of debate. You will very rarely simply be asked to explain or describe what you know about a certain area of the law. A good answer to an essay question will persuade the examiner. Simply ask yourself: 'Am I answering the question set?'.

A common mistake in an essay question is the 'shotgun' approach—simply stating everything you know about a topic. This type of answer lacks focus. Essay questions are often regarded as more difficult than problem questions, because you have to decide the parameters of your answer rather than being dictated to by the facts of the problem. You do need to be familiar with the literature in the area, and be familiar with areas due for or in need of reform. There is, however, no reason why you cannot do well in them as long as you have prepared the topics. You should never attempt an essay question if you do not know the case or the article from which it is taken! Usually, you are provided with a quote from a case or an article which represents one view of the current state of the law. Your task is to say whether or not you agree with that interpretation. You may feel that you have nothing to contribute at this stage to an academic discussion on, say, the effect of the law following the **Coroners and Justice Act 2009** on victims of domestic abuse. However, this is a topic which has been discussed at length by legal academics and judges—so refer to these discussions.

In summary, the difference between essay questions and problem questions is this—in a problem question you are being asked to use your legal knowledge to apply to a very specific set of facts and to reach a reasoned conclusion in which you provide legal advice. In an essay question, you are being asked to analyse a legal problem, and attempting to reach a conclusion on a point of law which is uncertain and the subject of debate. In other words, you need to know what the law is, what it was previously, and how it might be changed.

Summary

The importance of exam technique cannot be overstated. Criminal law is a very technical subject, and answers can appear muddled if they are not properly planned and structured. The general structure of *actus reus, mens rea*, and defences should be adopted. For problem questions, focus on the issues straight away, and apply the law to the facts given throughout, using relevant authorities. Focus on the *ratio* of cases and the effect of statutory provisions. Don't forget to conclude. If you have several options, discuss these in turn. Finally, make sure you have answered the correct number of questions, and allocated the requisite amount of time to each one. In essay questions, ensure any points you have made are supported by evidence, that you have weighed up any proposals for reform, and that you have focused on the question set.

 TAKING THINGS FURTHER

■ McVea, H. and Crumper, P., *Exam Skills for Law Students* (2nd ed., OUP, 2005).
■ Strong, S. I., *How To Write Law Essays and Exams* (2nd ed., OUP, 2006).

Fundamental Principles of Criminal Liability— *Actus Reus* and *Mens Rea*

2

ARE YOU READY?

In order to answer questions on this topic, you will need an understanding of the following:

- criminal liability for acts and omissions
- factual and legal causation and the rules on *novus actus interveniens* in causation, including the impact of the decision in ***R v Kennedy* [2007] UKHL 38**
- intention (direct and oblique)
- the development of the idea of recklessness
- negligence
- the coincidence of *actus reus* and *mens rea*

 KEY DEBATES

Debate: criminalising omissions

It is easy to say that we should be guilty of committing criminal acts, but less easy to find someone guilty of all the things that he does not do. Is killing the same as letting die? There is considerable debate on the topic of the 'Good Samaritan', or the duty to rescue. Ashworth holds that failing to help someone in danger should be criminalised on the grounds of social responsibility. However, other commentators such as Smith argue that the line between an act and an omission is too fine to place any great weight on and the focus ought to be on whether the defendant has caused the death of the victim, rather than any wider duty.

David is 35 years old and lives with Mona, his mother, who is bedridden. David cares for Mona by providing her with food and changing her medical dressings. Mona gives David money to cover the costs of the food, and pays the mortgage on the house. David begins a relationship with Jane. After five weeks Jane starts to stay at David's house at the weekends. One night, Jane surprises David by telling him that she has booked a holiday for them both—two weeks in Spain, departing the next day. David expresses his concern about who will look after his mother. Jane says that he has 'done his bit' and that David's sister Vera, who lives ten miles away, should help out for once. David telephones Vera and leaves a message on her answer phone telling her that she will have to look after Mona for the next two weeks. When Vera arrives home she accidentally erases her telephone messages before she has the chance to replay them. Whilst David and Jane are on holiday, Mona's condition worsens considerably. When they arrive home they find her unconscious, having become ill through lack of food and from infections caused by unchanged dressings. Shocked, David rushes her to hospital, where she is seen briefly by a harassed doctor, Simon, but is then left unattended in a hospital corridor. Mona dies shortly afterwards.

David and Jane have been convicted of manslaughter and wish to argue that there is no criminal liability for a failure to act, and that, furthermore, they did not cause Mona's death. Discuss.

CAUTION!

- Read the rubric to questions carefully, noting who it is you are asked to advise or comment on. With this type of question candidates have been known to waste valuable time detailing the liability of the doctor!

- Remember also that *actus reus* consists of both an act/omission plus evidence of causation. With causation, even if the medical treatment is negligent, it is unlikely to break the chain of causation.

- Be sure that you do not jump to the conclusion that David is liable simply because he is Mona's son—whilst familial relationships count for the purposes of a duty of care, the courts still operate a restrictive approach.

DIAGRAM ANSWER PLAN

Identify the issues
- ■ The question raises issues of *actus reus* and *mens rea* in the context of homicide.
- ■ Is there a omission giving rise to a duty of care in criminal law? If so, does that omission cause the death of the victim?

Relevant law
- ■ No general liability for omissions; however does a duty arise either by contract (*R v Pittwood*) or via a voluntary assumption of care (*R v Stone and Dobinson; R v Instan*)?
- ■ *Novus actus interveniens*. Medical cases. *R v Smith. R v Cheshire.*

Apply the law
- ■ Duty of care and death caused in fact and in law. Does the duty of care arise due to David's relationship, or is there a wider duty?

Conclude
- ■ Gross negligence manslaughter based on the above. Principles in *R v Adomako*.

SUGGESTED ANSWER

The first question to consider is whether David and Jane have committed a criminal act or omission which has caused Mona's death. As there is no positive act by either of them that causes death, the court would need to investigate whether or not liability can be based on the failure of either or both of them to prevent Mona's death.[1]

The question as to whether an omission, as opposed to an act, can actually cause a consequence is a moot point. Traditionally, the criminal law has always drawn a clear distinction between acts and omissions, being loath to punish the latter. However, apart from the numerous statutes that impose a duty to act, e.g. **s. 170** of the **Road Traffic Act 1988**, it appears that the common law will impose a duty to act only in very limited circumstances.

There can be no criminal liability imposed on David and Mona in respect of their failing to care for Mona unless the prosecution can establish that they were under a positive legal duty to care for her. Such a duty can be imposed by statute, but that is clearly not the case here. As Mona gives David money to cover the cost of food, arguably a contract arises as in **R v Pittwood (1902) 19 TLR 37** where the defendant, a railway gate operator, was found guilty of manslaughter when a person was killed crossing a railway line as a result of the defendant leaving a gate open when a train was coming. On the other hand, in domestic relationships such as this one, there is a presumption that no legally enforceable relationship existed. There may be some liability for omissions on other grounds. In *R v Instan* [1893] 1 QB 450, liability for manslaughter was placed upon a niece who failed to care for her aunt with whom she was living, having been given money by the aunt to buy groceries. There might be a similar duty on David.[2]

[2] It is important to choose the case which provides for the correct form of duty.

With regard to David and Jane, a duty cannot be found on a family relationship. However the prosecution might wish to argue that a positive legal duty arises at common law because Mona has grown to rely on their help. Whilst five weeks may not be sufficient to create a duty in Jane's case, the fact that David changes her dressings and buys her groceries but then stops doing so may give rise to some liability. In *R v Stone and Dobinson* [1977] QB 354, the Court of Appeal upheld convictions for manslaughter by gross negligence on the basis that the defendants had allowed the victim to stay with them and had started to care for her. They then failed to discharge that duty and failed to summon any assistance. The court stressed that the duty to act arose not simply because of a blood relationship between one of the defendants and the deceased, but because of the reliance relationship. It can be argued here that David did not discharge his duty in looking after Mona. He could have done more than simply making a telephone call.[3]

[3] Here, you are showing the examiner that you are not following the law blindly, but are able to distinguish your case on its own facts.

It could also be argued that a duty arises following the principle in *R v Miller* [1983]. In this case the House of Lords upheld the defendant's conviction for criminal damage on the basis of the doctrine of 'supervening fault'. In other words, in creating a dangerous situation, and then failing to counteract it, the defendant had committed a culpable omission. In that case the defendant had inadvertently fallen asleep smoking in bed, setting fire to the room. When he realised what had happened, he moved away rather than taking any action to stop the fire spreading. It might be said that going on holiday and leaving Mona without checking that Vera, could, in fact, take over responsibility for her care created a dangerous situation, which they failed to counteract.[4]

[4] Quoting directly from the case raises the bar of your answer.

The prosecution will now need to establish that David and Jane's omission caused Mona's death. Causation in criminal law is established by way of the 'but for' test established in *R v White* [1910] 2 KB 124.[5] Would Mona have died but for David and Jane's departure?

[5] In proving causation, look at factual causation first, then legal causation.

It seems clear that she would not as David would have been tending to her. This stage is known as causation in fact. It is not necessary for the prosecution to prove that the omission was the sole or main cause of death, merely that it contributed significantly to the victim's death.

The defendants here will argue that a number of different events occurred to make their omission insignificant in terms of liability. Vera did not get the message, and Simon, the harassed doctor, left Mona unattended in a hospital corridor. With regard to the first point, the defendants will argue that the defendant's conduct must be a substantial and an operating cause of death. Here, they might argue that the death of the victim was unforeseeable and they could not be expected to know that Vera would delete her phone messages.[6] To be legally significant, the defendant's conduct must be more than trivial, in accordance with the *de minimis* rule (the defendant's contribution must be more than minimal). The defendant's conduct does not need to be the sole cause of death. The question is only whether the defendant made a significant contribution. The fact that there might be two competing causes of death does not prevent the defendant from being responsible. It suffices that the defendant's contribution is more than merely trivial.

Any argument on the part of the defendants that they are not to be held responsible on the grounds that Simon, the doctor, was negligent, is also likely to fail. In *R v Smith* [1959] 2 QB 35 it was held that if, despite the medical treatment, the original injury was still an operating and substantial cause of death, the chain of causation would not be broken.[7] The chain would only be broken if the original wound was 'merely the setting in which another cause operates' or 'if the second cause is so overwhelming as to make the original wound merely part of the history'. In *R v Cheshire* [1991] 3 All ER 670, a guideline case on this matter, the court stated that negligent medical treatment would only break the chain of causation if it were 'so independent of the defendant's acts, and in itself so potent in causing death' that the contribution made by D's acts in causing death was rendered insignificant. Here, Mona is in hospital because she has become ill due to the lack of food normally provided by David, and, more recently, Jane. The fact that Simon has left her unattended, whilst clearly negligent, will not be sufficient to break the chain of causation based on these cases.

David and Mona have a duty of care towards Mona and the prosecution are likely to succeed in arguing that they have caused Mona's death.[8]

[6] Don't forget to apply the law to the facts at each stage.

[7] Medical treatment, however negligent, does not break the chain of causation.

[8] Provide an overall conclusion summarising the law and drawing a conclusion on the likely outcome.

LOOKING FOR EXTRA MARKS?

- In areas such as causation, structure is key. Ensure you deal with each defendant separately. You can build up a strong argument by quoting from cases and considering (or distinguishing) any potential argument on the part of the defence.

- Use the cases wisely, identifying the class of duty, and do not apply the law blindly. For example, even if there is a voluntary assumption of care, it may not apply in these particular circumstances.

QUESTION | 2

To what extent is a defendant criminally liable for a failure to act?

CAUTION!

- You should avoid simply describing the law in a question like this. Try to ensure that some comment is made on the examples given, that adds value to the points being made. In particular, don't describe the facts of cases.

- Some clear reference to the question set is crucial in a question like this. This is a straightforward question on general principles, but an excellent structure will produce a clear reasoned argument. This question is quite broad, so you can set your own parameters. You can explain this choice in the introduction.

DIAGRAM ANSWER PLAN

Outline the law: the general rule is that there is no criminal liability for omissions. However, in certain closely defined circumstances the law will create a duty of care. These circumstances are quite limited.

Provide case law examples: In *R v Pittwood* it was held that a duty of care arose when a death occurred due to a breach of contract. The law was extended in *R v Stone and Dobinson*—where there has been a voluntary assumption of care which is subsequently abandoned, the law will create a duty. You can and should include recognised academic views on liability. Here, there are two clear opposing positions.

Conclusion—although there are limits on the duty of care (e.g. in *R v Khan and Khan*), the courts may be widening the concept.

SUGGESTED ANSWER

Every offence in criminal law requires proof of an *actus reus* on the part of the accused. In the vast majority of cases, statute or common law defines this *actus reus* in terms of a positive act.

The basic rule in English criminal law is that there is no general positive duty to act to prevent the commission of criminal offences or to limit the effect of harm caused by the actions of others. This position reflects what is sometimes referred to as the individualistic approach to liability. If D is at a swimming pool, and he sees P (a young child with whom he has no connection) drowning in the deep end, why should D be required to go to P's aid? D has no special responsibility for P, and did not cause the risk to arise. It is pure chance that D is in a position to help. Why should fate be the basis for imposing a liability for failing to prevent P's death? Ashworth argues for a 'social responsibility' approach. This view proposes that liability should arise for failing to attend those in peril partly because of the moral obligation to do so, but also because it reflects a more complex social pact.[1] A positive duty to aid others would impose a responsibility but would also confer a corresponding benefit. D might one day find himself compelled to help P, but the next day he might be the beneficiary of the duty on P to aid D where D is in peril. Society benefits because less harm is suffered by individuals.

In reality, English criminal law does impose criminal liability for failing to act, but it does so on the basis of exceptions. Thus D will not incur liability for failing to act unless the prosecution can point to a positive legal duty to act.

The most obvious source of such legal duties will be statute. Parliament creates liability for failing to act in two ways. At a very simple level it creates offences of omission. Perhaps the best known example of this is provided by the **Children and Young Persons Act 1933**, which places parents and guardians under a legal duty to care for children. Suppose that parents go out for the evening leaving a four-year-old child alone. Whilst they are out he falls onto a fire and is killed. It is likely that the court would find that there was a culpable omission based on the breach of statutory duty, and liability could be imposed if causation and fault are also established.

An alternative basis for establishing a legal duty to act is where D is subject to a contractual duty or holds an office that suggests the imposition of a duty. In the case of employees the court will look at the express or implied terms of the contract to determine the extent and nature of the duties imposed on D. In *R v Pittwood* (1902) 19 TLR 37, a railway crossing gatekeeper opened the gate to let a cart pass,

[1] In an essay question like this, try to go beyond the case law and include academic opinion.

but then went off to lunch, forgetting to close the gate. A hay cart crossed the line and was hit by a train. The defendant was convicted of manslaughter. He argued that the only duty he owed was to his employers, with whom he had a contract. It was held, however, that his contract imposed a wider duty upon him to users of the crossing. Thus the duty arising under a contract inures to the benefit of those who are not privy to the contract—i.e. the passengers on the train.[2] In *R v Instan* [1893] 1 QB 450, D was given money by her aunt to buy groceries. D failed to care for her aunt who subsequently died. It is unlikely that any contractual duty existed in this case, as the agreement was a domestic one—hence there would have been no intention to create legal relations.

[2] A more in-depth discussion of the reasons for establishing the duty will attract more marks.

There are situations where, despite the absence of any statutory or contractual duty to act, it is felt that liability ought to be imposed. In such cases it falls to the common law to perform its residual function of supplying the omission. Judges 'discover' new common law duties to act because it is felt they ought to exist. *R v Instan* is a case in point.[3] For the last 12 days of her life the aunt was suffering from gangrene in her leg and was unable to look after herself. Only D knew this. D did not provide her aunt with food nor did she obtain medical attention. This omission accelerated the aunt's death. D's conviction for manslaughter was upheld, the court proceeding on the basis that a common law duty was simply a moral duty so fundamental the courts had to enforce it. As Lord Coleridge CJ observed, a legal common law duty is nothing else than the enforcing by law of that which is a moral obligation without legal enforcement.

[3] *R v Instan* was decided on a quasi-contractual basis. However it was also held that there was a legal duty, rather than a moral one.

The problem with the common law is that it is reactive—it only develops because cases come to the courts on appeal. The court in *R v Gibbins and Proctor* (1918) 13 Cr App R 134, accepted that a duty could be imposed upon a common law wife to care for her partner's child because, although the child was not hers, she had assumed a duty towards the child by choosing to live with the child's father and accept housekeeping money to buy food for them all.

Imposing liability for omissions where D undertakes to care for P and P becomes reliant on D may even be counter-productive. In *R v Stone and Dobinson* [1977] QB 354, the defendants were convicted of the manslaughter of Stone's sister Fanny because they took her in but failed to care for her adequately. With hindsight they might have been advised not to help her in the first place. The law therefore sends mixed messages.[4]

[4] The scope of the law was extended in this case, on the grounds of a voluntary assumption of care.

One ought to care for others, but one should not start to do so unless one is able to discharge that duty properly.

The common law duty to act was developed further by the important House of Lords' decision in *R v Miller* [1983] 1 All ER 978. D, who was squatting in an empty house, fell asleep whilst smoking a cigarette. Whilst he was asleep the cigarette set fire to the mattress. D woke, realised the mattress was on fire, but took no steps to douse the fire. The house was damaged in the ensuing blaze. He was obviously not under a statutory duty to put the fire out, nor was he under a contractual duty to do so. At the time the common law duties to act were based on duties owed to blood relatives, or arising from reliance. The House of Lords had little choice but to 'discover' a new legal duty at common law. Such a duty arises where D accidentally causes harm, realises that he has done so, and it lies within his power to take steps, either himself or by calling for assistance, to prevent or minimise the harm. The doctrine has since been applied to killing by gross negligence in *R v Evans (Gemma)* [2009] EWCA 650,[5] where it was held that awareness of having caused a dangerous situation could of itself give rise to the duty of care (effectively the duty to act) that forms the basis of the offence. Whilst the ruling in *R v Miller* is socially desirable—there is great social utility in D being required to limit the effect of his careless actions—there are many uncertainties. What is it that D is required to do once he realises he has caused harm? Must he act as the reasonable person would have done, or does he simply have to do his best?

Even where a positive legal duty to act can be identified, uncertainties may arise as to whether D has been or can be absolved from that duty. Some clarification is provided by the House of Lords' decision in *Airedale NHS Trust v Bland* [1993] AC 789, where it was held that doctors were under a duty to treat a patient where it was in the patient's best interests to do so. Where, however, all hope of the patient recovering had disappeared, the duty to nourish and maintain the patient would also cease.[6]

The courts are prepared to recognise the existence of a duty where it would be fair to do so. Williams and Hogan argue that the duty should be limited, due to the fine line between acts and omissions and the fact that causation is a crucial element of criminal liability. Ashworth, however, would extend the duty. It is submitted that the French model of a general statutory duty of easy rescue would be a good compromise. This would not lead to liability for manslaughter, but criminalises the omission itself, on the basis of social responsibility.[7]

[5] It is useful to explain how the law has been applied recently.

[6] The 'best interests' doctrine has been criticised on the grounds that it does not respect patient autonomy.

[7] It is useful if you can present alternatives or proposals for reform in your conclusion.

LOOKING FOR EXTRA MARKS?

▪ In an essay of this nature, refer to academic argument such as the debate between Williams and Ashworth. You should also ensure that you discuss what the limits of the law are. For example, in *R v Khan and Khan* **[1990] 1 WLR 15**, the House of Lords was careful to state that it was not prepared to extend the class of duty for criminal omissions.

▪ There are relatively few proposals for reform in this area so concentrate on the anomalies contained within the cases. Judges have created new precedents in this area of law. Quotes from the judgment will raise the bar of your answer, and will show that you can appreciate the reasons for the development of the law.

QUESTION | 3

Darren deals regularly in drugs. He meets Viv, his friend's daughter, at his flat one evening and gives her a quantity of heroin, which she injects into her own arm. He also injects himself. Viv, who is 15, has never tried heroin before. They carry on chatting that evening, and Viv falls asleep on the sofa. In the morning, she is unconscious. Darren sees this, but is late for work. He covers Viv up with a blanket, and leaves the flat, intending to call an ambulance on the way. As there is no one on the road, he decides to speed up and is soon travelling at 60 miles an hour through the centre of town. He is in a built up area. Unfortunately, he runs out of petrol and the car stalls, running into Maisie, another driver. Maisie is also travelling to work, and sees Sam trying to cross at a pedestrian crossing. She tries to stop but ends up hitting him. Sam is seriously injured and an ambulance is called. By now the streets are very busy and the ambulance is delayed. Sam eventually arrives at hospital where he is given a transfusion of the wrong type of blood by Bo, a junior doctor, and injected with an antibiotic for which he has an allergy. Sam dies. In the commotion, Darren forgets to call an ambulance for Viv and runs off. The police follow him into a disused warehouse. Unknown to him or the police, the warehouse is being used by Annie, an artist. Annie is walking along the corridor to get some more supplies when she bumps into Darren and screams. When he sees Annie, he grabs her and shouts out that he has a knife. The policeman, John, sees a shape at the end of a corridor and shoots, killing Annie instantly. When the police go to Darren's flat, they find Viv dead.

Discuss any criminal liability arising from these facts, concentrating especially on *causation*.

CAUTION!

▪ This question tests your ability to extract the rules on causation. Be systematic, working through the steps of factual and legal causation.

▪ Be sure that you do not confuse causation with *mens rea*, and that you are able to distinguish all the elements of constructive and gross negligence manslaughter. Advise the defendant only, not the other characters!

DIAGRAM ANSWER PLAN

Identify the issues	■ Liability for gross negligence manslaughter and manslaughter by an unlawful and dangerous act. ■ Causation—*R v Pagett/R v Kennedy*

Relevant law	■ The criteria in *R v Adomako* to be discussed and outlined. ■ The decision in *R v Kennedy*. ■ Causation and *novus actus interveniens*.

Apply the law	■ Whether there is a duty of care. ■ Whether Darren caused the deaths in fact and in law. ■ Whether there is liability for gross negligence manslaughter.

Conclude	■ Liability for gross negligence manslaughter and manslaughter by an unlawful and dangerous act on the facts above.

SUGGESTED ANSWER

In order to prove criminal liability for involuntary manslaughter (there does not appear to be sufficient evidence of *mens rea* here for murder), the prosecution will have to satisfy the court that the defendant, Darren, has committed an act or omission which caused a death. There are three recognised types of this type of manslaughter: manslaughter by gross negligence, manslaughter by an unlawful and dangerous act, and subjectively reckless manslaughter. Objectively reckless manslaughter no longer exists after the House of Lords' decision in *R v Adomako* **[1995] 1 AC 171**.

In relation to Viv, Darren may have committed manslaughter by gross negligence. The first thing to be satisfied is whether he owes a duty of care to Viv. If he does, the court will need to be satisfied that this duty has been breached, that a risk of death was reasonably foreseeable, that death was caused by the defendant, and the negligence was 'gross' – i.e. capable of amounting to a criminal act or omission.[1]

Whether a defendant owes the victim a duty of care is dictated by the principles governing duty of care in tort.[2] In the specific situation

[1] Set out the criteria for the relevant offence. This creates a structure for the rest of your answer.

[2] Note that the criminal standard of duty of care mirrors the tortious standard. There is some lack of clarity in the law here, as the criminal law espoused a narrow approach until *R v Adomako* (see later).

of the supply of drugs, in *R v Khan and Khan* [1998] **Crim LR 380**, the defendants' appeals were allowed even though they had not summoned assistance. The court did not wish to extend the class of duties in criminal law on the grounds that to do so would unnecessarily widen the law. In Darren's situation, however, the court may be inclined to draw parallels with *R v Evans (Gemma)* [2009] **1 WLR 1999**. In this case, the defendant gave heroin to her sister. A duty was created when she realised that her sister had succumbed to an overdose. As Darren puts a blanket over Viv, this situation may be similar. Lord Judge CJ held:

> when a person has created or contributed to the creation of a state of affairs which he knows, or ought reasonably to know, has become life threatening, a consequent duty on him to act by taking reasonable steps to save the other's life may reasonably arise.

A similar point arose in *R v Miller* in which a defendant caused a fire by falling asleep in bed holding a cigarette. He did not do anything about it even when he realised. The fact that he had created a dangerous situation which he then failed to counteract created a duty of care.

The next question is whether Darren has breached the duty. This is not difficult to establish in criminal law when there is a death. The prosecution must prove that Darren caused the death. The breach of duty must involve a risk of death which is obvious to the reasonable person, even if the defendant does not personally appreciate it. In *R v Misra and Srivastava* [2005] **1 Cr App R 21**, it was held that the circumstances must be such that a reasonably prudent person would have foreseen a serious and obvious risk of death.[3] This seems clear here, and in any event, Darren intends to call an ambulance.

[3]Note that this test is an objective one.

Finally, the jury must be convinced that the breach amounts to 'gross' negligence.

In *R v Adomako* [1995] **1 AC 171**, the court held that the question to be asked is as follows: was the defendant's conduct so bad in all the circumstances as to amount to a criminal act or omission? The test can be viewed as 'circular' in this definition of 'gross' negligence (a defendant's conduct is criminal if it is 'gross' negligence, and is classified as 'gross' negligence if it is a crime). This circularity was acknowledged by Lord Mackay in the judgment in *Adomako*, who emphasised that the decision is one for the jury, and is a question of fact.[4] The key issue is whether the defendant's conduct goes beyond a mere matter of compensation between the parties.

[4]Some critique adds depth to your answer here.

Applying these concepts to Darren's case, it is clear that his breach of duty satisfies the above requirements. His negligence in failing to act beyond throwing a blanket over Viv, thereby causing her death, is criminally negligent given the existence of the duty of care.[5]

[5]Apply the law to the facts, making it clear how the circumstances amount to a duty of care.

The next question is whether Darren has caused Sam's death. If so, he may be liable for constructive manslaughter (manslaughter by an unlawful or dangerous act). Has Darren committed an act which causes death?[6] The first condition is that an unlawful act has been committed. Driving at speed in a built up residential area is unlawful, and this is an act, not an omission. Causation is established by means of the two stage tests of factual and legal causation.

[6]Note that an omission cannot form the basis of this offence.

The factual causation test is as follows. The prosecution must establish that the victim would not have died but for the defendant's actions (*R v White* [1910] 2 KB 124). Here, Sam would not have died if Darren's car had not stalled. A further key factor in causation is whether an act is reasonably foreseeable to occur. Is there an unbroken chain of causation between Darren's bad driving and Sam's death in the sense that death or serious bodily harm was reasonably foreseeable in the circumstances? Darren will want to argue that he could not help stalling, and that it was not reasonably foreseeable that he would then drive into Maisie, killing Sam. Only the free, deliberate, and informed act of a third party can break the chain of causation. In *R v Pagett* (1983) 76 Cr App R 279, a case in which the police shot at D, who was holding his girlfriend hostage, killing her instantly, the court said that although there were circumstances in which the act of a third party might break the chain of causation, a reasonable act performed in self-preservation does not. Here, Maisie was acting as a reasonable, legal driver might act. Darren will therefore not be able to argue that the chain of causation was broken. It is not an unforeseeable event for a car to stall. Maisie was not acting voluntarily in hitting Sam. She was acting in self preservation, or to prevent a worse harm. To succeed here, Darren will have to show that Maisie was also driving dangerously. This does not appear to be the case here, but we cannot be sure.[7]

[7]You can offer alternative arguments.

Darren will try to argue, further, that Bo's possibly negligent medical treatment has caused Sam's death rather than Darren. The first question will be whether the doctor was acting negligently in administering a transfusion of the wrong type of blood, and in giving Sam an antibiotic to which he is allergic. The rules on medical negligence as a potential *novus actus interveniens* were considered in the cases of *R v Smith* [1959] 2 QB 35, *R v Jordan* (1956) 40 Cr App R 152, and *R v Cheshire*. Medical negligence will not break the chain of causation provided the original injuries were a substantial and operating cause of death. Darren may try to rely on *R v Jordan* (1956) 40 Cr App R 152 in which the chain of causation was held by the Court of Appeal to have been broken by the 'palpably wrong' administration of large doses of an antibiotic to which D is allergic.[8] This was considered to be 'independent' of D's original wounds. It is

[8]Set out the law, but here again, note that there are contrasting arguments.

unlikely that in this case, much was known about Sam's blood group or drug tolerance in an emergency situation like this. In any event, it is unlikely that medical negligence will break the chain of causation. In **R v Cheshire [1991] 1 WLR 844** the Court of Appeal held that even though medical negligence was the immediate cause of the victim's death, it did not exclude the defendant's responsibility. The negligence was not so independent of the defendant's acts, and in itself so potent in causing death, that the defendant's acts could be regarded as insignificant.[9]

[9]This case is useful if you cannot decide between the contrasting arguments above.

The subsequent events in the warehouse mirror the facts of **R v Pagett** (explained earlier). As stated earlier, any argument on Darren's part that he did not cause Annie's death, but that the police officer did, will fail.

Darren may be found guilty of manslaughter by gross negligence with regard to Viv, and manslaughter by an unlawful and dangerous act with regard to Sam and Annie.

+ LOOKING FOR EXTRA MARKS?

■ This question is deceptive in that it only deals with the essential principles of criminal liability. However causation in particular has some conflicting case law decisions. You can use these to your advantage to build up a strong argument. If you can include an awareness of weaknesses in the law, this will show that you have really understood the topic. Here, the common argument that gross negligence manslaughter is 'circular' is included.

■ The structure of this type of question is crucial. Deal with evidence of the act or omission before moving on to factual and legal causation in turn. In looking at the intervening act, choose your authorities carefully.

Q QUESTION 4

Whatever doubts there may have been in the past, the definition of intention in English Criminal Law is now settled.

Critically assess the validity of this statement with reference to relevant case law.

! CAUTION!

■ In intention, the current judicial guidelines are contained within the case of **R v Nedrick**. You will need to consider previous case law in order to answer an essay question on this topic, but bear in mind the older cases are no longer current.

■ Ensure that you refer to the question set, and provide some critical analysis.

DIAGRAM ANSWER PLAN

Outline the law: Provide a brief definition of direct and indirect intention and its development and in particular the decision of *R v Moloney* distinguishing between intention and foresight. How far have the courts settled on a meaning of intention?

▼

Provide case law examples: Explanation of the decision in *R v Nedrick* and reference to the House of Lords decision in *R v Woollin* and in *R v Matthews; R v Alleyne*—do these cases settle the debate?

▼

Conclude with an analysis and discussion of the role of foresight in intention. The changes made by *R v Woollin*. The Law Commission's recommendations.

 SUGGESTED ANSWER

[1] Identify the key arguments from the outset and avoid excessive description.

The concept of intention in English criminal law has been the subject of considerable debate and discussion. There is no statutory definition of intention, and the courts have not shown much consistency to date in attempting to define it. [1]

As intention is obviously a matter of the defendant's state of mind, it is of course difficult for the jury to assess it. Therefore, guidelines from the judge are needed. In the majority of cases, the word can be used in its ordinary meaning—that is, when it is the person's aim to bring about a particular consequence. Thus, in **Steane [1947] 1 All ER 813**, the accused, who assisted the enemy during the war, had his conviction quashed as the court decided that he did not intend to assist the enemy. He had argued that he was trying to protect his family, who would have been harmed had he not cooperated. This type of intention—which must be distinguished from motive—applies where a defendant intends a consequence if he aims, and acts in order to, make that consequence happen. This type of intention is clear and easy enough for a jury to follow on the facts of the case.

However, in some circumstances, a defendant may bring about a consequence that is different from that which he intended to achieve. This is known as indirect or oblique intention. The defendant, could, for example, put a bomb under the pilot's seat on a plane owned by the defendant in order to destroy the plane and claim the insurance money. The deaths of the pilot and the crew are not an essential part of his purpose, but are almost certain to occur if the defendant succeeds in his plan to destroy the plane. It is theoretically possible for the crew and the pilot to escape, but the possibility is remote. The question then is whether intention should include a situation in which the defendant does not directly aim or desire to cause death or serious injury, but death or serious injury are an inevitable consequence of the course of action he chooses to take. In this type of case, a jury needs very clear guidance on the meaning of intention, and in what circumstances they may decide on a verdict of murder rather than manslaughter.[2] This type of case is very rare, but the law must cater for it, nonetheless.

[2] The concept of oblique intent is not a matter of law, but a matter of evidence. You should avoid referring to the 'definition' of oblique intent.

In case law spanning three decades, the law has moved from an objective analysis of oblique intent to one which takes account of the defendant's knowledge at the time of the events leading to death. In this way, there is now a clear distinction between murder and manslaughter. This was not always the case. In *DPP v Smith* [1961] **AC 290**, a case regarding the killing of a police officer, the trial judge directed the jury that if they were satisfied that the defendant 'as a reasonable man must have contemplated that GBH was a likely result and that such harm did happen and that the officer dies as a consequence, then the accused is guilty of capital murder'. This case was heavily criticised on the grounds that such an objective test was not suitable for such a serious crime, and, furthermore, that it failed to take account of the defendant's state of mind, a crucial element in criminal liability.[3] This case led to the enactment of **s. 8 of the Criminal Justice Act 1967** which bound juries to look beyond the fact that the defendant had caused the result, and to draw inferences from all the evidence available to them.

[3] Note that this case is no longer considered to be good law.

The case law following *DPP v Smith* moved towards subjectivity, but seemed to confuse the concepts of foresight and intention. Thus in *Hyam v DPP* [1974] **2 All ER 241** the House of Lords upheld a conviction for murder where the accused had set fire to a victim's house by putting burning newspaper through her letterbox. This caused the death of the victim's two children, who, unknown to D, were in the house at the time. D stated that her intention had only been to frighten the victim. The House of Lords held that D would have the *mens rea* for murder if he knew that it was highly probable that her act would cause death or serious injury. The result of this case was that foresight of a high probability of death or serious harm resulting from her conduct would be enough for the *mens rea* for murder. This applied whether or not such foresight amounted to intention.

The issue of intention was debated by the House of Lords in *R v Moloney* [1985] **1 All ER 1025** and *R v Hancock and Shankland* [1986] **1 All ER 641**. In the former case, Moloney shot his stepfather from point blank range and was convicted of murder after the trial judge directed the jury that in law a man intends the consequence of his voluntary act when he desires it to happen (whether or not he foresees that it probably will happen) or when he foresees that it will happen, whether he desires it or not. The House of Lords quashed the conviction on the basis that this was a misdirection, Lord Bridge stating that:

the judge should avoid any elaboration or paraphrase of what is meant by intent, and leave it to the jury's good sense to decide whether the accused acted with the necessary intent, unless the judge is convinced that, on the facts and having regard to the way the case has been presented to the jury in evidence and argument, some further explanation or elaboration is strictly necessary to avoid misunderstanding.

This decision was followed by the House of Lords' ruling in *R v Hancock and Shankland*, where Lord Scarman also made the point that if intention required a detailed direction, it was best to leave this to the discretion of the trial judge. He added that the trial judge could not do as Lord Bridge suggested and simply direct the jury to consider whether the defendant foresaw death or serious injury as a 'natural consequence' of his actions. Instead, Lord Scarman stated that the trial judge must refer to the concept of probability—the more probable the consequence, the more likely the accused foresaw it and intended it. However, these do not always amount to the same thing. The defendants in this case may well have foreseen that throwing the blocks would result in injury, but this did not mean they intended to kill.[4]

[4]It is crucial to distinguish between foresight and intention clearly as it is central to the debate. It is also the issue that has produced the most uncertainty.

Despite clear House of Lords *dicta* to the contrary, the Court of Appeal in *R v Nedrick* [1986] 3 All ER 1 did lay down some guidelines to the effect that the jury should not infer intention unless they considered that the accused foresaw the consequence as a virtual certainty. However, this decision has attracted criticism, and the Court of Appeal in *R v Walker and Hayles* [1989] 90 Cr App R 226 stated 'we are not persuaded that it is only when death is a virtual certainty that the jury can infer intention to kill'. The most current interpretation of oblique intent, therefore, may still be open to criticism.[5]

[5]At this stage, refer back to the question. This case casts doubt on the assertion in the quote that the 'definition' is settled.

Nevertheless, the status of *Nedrick* was confirmed by the House of Lords' discussion in *R v Woollin* [1998] 4 All ER 103. The House stated that where the simple direction was not enough, the jury should be further directed that they were not entitled to find the necessary intention unless they felt sure that death or serious bodily harm was a virtually certain result of D's action (barring some unforeseen intervention) and that D had appreciated that fact.

This decision also illustrates one of the difficulties of the present approach, i.e. when is the issue of intention so complicated as to warrant a detailed direction? In *R v Walker and Hayles*, the Court of Appeal decided that 'the mere fact that a jury calls for a further direction on intention does not of itself make it a rare and exceptional case requiring a foresight direction'. On the other hand, in **R v Hancock and Shankland**, the House of Lords confirmed that the trial judge was right to give a detailed direction, even though the content of the direction was wrong.

A further problem is that different juries may have different ideas as to what constitutes intention, some insisting on purpose being necessary, while others are prepared to accept that only foresight of a probable consequence is required. There is clearly the risk of inconsistent decisions and it is therefore not surprising that the Law Commission (Nos 122 and 218) have recommended that the following standard definition of intention be adopted:[6]

[6]An alternative option is to adopt the Law Commission's recommendation.

a person acts intentionally with respect to a result when:

(i)   it is his purpose to cause it; or

(ii) although it is not his purpose to cause that result, he knows that it would occur in the ordinary course of events if he were to succeed in his purpose of causing some other result. In fact, it was described as a 'tried and tested formula'.

It can be argued that there is still some ambiguity in the direction. In 1998, JC Smith described the Nedrick formula as involving 'some ineffable, indefinable notion of intent locked in the breasts of jurors'. In conclusion, it can be said that given the criticisms of **R v Nedrick** in subsequent cases as described earlier, the guidance given in that case does not necessarily settle the definition.

LOOKING FOR EXTRA MARKS?

■ The key issue in oblique intent (and the issue which has caused the courts the most difficulty) is in the distinction between foresight and intention. Make sure that you can explain this carefully, using the case law.

■ Think about providing some alternative to the current definition, for example by discussing proposals for reform. The Law Commission has considered homicide and intention a number of times but suggested a definition in its 2006 report (*Murder, Manslaughter and Infanticide* (Law Com. No. 304 HC 30)). Note also the development of the concept in the leading judgments.

QUESTION | 5

Explain why the House of Lords in **R v G and Another** [2003] 4 All ER 765 settled on a definition of subjective recklessness in the context of **s. 1** of the **Criminal Damage Act 1971**.

! CAUTION!

- This is a classic case of the criminal law's struggle between an objective and a subjective approach to liability.
- Ensure that you address the reasons for the definition and do not simply describe the decision.

○ DIAGRAM ANSWER PLAN

The development of recklessness in the courts and in particular the interpretation of recklessness in the **Criminal Damage Act 1971**.

▼

Outline the law: Provide a brief definition of recklessness and the difference between objective and subjective liability.

▼

Problems caused by the subjective definition. *R v Cunningham* and *R v Stephenson*.

▼

The decision in *R v Caldwell* and the objective test [1981].

▼

The decision in *R v G and Another* and the reasons for overuling *R v Caldwell*.

▼

Conclusion—the return to a subjective analysis of recklessness.

A   SUGGESTED ANSWER

The concept of recklessness is distinguished from that of intention. A defendant may be considered to be reckless if it is not his aim to achieve a result or where he is not aware that it is virtually certain to occur. Instead he may simply foresee that it may occur, without any degree of certainty.

The distinction between a subjective approach and an objective approach is crucial in understanding the development of the law of recklessness. The current definition is contained in the case of *R v G and Another* [2003] UKHL 50.

[1]Give a brief summary of the current state of the law.

Subjective recklessness requires the court to determine the defendant's state of mind and level of knowledge at the time of committing the offence.[1] In *R v Cunningham* [1957] 2 All ER 412, the Court of

Appeal held that a defendant was reckless only if he took an unjustifiable risk and was aware of the possibility of that risk. The defendant took a gas meter from an empty house to steal money from it. He left behind a broken pipe from which gas escaped. He was convicted of maliciously administering a noxious substance so as to endanger life under **s. 23** of the **Offences Against the Person Act 1861** as he was aware of the risk in dislodging the pipe, but continued to take that risk.

[2] Identify problems with the existing law.

A problem could arise if the defendant failed to see that there was a risk.[2] If the defendant was not aware of the risk, he could not be convicted of an offence for which the *mens rea* is subjective recklessness. In *R v Stephenson* [1979] QB 695 a defendant was found not guilty of criminal damage when he set fire to a haystack to keep warm. The defendant was schizophrenic and did not recognise the risk of the fire spreading—he was not, therefore, reckless.

[3] Add some critical comment to your discussion, to add value and analysis to what you are saying.

This seems a fair decision. It does not take account, however, of a defendant who deliberately closes his mind to the risk, or one who cannot see the risk because he is intoxicated.[3] The judicial approach of subjective recklessness was changed in the case of *Metropolitan Police Commissioner v Caldwell* [1981]. The defendant's conviction for criminal damage (under **s. 1(2)** of the **Criminal Damage Act 1971**) was upheld by the House of Lords. The offence is that of damaging property with intent to endanger life. The defendant had got drunk and set fire to a hotel as an act of revenge against the owner. The defendant alleged that he was so drunk at the time of the event that it had not crossed his mind that he may be endangering life. Intoxication cannot be a defence to a basic intent crime, such as criminal damage. The judges took the opportunity to redefine recklessness in objective terms. Lord Diplock stated that:

a person is reckless if (1) he does an act which in fact creates an obvious risk that property will be destroyed or damaged and (2) when he does that act he either has not given any thought to the possibility of a risk or has recognised that there is some risk involved and has nonetheless gone on to do it.

[4] This highlights the development of the law.

This ruling changed the approach of the courts to recklessness in the context of criminal damage from a subjective one to an objective one.[4] This seemed to resolve the problem of the previous rule in that it took account of a defendant who refused to see the risk, but it risked being unfair to a defendant who was not able to see the risk. In *Elliott v C (A Minor)* [1983] 2 All ER 961 the Divisional Court held that no account should be taken of the fact that the defendant was a 14-year-old girl of limited intelligence, who was tired and hungry. She had spilt some inflammable spirit on the wooden floor of a garden shed, and then dropped a lighted match. A reasonable person would have recognised the risk, and it did not matter that even if D had thought about it she might not have been able to recognise it.

The decision in *MPC v Caldwell*, thus, narrowed the scope of recklessness, but meant an unfair decision in circumstances such as that described above. Secondly, there was the argument that '*Caldwell* recklessness' was not acceptable as a form of *mens rea* because it was not based on the defendant's state of mind. Whilst many might have applauded Lord Diplock's efforts to penalise thoughtlessness in terms of a social policy initiative, the real question was whether he was right to pursue this via a radical judicial reinterpretation of the term 'recklessness'.

[5] Try to identify the overall impact of changes in the law.

As far as recklessness is concerned the subjectivist argument has found favour again, as evidenced by the House of Lords' decision in *R v G* [2003] **4 All ER 765**, where it was held that a defendant could not be properly convicted under **s. 1** of the **Criminal Damage Act 1971** on the basis that he was reckless as to whether property was destroyed or damaged when he gave no thought to the risk and, by reason of his age and/or personal characteristics, the risk would not have been obvious to him, even if he had thought about it.[5] Lord Bingham observed that recklessness should at least require a knowing disregard of an appreciated and unacceptable risk of, or a deliberate closing of the mind to, such risk. In his view it was not clearly blameworthy to do something involving a risk of injury to another if one genuinely did not perceive the risk.

R v G reflects a general judicial trend in favour of subjectivity, as evidenced in decisions such as *B v DPP* [2000] **1 All ER 833**.

As a result of the decision in *R v G and Another*, the test for recklessness in criminal damage has returned to a subjective test—the court must take into account any relevant characteristics in assessing the defendant's state of mind. The rule in Caldwell applied only to criminal damage.

[6] The *ratio decidendi*, or reasons for the decision, are important here, as the House of Lords overruled itself on this issue.

Lord Bingham's reasons were as follows:[6]

1. In serious crimes, the defendant's state of mind must be culpable. An objective test effectively makes the crime one of strict liability. Lord Bingham asserted that it is not clearly blameworthy to engage in conduct where there is a risk of injury if the defendant does not genuinely perceive that risk.

2. The approach from *Caldwell* sometimes compelled juries to commit what they perceived as obvious unfairness towards defendants

3. The decision in *Caldwell* itself was held to be a misinterpretation of the law contained in the **Criminal Damage Act 1971**.

4. Lord Steyn condemned the consequences of the decision as impractical: 'the surest test of a new legal rule is not whether it satisfies a team of logicians but how it performs in the real world. With the benefit of hindsight the verdict must be that the rule laid down in *Caldwell* failed this test . . . experience suggests that in *Caldwell* the law took a wrong turn'.

LOOKING FOR EXTRA MARKS?

- Analysis is crucial in a question like this.
- A direct comparison of Lord Bingham's judgment in *R v G and Another* and Lord Diplock's judgment in *R v Caldwell* will help to add real weight to your answer.

TAKING THINGS FURTHER

- Amirthalingam, K., '*Caldwell* Recklessness is Dead, Long Live *Mens Rea's* Fecklessness' [2004] MLR 491.

  This article argues that whilst the return to subjective recklessness in R v G is desirable as it assesses the individual defendant's liability, an element of objectivity is needed to assess guilt.

- Ashworth, A., 'The Scope of Criminal Liability for Omissions' [1989] LQR 105 424–9.

  This article proposes a duty of easy rescue based on social responsibility.

- Hart, H. L. A. and Honore, T., *Causation in the Law* (2nd ed., OUP, 1985).

  An in-depth discussion of the meaning of causation in the criminal law.

- Norrie, A., 'After Woollin' [1999] Crim LR 532.

  *This article examines the meaning of the term 'intention' in the criminal law following the case of **Woollin** and further discussion of the distinction between foresight and intention.*

- Williams, G., 'Criminal Omissions: The Conventional View' (1991) 107 LQR 86.

  This article discusses the scope of criminal omissions and discusses the differences between acts and omissions. Analyses the law/morality debate in the context of omissions and takes issue with Ashworth's social responsibility argument.

Online Resource Centre   www.oxfordtextbooks.co.uk/orc/qanda/

Go online for extra essay and problem questions, a glossary of key terms, online versions of all the answer plans and audio commentary on how selected ones were put together, and a range of podcasts which include advice on exam and coursework technique and advice for other assessment methods.

Murder and Manslaughter

3

ARE YOU READY?

In order to answer questions on this topic, you will need an understanding of the following:

- the key distinctions between murder, voluntary manslaughter, and involuntary manslaughter
- the *actus reus* for murder (refer to causation in the previous chapter)
- the *mens rea* for murder—direct and oblique intent (refer to *mens rea* in the previous chapter)
- the statutory provisions in the **Coroners and Justice Act 2009** on the defences of diminished responsibility and loss of control
- the differences between gross negligence manslaughter, reckless manslaughter, and manslaughter by an unlawful and dangerous act manslaughter
- the effect of the decision in *R v Kennedy* **[2007] UKHL 38** in relation to the chain of causation in drugs cases

KEY DEBATES

Debate: abused partners who kill

In the previous law contained in the **Homicide Act 1957**, an abused partner who killed had to do so suddenly in order to benefit from the defence, with no time lapse between the last provocation and killing. This was thought to be unfair to women, who tend not to react immediately to provocation.

The new defence of loss of control, in the **Coroners and Justice Act 2009**, abolishes this requirement. Whilst the Act has improved this situation, in *R v Clinton* **[2012] EWCA Crim 2**, the Court of Appeal ruled that whilst **s. 54(4)** of the Act excludes sexual infidelity as a trigger for the

⊙

loss of control defence, it should not be read as excluding evidence of sexual infidelity as part of the context for the qualifying trigger. In two articles in the Criminal Law Review, Alan Norrie and Ronnie Mackay provide a thorough analysis of the effect of the legislative changes contained in the **Coroners and Justice Act 2009**, as well as reviewing the problems in the previous law on provocation and diminished responsibility, in particular towards abused women.

QUESTION | 1

Tim and Karen had been married for six years. Recently Karen had made a new set of friends and had become withdrawn from Tim and their relationship. She regularly went out to nightclubs without him and was drinking heavily. As a result, Tim was receiving treatment from his doctor for clinical depression. One night he decided to follow Karen to the nightclub and found her dancing and kissing another man. At home, Karen told Tim that she had found a much better lover and that Tim bored her. Tim, furious and humiliated, reached for the poker next to the fire and hit Karen several times on the head with it. She collapsed. When Tim realised what he had done, he called the police and Karen was taken to hospital. When she regained consciousness, she took an overdose of painkillers which had been accidentally left next to her bed by an absent-minded nurse, and she died. Tim says that he did not want to kill Karen but was confused and angry.

Discuss Tim's criminal liability for murder, including the effect of any defences he may have.

CAUTION!

■ Adopt a logical structure throughout, working your way through causation and the *novus actus interveniens*, then direct and oblique intent, including causation, then the partial defences to murder contained in the **Coroners and Justice Act 2009**.

■ Do not confuse the issue of intent with the issue of a defence of diminished responsibility.

DIAGRAM ANSWER PLAN

| Identify the issues | ■ The question raises the issue of murder and the relevant partial defences of loss of control and diminished responsibility. |
| | ■ There is also an issue of intoxication, relating to *mens rea*. |

| Relevant law | ■ Discuss the actus reus of murder and work through the principles of causation. Is there an argument relating to *novus actus interveniens*? |
| | ■ Discuss the mens rea of murder, including oblique intent. |

| Apply the law | ■ Tim's intoxication may affect *mens rea* (*DPP v Majewski*) |
| | ■ Apply the provisions of **Coroners and Justice Act 2009**. |

| Conclude | ■ Conclude on murder or manslaughter by reason of loss of control or diminished responsibility. |

SUGGESTED ANSWER

[1] It is a good idea to start your discussion with a definition.

[2] Always start with factual causation as this establishes the logical link between the defendant's act and the victim's death

[3] Even though the case of *R v Jordan* suggests that the chain could be broken, this is very rare. Even if the medical treatment is severely negligent, it is unlikely to break the chain of causation if the 'operating' cause—that is, the reason that the victim is in the hospital—is the defendant's original action.

This question raises issues of Tim's liability for murder and any defences which may be available to him. The *actus reus* of murder is the unlawful killing of a human being.[1] The concepts of unlawful and human being are easily satisfied here. The first issue to discuss is causation. Tim is clearly the factual cause of Karen's death. Karen would not have died if Tim had not hit her on the head with the poker: *R v White* [1910] 2 KB 124.[2] A question arises over whether Tim's contribution to her death is too remote. In other words, will Tim's defence team be able to argue that the forgetfulness of the nurse forms a sufficient contribution to Karen's death, and makes Tim's contribution insignificant: *R v Smith* [1959] 2 QB 35, and *R v Cheshire* [1991] 3 All ER 670.

As a general rule, negligent medical treatment does not break the chain of causation. This is true even if the treatment is severely negligent. The key point is whether Tim can be considered to be a substantial and operating cause of Karen's death.[3] The common law defines the *mens rea* of murder as 'malice aforethought'. This is now widely understood as meaning an intention to kill or to do grievous bodily harm. If it cannot be shown that his purpose was to cause serious injury, then the judge will direct the jury that they are only entitled to infer intention where death or serious injury is a virtually certain consequence of Tim's actions, and that Tim appreciated this to be the case. It seems likely that at least one of these circumstances will be satisfied. In order for him to be found guilty of murder the prosecution must prove that Tim had either the intention to kill or to do grievous bodily harm. Intent can be based on 'purpose/desire' or on evidence of foresight. It would appear to have been Tim's purpose to do some grievous bodily harm—this would suffice for the *mens rea* of murder. If necessary the trial judge could give a **'Nedrick'** direction— **R v Nedrick [1986] 3 All ER 1**. This would involve asking the jury to consider whether or not there was evidence that Tim foresaw death or grievous bodily harm as virtually certain to result from his action.

[4] Don't forget to deal with both elements of the **Nedrick** direction.

Only if there was evidence that Tim foresaw death or grievous bodily harm as virtually certain to result from his actions would a jury be entitled to infer that he intended death or grievous bodily harm.[4]

[5] Answer only the question you have been set!

As the question asks you to focus on murder rather than involuntary manslaughter, you should now turn to the defences.[5]

The loss of control defence is constructed in such a way that Tim will need to provide evidence that he acted as he did because of a qualifying trigger.

The first of these under the **2009 Act** (sometimes referred to as the 'fear trigger') is that he acted as a result of his fear of serious violence by Karen. This is not the case here. The Act provides a second possibility—that Tim's loss of self-control was attributable to things said by Karen that constituted circumstances of an extremely grave character such that they caused Tim to have a justifiable sense of being seriously wronged. A number of matters need to be considered here. First,

[6] Do not forget to apply the law to the facts throughout.

the legislation is clear that Karen's words alone can be sufficient.[6] Second, it would be for the prosecution to prove beyond all reasonable doubt that the words spoken did not amount to circumstances of an extremely grave character.

The prosecution may still argue that the 'anger' trigger is not available because **s. 55(6)(c)** expressly precludes its operation in circumstances where the thing said or done that is claimed to have triggered D's action constitutes sexual infidelity. However, in *R v Clinton* [2012] **EWCA Crim 2**, the Court of Appeal ruled that whilst **s. 54(4)** of the **2009 Act** excludes sexual infidelity as a trigger for the loss of control defence, it should not be read as necessarily excluding evidence of sexual infidelity (as part of the context in which the issue of whether or not there was a qualifying trigger could be considered).

If the jury is satisfied that there is a qualifying trigger for Tim's actions, it will then have to consider whether a person of Tim's sex and age, with a normal degree of tolerance and self-restraint, and in Tim's circumstances, might have reacted as Tim did, or in a similar way. The purpose of this formulation is to prevent a defendant citing any personal characteristics that might affect his self-control. In doing so, it reflects the approach taken by the Privy Council in *Attorney-General for Jersey v Holley* [2005] UKPC 23,[7] in relation to the common law defence of provocation (since abolished by the **Coroners and Justice Act 2009**), which endorsed the view that a defendant pleading the defence of provocation had to be judged by the standard of a person having ordinary powers of control. Hence Tim's depression would not be relevant for these purposes. What the jury would be entitled to take into account are Tim's personal circumstances in so far as they explain the gravity of the words or actions causing him to lose his self-control, for example his marital difficulties and the fact that Karen has become withdrawn from the relationship. In summary, therefore, if there is evidence that Tim lost his self-control, was not acting out of revenge, that his actions came within the 'anger' qualifying trigger, and were those that might have been displayed by a reasonable person in his circumstances, his liability for the death of Karen could be reduced to manslaughter.

Bearing in mind that characteristics such as mental illness that have a bearing on the temperament of a defendant are excluded from the statutory defence of loss of control, Tim would be better advised to plead the defence of diminished responsibility, established under **s. 2** of the **Homicide Act 1957**, as subsequently amended by **s. 52** of the **Coroners and Justice Act 2009**.[8] Under the amended **s. 2(1)** Tim would have to prove that, at the time of the killing, he was suffering from an abnormality of mental functioning arising from a medical condition. The facts indicate that he had been diagnosed and is being treated by a doctor for his depression.

Tim would further have to establish that this abnormality of mental functioning caused a substantial impairment in: (a) his understanding of the nature of his conduct; (b) his ability to form rational judgment; or (c) his ability to exercise self-control. The Court of Appeal has confirmed that, for the purposes of the **2009 Act**, the concept of substantial impairment should be approached in the same way as was the case under the **Homicide Act 1957**; see *R v Brown* [2011] **EWCA 2796**. Hence there should be evidence of more than some trivial degree of impairment but there does not have to be evidence of total impairment; see *R v Lloyd* [1967] **1 QB 175**.

Of these three options the impairment of self-control option is likely to prove the most fruitful for Tim,[9] provided the jury is satisfied that the impairment is substantial and, further, that the abnormality of mental functioning provided an explanation for Tim's actions in the sense that it was the cause or a contributory factor in making Tim act as he did. As indicated earlier, there is every prospect of this defence

---

[7] Show knowledge of the development of the law.

[8] Try to reach a proper conclusion, based on your assessment of the facts.

[9] The new legislation has substantially improved the law in these area by providing three distinct scenarios. Make sure you specify which one is most appropriate.

[10] Try to give practical legal advice based on your argument.

succeeding, and in consequence reducing Tim's liability to manslaughter, provided the expert evidence is sufficiently compelling. Tim should be advised that he is likely to be convicted of manslaughter by reason of diminished responsibility.[10]

LOOKING FOR EXTRA MARKS?

- Better answers may identify that responses to sexual infidelity are excluded by the Act in **s. 54(4)**—however the case of **R v Clinton** casts some doubt on this, and it should not be read as excluding evidence of sexual infidelity as part of the context of whether or not there was a qualifying trigger.

- Can you say which the better defence is, and conclude on the issue of whether Tim will be guilty of murder or manslaughter?

QUESTION | 2

The **Coroners and Justice Act 2009** aimed to create a more 'effective, transparent and responsive' justice service for victims, providing greater clarity and fairness. (**Explanatory Notes to the Coroners and Justice Act 2009**).

Discuss this statement in relation to the defences of loss of control and diminished responsibility by abused women who kill.

CAUTION!

- With essay questions such as this, make sure you do not simply describe what the law is. You need to say whether you agree or disagree with the statement, based on evidence.

- The previous law on the characteristics of the defendants should not now be needed. However, in discussing the effectiveness of the new law, previous cases can expose some of the mischief the Act was trying to address.

DIAGRAM ANSWER PLAN

Explain the effect of the Coroners and Justice Act on the two partial defences to murder: loss of control and diminished responsibility. The Act amends **s. 2** of the **Homicide Act 1957** and creates a new defence of loss of control.

⬇

Diminished responsibility and the medical requirement.

⬇

Loss of control. Consider the subjective test. The Act removes the sudden requirement.

▼

Exclusion of sexual infidelity—*R v Clinton*.

▼

Consider the objective test—development of the law. A return to an objective test.

▼

Conclusion. The Act still has some problems.

 SUGGESTED ANSWER

The defences to murder under the **Coroners and Justice Act 2009** amended the law in relation to diminished responsibility, and changed the law in relation to the defence of provocation, replacing it with a new defence of loss of control. These changes were brought about as a result of inconsistencies in case law, and were the culmination of three Law Commission reports: 'Partial Defences to Murder' (LC no 290, 2004), 'A New Homicide Act for England and Wales' (LC no 177, 2005) and 'Murder, Manslaughter and Infanticide' (LC No 304, 2006).

Diminished responsibility is now defined under **s. 2** of the **Homicide Act 1957** as amended by **s. 52** of the **Coroners and Justice Act 2009**. The **Coroners and Justice Act 2009** provides for a new defence of loss of control, replacing the previous law of provocation, which was previously contained in the common law and in the **Homicide Act 1957**.

[1] In the introduction, refer to the rubric and state what you intend to do.

The changes in the **CJA 2009** will be discussed, and the effectiveness of the changes will be analysed.[1]

In relation to diminished responsibility, **s. 52(1)** states that a person will not be convicted of murder if he was suffering from such abnormality of mental functioning which arose (a) from a recognised medical condition; (b) which substantially impaired his responsibility to do one of three things mentioned in **s. 52(1)(A)**; and (c) which provides an explanation for his acts and omissions in doing the killing. There must be a causal link between the defendant's condition and the killing. The definition of abnormality of mind requirement in the previous law was much wider. The new law requires a 'recognised medical condition'.

[2] Back up and analyse your opinion, giving reasons for your answer. Here, the law has improved due to a tightening of the definition.

This amendment appears to be an improvement to the law. It was not always clear which conditions were included in the definition. With particular reference to victims of abuse, battered wife syndrome will continue to be part of the definition.[2]

The defendant has to establish that this abnormality of mental functioning caused a substantial impairment in (a) his understanding of the nature of his conduct; (b) his ability to form a rational judgment; or (c) his ability to exercise self-control. There does not have to be evidence of total impairment.

Loss of control has replaced the defence of provocation. To begin with, the judge will determine whether there is sufficient evidence of loss of control to put before a jury. In **ss. 54** and **55** of the **Coroners and Justice Act 2009**, there must be a loss of control (**s. 54(1)(a)** due to a qualifying trigger (**s. 54(1)(b)**) due to a fear of serious violence from the victim or a thing done or said which constituted circumstances of an extremely grave character and caused the defendant to have a justifiable sense of being seriously wronged (**s. 55(4)**). It excludes situations of revenge or violence by the defendant.

Parliament was keen to make a clear distinction between genuine cases of loss of control and so called revenge killings.[3]

The subjective test had been criticised in the past due to its unfairness towards women. The requirement for a 'sudden' loss of control required a 'snap' reaction, which is typically the reaction of men rather than women. In cases such as *R v Thornton* and *R v Ahluwalia* [1993] any delay between the last abuse and the killing, was interpreted by the courts as the conscious formulation of a plan for revenge. Although some attempt was made by the Court of Appeal to recognise 'cumulative provocation' in cases of domestic violence, the delay often meant that the defence was rejected. In cases such as these, the defendant was not successful in pleading provocation, but had to plead diminished responsibility instead, effectively labelling the defendant as mentally ill.[4]

In this respect, the **Coroners and Justice Act 2009** has improved the law. A defendant who has been abused will no longer need to prove that the loss of control was sudden, and will not be forced to plead the defence of diminished responsibility instead of loss of control. However, the law excludes cases of sexual infidelity, **s. 55(6)(c)**. It might be argued, for example, that honour killings should be excluded from the defence. A further criticism may be that the qualifying trigger of fear may be too close to self-defence.

The second area in provocation to be considered is the objective test. The **Homicide Act 1957** had stipulated that the jury had to ask whether a reasonable man would have acted as the defendant did. This raised the question of whether any particular information about the defendant could be put to the jury in order to help them to establish this. If certain characteristics could be put to the jury, then the defendant could be judged by his own reduced powers of self-control and not those of the reasonable man.[5] The case law on this point was

[3] Referring to the rationale for a particular legislative provision can help you to see whether it has achieved its aims. *Hansard* can be a useful research tool here.

[4] You can comment on the law in its social context. Here, this was a particular disadvantage of the unavailability of the defence to certain groups of people.

[5] The debate on which characteristics of the defendant could be taken into account for the purposes of the objective test was wide ranging. Comment on whether the Act has helped in this.

far from clear. If the offensive conduct from the victim signified increased gravity to the defendant because it was aimed at a particular characteristic, then this characteristic could be taken account of by the jury. If the taunt was not about the particular characteristic the defendant was sensitive about, then it could not be put to the jury. Later cases, however, dispensed with this idea of the mode of provocation and allowed nearly all characteristics to be put to the jury. This was the case even if this knowledge was prejudicial, and even if it was likely to reduce self-control. As long as it increased the gravity of the provocation to the defendant, it was admissible. Thus, in *R v Smith* **(Morgan)**, the defendant's alcoholism and depression, which affected his powers of self-control, was admitted.[6] However, in the case of *Attorney General v Holley* **[2005] UKPC 23**, the court stated that the test should be an objective one. The defendant's reaction will be compared to that of a normal person of the defendant's sex and age with normal tolerance and self-restraint. This endorses the view that a defendant pleading this defence is to be judged by the standard of someone having ordinary powers of self-control.

> [6] Try to give case law examples wherever possible, even in an essay.

Does the new law retain a purely objective test? At face value, it seems to. This is evident in the use of the words 'a person with a normal degree of tolerance and self-restraint'. However the provision includes the term 'in the circumstances of the defendant'. The jury are entitled to take into account the personal circumstances of the defendant to the degree that it affects the gravity of the provocation to him. If there is evidence that the defendant was not acting out of revenge, that his or her actions came within the qualifying trigger, and that they were those that might have been displayed by a reasonable person in his or her circumstances, then the defence of loss of control may be made out.

In conclusion, it can be said that although the **Coroners and Justice Act 1999** has attempted to help victims of domestic violence who kill, problems remain, particularly in cases of sexual infidelity. This is evident from the cases of *R v Clinton* and *R v Dawes*. In relation to the objective test, it is still difficult for juries to be able to establish exactly what they are allowed to take account of when asking whether a person with a normal degree of tolerance and self-restraint would have acted as the defendant did. The introduction of the **CJA 2009** was meant to eradicate the obstacles faced by battered women who kill but it appears they have only been reduced.[7] It is the education of the jury which appears to be an important factor in the success of the partial defence of loss of control, particularly due to the jury's understanding of what characteristics should be considered.

> [7] Refer back to the question.

It remains the woman's responsibility to prove her actions were justifiable, which is difficult when comparing it to the reasonable man. Without personally experiencing domestic abuse it remains difficult for a judge or jury to understand the actions of an abused woman so using the partial defence of loss of control remains a risk. Due to the objective test, many women have to resort to the partial defence of diminished responsibility, which is not a viable option as without a recognised medical condition this defence does not apply, leaving no further options. The **Coroners and Justice Act 2009** has not corrected this problem, leaving many victims of abuse without the necessary available defences.

It appears that the **Coroners and Justice Act 2009** has not addressed the problems regarding statutory interpretation, as it remains open.

Despite the continuing issues which have been raised regarding the 'loss of control' requirement, the introduction of fear has been welcome. The interpretation of the Act still remains wide and the requirement of loss of control still remains impossible for many to show. Without recognising the full extent of the effect of the abuse, outside the requirement of a reasonable man, the defence will remain unavailable to many. The Law Commission, whose recommendations led to the **Coroners and Justice Act 2009**, has proposed that the 'loss of self-control' requirement be abolished, but it still appears in the Act. This is confusing as 'loss of self-control' implies an impulsive reaction. Sexual infidelity is not defined and nor is 'a considered desire for revenge'.

In conclusion, it can be said that although the new law has attempted to iron out some inconsistencies, it may have created new ones. It may be no easier for juries to understand.

LOOKING FOR EXTRA MARKS?

- Try to use the law in its social and political context, but always back up with case law principles wherever possible.
- Refer to academic comment in this area. For example, the debate on which characteristics should be put to the jury has attracted prolific commentary.

Sid, who is 75 years old and quite frail, is queuing for his pension at the post office one morning. He is not feeling very well and has forgotten to take his medication for his heart condition. Jim enters the post office, furious that his unemployment benefit has not been paid on time. He is determined to speak to the cashier and so pushes to the front of the queue. In doing so he pushes Dee, an elderly lady also waiting to pick up her pension, out of the way. Dee falls on Sid, who falls over. Jim leaves the post office.

Meanwhile Sid has a heart attack. The cashier calls an ambulance and Sid is taken to hospital, where he is seen by Dr Peach, who advises that Sid should be kept under observation. Unfortunately, Sid develops a chest infection and he is connected to a ventilator. Dr Peach is too busy to check on Sid regularly, and so does not realise that the tube has become blocked. Sid dies of asphyxia.

Advise the Crown Prosecution Service on the liability of Jim and Dr Peach for Ned's death.

CAUTION!

- Structure is very important in this question as there are two different types of manslaughter to be considered.

- The element of dangerousness in constructive manslaughter must be discussed very carefully. It cannot be confused with causation.

DIAGRAM ANSWER PLAN

Identify the issues	▪ Identify the potential charges of constructive manslaughter and manslaughter by gross negligence.
Relevant law	▪ Is there an unlawful act? Does it have to be directed at the victim? Has Jim caused the death of Sid?
Apply the law	▪ Discuss whether the doctor may be guilty of gross negligence manslaughter.
Conclude	▪ The chain of causation is unlikely to be broken.

Jim's liability for the death of Sid will be involuntary manslaughter rather than murder, as there is no evidence that he has the *mens rea* for murder. The type of manslaughter will depend on the initial act or omission which led to Sid's death. Manslaughter by an unlawful or dangerous act (also known as constructive manslaughter) requires, firstly, an unlawful act. The unlawful act must be a crime and not a tort. In pushing Dee, Jim has committed a battery.[1] A battery is defined as the unlawful application of unlawful personal violence. This can be committed directly or indirectly. The result of this is that Sid was knocked over. In *R v Mitchell* **[1983] 2 All ER 427** the accused was found guilty of manslaughter when he hit a man who fell against an old woman, knocking her over, causing her death.

[1] The *actus reus* and the *mens rea* of the unlawful act must be proven as the basis for this offence.

Furthermore, Jim may try to argue that it is not necessary that the unlawful act is directed at the victim. In *R v Dalby* **[1982] 1 All ER 916**, the Court of Appeal appeared to introduce a third condition into constructive manslaughter—that the act must be directed at the victim.[2] However it now seems clear, following *R v Mitchell* and *R v Goodfellow* **(1986) 83 Cr App R 23**, that this is unnecessary. Given that Jim pushed Dee out of the way, the court will conclude that Jim's unlawful act did not have to be directed at the eventual victim.

[2] It was thought that the unlawful act needed to be directed at the victim: it is now settled that it does not.

The unlawful act must be dangerous. In *R v Church* **[1965] 2 All ER 72** it was held that an act is dangerous if a sober and reasonable person would foresee the risk of some harm.[3] Following *R v Dawson* **(1985) 81 Cr App R 150** the jury can conclude that the criminal act is 'dangerous' for these purposes if a sober and reasonable person at the scene of the crime, watching the unlawful act being performed and seeing what the defendant sees, would have foreseen the risk of some physical harm. If Sid is obviously frail, then Jim would have been aware of the risk. The reasonable person does not have the benefit of hindsight. Hence, in assessing the dangerousness of pushing Dee, the jury must ignore the fact that Sid had a weak heart, as this fact was not known to Jim. This area of law is not abundantly clear.

[3] The concept of dangerousness has caused the courts some problems. Is it to be assessed subjectively or objectively? The case of *R v Dawson* appears to have been decided on its own facts. In any event, it must not be confused with causation.

Jim may argue that he did not know that his actions were dangerous, but this contention will not succeed as the House of Lords in *DPP v Newbury* and *Jones* **[1976] 2 All ER 365** confirmed that, as a question of fact for the jury, the prosecution does not have to prove that the accused recognised the risk of danger.

The next question to consider is whether Jim's actions have caused Sid's death. Sid would not have died if Jim had not barged into the post office—this satisfies the requirement of factual causation

[4]Raise the defendant's likely argument—then deal with how successful it is likely to be, given the decided case law.

(*R v White* [1910] 2 KB 124). Jim is likely to want to argue that Dr Peach was negligent in looking after Sid once he was in the hospital; and that therefore the chain of causation is broken by the *novus actus interveniens* of negligent medical treatment.[4] The prosecution do not have to prove, however, that Jim's actions were a sole or even a main cause of the victim's death, merely that they made a significant contribution. In *R v Smith* [1959] 2 All ER 193 the accused's conviction for murder was upheld as the court held that as the original wound was still an operating cause of death the chain of causation was not broken. Similarly in *R v Cheshire* [1991] 3 All ER 670, Beldam LJ stated 'it will only be in the most extraordinary and unusual case that such treatment can be said to be so independent of the acts of the accused that it could be regarded in law as the cause of the victim's death to the exclusion of the accused's act'. The question will be whether the chest infection suffered by Sid is 'independent' of Jim's initial act.

[5]This is a different issue to Dr Peach's liability.

Furthermore, Jim might argue that Dr Peach's failure to check up on Sid breaks the chain of causation, especially as he was on a form of life support.[5] This argument was rejected by the House of Lords in *R v Malcherek*; *R v Steel* [1981] 2 All ER 422, where Lord Lane CJ stated 'the fact that the victim has died despite or because of medical treatment for the initial injury given by careful and skilled medical practitioners, will not exonerate the original assailant from responsibility for the death'. Given that the treatment is probably not the sole cause of Sid's death, it is submitted that Jim has 'caused' the death.

The *mens rea* for this offence is the *mens rea* for the unlawful act. If this is battery then what is required is evidence that Jim either intended or was reckless as to the infliction of unlawful personal violence.

[6]Don't forget that recklessness is always assessed subjectively.

In barging into the post office, he must have foreseen a risk of harm (*R v G* [2003] 4 All ER 765).[6]

The prosecution would appear to be able to satisfy the requirements of manslaughter by an unlawful and dangerous act. Alternatively, the prosecution may argue that Jim has committed manslaughter by gross negligence or by reckless manslaughter. It may be argued that Jim has created a dangerous situation by leaving the post office without summoning help. In *R v Miller* [1983] 1 All ER 978 the House of Lords upheld the accused's conviction for criminal damage where he had inadvertently caused a fire and then, when he realised what he had done, simply left without doing anything to summon help. As such, Jim may, at this point, have a duty of care towards Sid.

[7]Would a reasonable person have appreciated a risk of death?

The question will be whether the other remaining criteria in *R v Adomako* [1994] 3 All ER 79 are also satisfied.[7] In particular the jury will have to decide whether Jim's behaviour was grossly negligent.

The same criteria will be applied to Dr Peach. Doctors clearly owe their patients a duty of care but it is likely that in this instance the doctor will not be found to be grossly negligent. According to *R v Adomako* [1994] 3 All ER 79 the requirements for the operation of this offence are as follows:

- the defendant owes the victim a duty of care;
- the defendant acted in breach of that duty;
- the defendant's conduct was grossly negligent;
- the conduct carried a risk of causing death.

[8]This seems unlikely. Apply the law to the facts.

In relation to Dr Peach the jury will have to, according to Lord Mackay, consider 'whether in all the circumstances the extent to which the accused's conduct departed from the proper standard of care incumbent upon him involving as it must have done a risk of death to the victim was such that it must be judged to be criminal'.[8] In the circumstances of a busy casualty department, it might be said that the doctor did not depart from those standards sufficiently to fall into this category.

+ LOOKING FOR EXTRA MARKS?

- A discussion of whether the unlawful act needs to be directed at the victim will add depth to your answer in this type of question.
- Try to show an ability to argue in the alternative.

Q QUESTION | 4

Don is in a relationship with Sally. One day, Sally tells Don she is leaving him for Rob, who is the best lover she has ever had. Don is diagnosed with depression. That evening, Don angrily throws a burning paraffin-soaked rag through Rob's open window. He does not check whether anyone is inside. The fire spreads rapidly, trapping Millie, Rob's little sister, on the top floor. Bert, a neighbour, hears Millie's screams, but does nothing. Eventually, the fire brigade arrives. Fireman Fred discovers that he has forgotten to bring a tall enough ladder. Millie jumps from an upper window into the arms of the crowd gathering below. She suffers severe injuries. In hospital, Dr John gives Millie a blood transfusion of the wrong blood-type. She dies a week later. In his statement to the police, Don said that he thought it possible that someone would be injured but he had not wanted anyone to die. His aim was to frighten Rob into leaving Sally alone.

CAUTION!

■ This question is more difficult than it looks. You need to distinguish carefully between murder and manslaughter. This discussion hinges on *mens rea*. It is also a prime example of a question in which structure is of the utmost importance as there are a number of issues to cover, with multiple defendants, offences, and potential defences.

■ Make sure that you deal with the defences separately, but with all the technical requirements.

DIAGRAM ANSWER PLAN

Identify the issues	■ Identify the possible offences: murder or manslaughter. *Actus reus* and *mens rea* issues. ■ Partial defences to murder—loss of control/diminished responsibility.
Relevant law	■ Murder as defined by Coke. *Actus reus* of murder and causation. *Novus actus interveniens*. *Mens rea* of murder. ***Nedrick***.
Apply the law	■ Does medical treatment count as a break in the chain of causation? ***R v Cheshire***. Do both limbs of the ***Nedrick*** test apply? The objective test in loss of control. ***Holley***.
Conclude	■ Result of a successful plea of loss of control. Conclusion.

SUGGESTED ANSWER

Where there is a death, the only possible offences are murder and manslaughter. Murder is defined as the unlawful killing of a human being within the Queen's Peace with intention to kill or to cause grievous bodily harm.

Would Millie have died if Don had not put the rag through the letter box? The answer is negative: *R v White* [1910] 2 QB. Don may wish to argue that other factors contributed to Millie's death.[1] In other words, rather than him being responsible, he might want to argue that Fireman Fred's negligence, Bert's failure to act, and Dr John's negligent medical treatment have been a greater contributory factor to

[1] *Novus actus interveniens* should be discussed at this point, even though the issues appear later in the question. Do not get sidetracked by the liability of the other defendants.

Millie's death than Don's action of putting the paraffin-soaked rag through the letter box. As Bert has no duty to act (given that he does not fall into any of the recognised categories), he is unlikely to break the chain of causation. Fireman Fred has a duty of care to the public as a contracted employee. However, the actions of a third party, especially when acting under a legal duty or a duty of self-preservation, will not break the chain of causation: **R v Pagett**. Finally, the court must consider whether the actions of Dr John have broken the chain of causation. The cases of **R v Smith** and **R v Cheshire** are clear on this issue. Even severe medical negligence does not break the chain of causation as long as the defendant is still a substantial and operating cause of death. In this case, Millie would not have been receiving medical treatment if it had not been for Don's action. The fact that she receives a blood transfusion of the wrong type does not change this fact.

[2] Having established causation, you can now turn to intention.

Don states that he did not intend to kill anyone.[2] Therefore, it is appropriate to consider oblique intention. The **Nedrick** direction must be considered here. This states that the jury are not entitled to infer intention unless death or serious injury is virtually certain to occur, and that the defendant foresees this as a possibility. Applying this to the facts of the question, it can probably be said that although the first part of the test may be satisfied (it is likely that if a burning petrol-soaked rag is put through a letter box that someone will be seriously injured), it may not be said to be virtually certain that Don knew this.

[3] Be prepared to consider defences in the alternative. If the facts of the question suggest the defences to murder, then discuss these accordingly.

If he is found to be reckless, then you may be able to consider reckless manslaughter or manslaughter by an unlawful or dangerous act. Recklessness is defined subjectively—that is, according to the knowledge of the defendant in question.[3]

Don's defences will depend on the level of *mens rea* decided. If he is found guilty of murder, then the partial defences to murder will need to be considered. The **Coroners and Justice Act 2009** covers the partial defences to murder. To begin with, it will need to be established whether there was a qualifying trigger which made Don act as he did. The qualifying trigger can be a fear of serious violence, or a

[4] Only choose to discuss the part of the test which applies in this scenario.

thing done or a thing said. In the instant case, Sally's statement that Rob is the best lover that she has ever had may suffice.[4] However, The prosecution may still argue that the 'anger' trigger is not available because **s. 55(6)(c)** expressly precludes its operation in circumstances where the thing said or done that is claimed to have triggered Don's action constitutes sexual infidelity. However, in **R v Clinton** [2012] **EWCA Crim 2**, the Court of Appeal rules that whilst **s. 54(4)** of the 2009 Act excludes sexual infidelity as a trigger for the loss of control defence, it should not be read as excluding evidence of sexual infidelity as part of the context in which the issue of whether or not there was a qualifying trigger could be considered.

If the jury is satisfied that there is a qualifying trigger for Don's actions, it will then have to consider whether a person of Don's sex and age, with a normal degree of tolerance and self-restraint, and in Don's circumstances, might have reacted in a similar way. The purpose of this formulation is to prevent a defendant citing any personal characteristics that might affect his self-control.[5] In so doing it reflects the approach taken by the Privy Council in *Attorney-General for Jersey v Holley* [2005] UKPC 23, in relation to the common law defence of provocation (since abolished by the **Coroners and Justice Act 2009**), which endorsed the view that a defendant pleading the defence of provocation had to be judged by the standard of a person having ordinary powers of control. In summary, therefore, if there is evidence that Don lost his self-control, was not acting out of revenge, that his actions came within the 'anger' qualifying trigger, and that they were those that might have been displayed by a reasonable person in his circumstances, his liability for the death of Millie could be reduced to manslaughter. The fact that Millie rather than Sally is the object of Don's anger should not matter: *R v Pearson*.[6]

As an alternative, and bearing in mind that characteristics such as mental illness that have a bearing on the temperament of a defendant are excluded from the statutory defence of loss of control, Don would be advised to plead the defence of diminished responsibility, established under **s. 2** of the **Homicide Act 1957**, as subsequently amended by **s. 52** of the **Coroners and Justice Act 2009**. Under the amended **s. 2(1)** Don would have to prove that, at the time of the killing, he was suffering from an abnormality of mental functioning arising from a medical condition. The facts indicate that he had been diagnosed by a doctor as suffering from depression. Hence this first requirement might be made out provided the expert evidence satisfied the balance of probabilities test.

Don would further have to establish that this abnormality of mental functioning caused a substantial impairment in: (a) his understanding of the nature of his conduct; (b) his ability to form rational judgment; or (c) his ability to exercise self-control. The Court of Appeal has confirmed that, for the purposes of the **2009 Act**, the concept of substantial impairment should be approached in the same way as was the case under the **Homicide Act 1957**.

Of these three options the impairment of self-control option is likely to prove the most fruitful for Don, provided the jury is satisfied that the impairment is substantial and, further, that the abnormality of mental functioning provided an explanation for Don's actions in the sense that it was the cause or a contributory factor in making Don act as he did.[7] As indicated earlier, there is every prospect of this defence succeeding, and in consequence reducing Don's liability to manslaughter, provided the expert evidence is sufficiently compelling.

[5] The objective test in loss of control precludes personal characteristics of the defendant.

[6] Third party provocation counts for the purposes of the Act: *R v Pearson*.

[7] Here, you can conclude, and advise on the best course of action.

LOOKING FOR EXTRA MARKS?

■ Excellent answers will not only describe the different requirements for the different offences and defences, but will attempt to reach a conclusion on the best defence available.

■ Don't forget to deal with all the requirements in a particular test and analyse on the facts.

QUESTION | 5

Although the abolition of objectively reckless manslaughter by the case of *R v Adomako* [1995] 1 A171 has simplified the law, there remain substantial problems in the law on involuntary manslaughter. Discuss.

CAUTION!

■ This is not an easy question. You will need to demonstrate that you can identify the different types of manslaughter, but also how the law developed to its current position. You will then need to assess whether the law is satisfactory in its current form.

DIAGRAM ANSWER PLAN

> Scope of the question—the types of involuntary manslaughter.

▼

> Constructive manslaughter—must the act be directed at the victim?

▼

> Constructive manslaughter—dangerousness.

▼

> Reckless manslaughter—the redefinition in *R v Adomako*.

▼

> Gross negligence manslaughter.

▼

> Challenges to gross negligence manslaughter.

▼

> Conclusion.

This question covers the concept of involuntary manslaughter. This type of manslaughter can be charged where the prosecution cannot prove *mens rea* for the killing. It is settled that there are three types of manslaughter—manslaughter by an unlawful and dangerous act (also known as constructive manslaughter), reckless manslaughter, and manslaughter by gross negligence.[1] These will be discussed below, and an assessment of the clarity of the law will be attempted.

[1] Begin by setting out the current law on the topic under discussion.

Manslaughter by an unlawful and dangerous act is committed when the defendant commits an unlawful act. This act must be a crime. The crime must also involve an act; an omission will not suffice. The unlawful act must be dangerous; furthermore, it must cause the death in fact and in law. The *mens rea* for the crime is that of the unlawful act.

[2] Set out what you are trying to achieve in the essay—here, a discussion of the problems across the categories of manslaughter.

This seems clear enough—however, there are a number of controversies contained in the law. These will be discussed below, and an assessment of the clarity of the law will be attempted.[2]

Secondly, it is not always clear what constitutes a 'dangerous' act. The court in *R v Church* [1965] 2 All ER 72 held that a dangerous act is one which is 'such as all sober and reasonable people would inevitably recognise must subject the other person to at least the risk of some harm'. This suggests an entirely objective test which would discount the views or knowledge of the defendant. However, in *R v Dawson* (1985) 81 Cr App R 150 the defendant was not guilty of manslaughter where the victim died of a heart attack when the defendant and two others threatened him with weapons during an attempted armed robbery. The defendants did not know he had a weak heart.[3] In *R v Watson* [1989] 2 All ER 865, the defendant could clearly see that the victim was a frail old man who was reacting badly to the experience. To the reasonable man armed with the knowledge acquired by the defendant during the burglary there would have been no doubt that the burglary created a risk of personal injury to the victim. The test, therefore, can be described as an objective one, with the knowledge of the defendant to be incorporated. This is not entirely clear.

[3] The key here is that the reasonable man is to be regarded as having the same knowledge as the defendant would have if he had been at the scene. This case is not easy to reconcile with the thin skull rule but it is about dangerousness, not causation.

The unlawful act itself can be difficult to establish. A further issue which the courts have considered is whether the unlawful act must be directed at the victim. In *R v Dalby* [1982] 1 All ER 916, the Court of Appeal appeared to suggest that the act had to be directed at the victim. However in *R v Goodfellow* (1986) 83 Cr App R 23, where the accused, intending to be rehoused by the council, set fire to his house causing the death of some of his family, this doctrine was rejected and the accused was convicted of unlawful and dangerous act manslaughter. Furthermore, in *Attorney General's Reference (No 3 of 1994)* Lord Hope confirmed that as long as there is an unlawful and dangerous act which causes the victim's death it does not matter if the act was directed to someone else.[4]

In addition to the unlawful act, the prosecution must establish that the defendant has caused the death in fact and in law. The House of Lords' decision in *R v Kennedy* **[2007] UKHL 38** now settles the debate over whether the victim's choice to self-inject with drugs supplied by the defendant breaks the chain of causation and thus exonerates the defendant. Thus, there is no liability in manslaughter in this situation. The court confirmed that provided the victim was a fully informed and responsible adult, it was never appropriate to find the supplier guilty of manslaughter.[5]

[5] This House of Lords case settled this debate. There is a break in the chain of causation in cases like this.

The debate over reckless manslaughter also now appears to be settled. This question has been problematic for the courts. The original position was that a defendant who was subjectively reckless, and caused death, was guilty of manslaughter. In *R v Pike* **[1961] Crim LR 114**, the defendant administered carbon tetrachloride to a woman in order to enhance sexual satisfaction, having done so to other women in the past without any ill effects. The woman in question died, and it was held that the trial judge had properly directed the jury that they should convict the defendant if they thought that he had been aware of the risk. In *R v Lidar* **[2000] 4 Archbold News 3**, the Court of Appeal accepted that a category of subjective recklessness still exists.[6] They were inclined to accept that the risk which the defendant foresees must be one of serious injury rather than just some injury. The case is inconclusive, however, because the court was able to uphold the conviction as it was satisfied that in any case the defendant's conduct created a risk of some injury. Whether this should still be a separate category is a moot point as the defendant could just as easily have been convicted of other types of manslaughter. Nonetheless the category differs from unlawful and dangerous act manslaughter as it encompasses lawful as well as unlawful conduct, and omissions as well as acts.[7]

[6] This case confirms the existence of a separate category of subjectively reckless manslaughter.

[7] It is important to highlight this issue, as otherwise there is no point having a separate category.

What is clear is that objectively reckless manslaughter has been abolished. In *R v Adomako* **[1994] 3 All ER 79**, the House of Lords overruled *R v Seymour*, which in turn had applied *R v Caldwell* to manslaughter. Since *R v G* has overruled *R v Caldwell* on the issue of recklessness, the only type of recklessness recognised in criminal law is subjective. If the defendant caused a death and there was a serious and an obvious risk of death, he was guilty of manslaughter even if he did not appreciate the risk. This is certainly an improvement in the law.

A defendant can be convicted of gross negligence manslaughter, according to *R v Adomako*, if the following criteria are satisfied. First, the prosecution must prove that the defendant had a duty of care towards the victim; secondly, that the defendant acted in breach of that duty; thirdly, that the defendant's conduct was grossly negligent, and lastly, that the conduct caused the victim's death. The key issue is that it must be shown that the defendant's breach of duty was 'gross'. This means that his omission must be so bad as to justify a criminal conviction.

There may be a number of issues surrounding this case. It may not be clear which type of duty must be established—a duty in crimi-

[8]Include academic debate where you can in an essay like this.

nal law (which is very narrow) or a duty in tort. Herring argues that both must be established, but Elliott argues that the duty should be based on the ordinary principles of negligence.[8] Furthemore, the jury are left with a wide discretion on whether to convict the accused. Finally, there may be a breach of the European Convention on Human Rights (ECHR). In *R v Misra* **[2004] EWCA Crim 2375** the ruling in *R v Adomako* was challenged on the grounds that it was inconsistent with the ruling in *R v G* on recklessness and secondly that it may be inconsistent with the ECHR.

In relation to establishing the risk of death it is not quite clear how great the risk must be. It might also be argued that the test for gross negligence is effectively circular, and given that the jury determine whether the negligence was sufficiently gross for liability it is uncertain.

[9]Conclude by summarising the issues, and referring back to the question.

[10]It is a good idea to highlight practical reasons for the anomalies you have highlighted.

In conclusion, the law on involuntary manslaughter has not been without difficulty.[9] The courts have grappled with the meaning of recklessness, dangerousness, and causation. For the most part, however, the law appears to be settled. Mitchell has argued that the development of the law may be based less on legal definitions than practical prosecuting decisions.[10]

LOOKING FOR EXTRA MARKS?

■ Try to make some critical comment as you proceed through the essay, referring to academic opinion. In particular, there is some uncertainty surrounding the definition of the duty of care in criminal law and the law of torts. The article by Herring and Palser (see Taking Things Further) refers to this.

■ Refer back to the question at the end of each paragraph. This ensures you will stay relevant.

TAKING THINGS FURTHER

■ Lacey, N., 'A Clear Concept of Intention: Elusive or Illusory?' [1993] 56 (5) 621 MLR, and Horder J., 'Intention in the Criminal Law: A Rejoinder' [1995] MLR 58, 678.
In these two articles in the Modern Law Review, Lacey and Horder discuss the 'moral elbow room' left by the definitions of oblique intent and the difficulties and desirability of achieving consistency and certainty, when ultimately decisions are made on a practical basis.

■ Law Commission, *Partial Defences to Murder*, LC290, CM6301 (2004).

Proposals for reform which led to the enactment of the **Coroners and Justice Act 2009**.

■ Norrie, A., 'The Coroners and Justice Act 2009—partial defences to murder (1) loss of control' [2010] Crim LR 275, and Mackay, R.D., 'The Coroners and Justice Act 2009—partial defences to murder (2): the new diminished responsibility plea' [2010] Crim LR 290.

These two articles provide good detailed comparisons of the new partial defences to murder under the **Coroners and Justice Act 2009** *and the* **Homicide Act 1957**.

■ Norrie, A., 'After Woollin' [1999] Crim LR 532–40.

The article examines the meaning of the term 'intention' in the criminal law following the case of **Woollin** *and further discussion of the distinction between foresight and intention.*

Online Resource Centre   www.oxfordtextbooks.co.uk/orc/qanda/

Go online for extra essay and problem questions, a glossary of key terms, online versions of all the answer plans and audio commentary on how selected ones were put together, and a range of podcasts which include advice on exam and coursework technique and advice for other assessment methods.

Non-Fatal Offences Against the Person

4

ARE YOU READY?

In order to answer questions on this topic, you will need an understanding of the following:

- common law assault and battery
- the statutory assaults—**ss. 18, 20,** and **47** of the **Offences Against the Person Act 1861**
- **sections 23** and **24** of the **Offences Against the Person Act 1861**
- the common law defence of consent
- self-defence under **s. 76** of the **Criminal Justice and Immigration Act 2008** and **s. 43** of the **Crime and Courts Act 2013**
- an awareness of the **Protection from Harassment Act 2007**

KEY DEBATES

Debate: biological grievous bodily harm

The transmission of sexually transmitted diseases has caused the courts some problems—is this form of harm to be treated in the same way as other forms of grievous bodily harm? Crucially, the *mens rea* can be difficult to establish in situations where a defendant is aware of infection but does not tell the sexual partner. Matthew Weait and Loveless and Derry examine the role of the criminal law here, discussing the exact role of recklessness and the difficulties inherent in consent.

Mike and Karen are both lecturers at Crammershire University. Karen is a member of the university's karate club and she persuades Mike to join. The day of the next karate club meeting is Karen's birthday. Before the club meeting she spends a few hours in the bar drinking with friends. By the time she leaves the bar to go to the training sessions Karen has drunk six pints of lager and several vodka 'shots'. During the training session Karen hits Mike in the face with her forearm. Mike falls awkwardly, hitting his head on a nearby bench. Mike's girlfriend Gaye, who had come along to watch the session, witnesses the attack on Mike and runs towards Karen screaming abuse. Karen, who is intensely jealous of Gaye's relationship with Mike, throws Gaye to the ground and kicks her in the head. Gaye suffers minor bruising and grazes. Karen, who is distressed, runs off to the changing rooms without bothering to attend to Mike. Other club members call for medical help. It later transpires that Mike has a broken leg and has lost the hearing in one ear.

The following week Mike sees Karen coming towards him in the corridor at the university. As she approaches Karen raises her arm, intending to give Mike a hug and apologise for what she has done. Mike fears that she is about to hit him again. He pulls his mobile telephone out of his pocket and thrusts it towards Karen's face with the result that Karen suffers several broken teeth. In the weeks following these incidents Gaye becomes increasingly depressed and neurotic and has to seek professional psychological help to cope with the trauma caused by Karen's attack.

Advise the Crown Prosecution Service as to the respective criminal liabilities of Karen, Gaye, and Mike.

CAUTION!

■ Don't forget to identify and discuss any causation issues in a question like this—the provisions of the **Offences Against the Person Act 1861** referring to statutory assaults all require it to be proven.

■ An omission as well as an act can trigger these offences.

DIAGRAM ANSWER PLAN

Identify the issues	■ The legal issues here are ss. 18, 20, 47 of the Offences Against the Person Act 1861. ■ The defences are consent and self defence. *Mens rea* may be affected by intoxication.
Relevant law	■ Discuss the *actus reus/mens rea* of the offences, starting with the most serious.
Apply the law	■ Discuss which defences apply, taking care to explain each requirement. ■ *R v Barnes* criteria. ■ Duty to act.
Conclude	■ What is the effect of the defences? *Majewski* test.

SUGGESTED ANSWER

This question relates to non-fatal offences against the person and the defences of self-defence, intoxication, and consent. Turning first to incidents arising out of the karate session, Mike suffers a broken leg and loss of hearing as a result of the fall. The broken leg and loss of hearing could each be classified as 'grievous bodily harm' (**R v Saunders [1985] Crim LR 230**). This opens up the possibility of charges under **s. 18** and **s. 20** of the **Offences Against the Person Act 1861**.[1] Section 18 requires proof that Karen caused grievous bodily harm—but for her actions Mike would not have suffered the harm. Causation in law requires proof that the harm was a reasonably foreseeable consequence of her actions. The fact that Mike falls and hits his head etc. will not break the chain of causation. The *mens rea* for **s. 18** is intent. On the facts it may be difficult to establish that Karen intended to do grievous bodily harm, given the factor of intoxication. A charge under **s. 20 of the Offences Against the Person Act 1861** could be brought as an alternative. The harm required is either grievous bodily harm, or wounding. The injuries suggest that he has suffered a wound. On the basis of **C v Eisenhower [1984] QB 331** this

[1] Note that not all possible non-fatal offences have been included here. The best approach is to start with the level of harm, then go to the *actus reus* of the relevant offence.

requires proof of a rupture of the dermis and the epidermis. Under **s. 20** the grievous bodily harm must be inflicted and there does not seem to be a problem here in that regard. The *mens rea* under **s. 20** is satisfied by proof that Karen was reckless: see *R v Mowatt* [1968] **1 QB 421**.[2] Karen must at least have been aware of the possibility of causing some physical harm. She does not need to have foreseen the harm actually caused.

[2] The *mens rea* of these offences can be tricky—note that it is only an awareness of the possibility of some physical harm, not harm of the gravity described in the section.

Turning to consider the defences that Karen might raise in respect of the harm done to Mike, she may seek to rely on his consent to harm. On the basis of *R v Donovan* [1934] **2 KB 498**, a victim cannot validly consent to physical harm if it amounts to actual bodily harm or worse unless the activity comes within a range of policy-based exceptions. The issue would be whether or not karate classes come within this exception. Even if they do, a further issue would be the extent of the harm or risk of harm consented to by participants. What was accepted in one sport, such as the physical contact inevitable in martial arts, would not necessarily be covered by the defence of consent in another.

In *R v Barnes* [2004] **EWCA Crim 3246**, Lord Woolf CJ observed that if the defendant's actions are within the rules and practice of the game and do not go beyond it, that will be a firm indication that what has happened is not criminal. Karen is, on the facts, a more experienced martial arts exponent and it could be argued that Mike consented to a restricted range of risks—i.e. that he did not expect to be hit by her.[3] The key point will be whether or not her actions can be regarded as having been so obviously late or violent as not to be seen as an instinctive reaction, error, or misjudgement in the heat of the contest. On the facts it is submitted that Mike will probably be regarded as having validly consented to the risk of being hit.

[3] This is a good example of applying the law and building up an argument on the facts.

If the defence succeeds, Karen will have a complete defence to charges under **s. 18**, **s. 20**, and **s. 47** of the **Offences Against the Person Act 1861**.

[4] Note that intoxication is not, strictly speaking, a defence, but a denial of one element of the offence—namely, *mens rea*.

The alternative defence would be self-induced intoxication.[4] If Karen was merely drunk she has no defence as such—intoxication requires evidence that she was incapable of forming, and did not form, the necessary intent. On the basis of *DPP v Majewski* [1977] **AC 142**, her voluntary intoxication could be a defence to crimes of specific intent but not crimes of basic intent. Section 18 of the **Offences Against the Person Act 1861** is a specific intent crime because the *mens rea* goes beyond the *actus reus*.[5] If Karen was charged under **s. 18** and successfully pleads intoxication her liability will be reduced to the 'lesser included' offence of **s. 20 Offences Against the Person Act 1861**—a basic intent crime. Hence if she is charged under **s. 20** or **s. 47 Offences Against the Person Act 1861** or charged with common assault or battery she will not escape liability on the grounds

[5] The terms specific and basic intent refer to the type of *mens rea* inherent in the definition of the crime. Crimes which require intention to prove liability are, generally speaking, crimes of specific intent. Crimes which have an element of recklessness in their definition are usually crimes of basic intent.

of self-induced intoxication, as these are all basic intent crimes. She cannot claim that her consumption of the alcohol was anything other than reckless: see *R v Hardie* **[1984] 3 All ER 848**. Her liability will, therefore, be imposed on the basis that she was reckless in becoming intoxicated and recklessness is sufficient *mens rea* in respect of any one of the basic intent offences.

Karen may also have incurred liability in respect of the harm caused to Gaye. Psychological harm can amount to grievous bodily harm or actual bodily harm depending on its seriousness: see *R v Burstow; R v Ireland*.[6] The prosecution will have to produce medical evidence to show that the harm is not transient and minor. On the facts, bearing in mind the *mens rea* requirements outlined previously, a charge under **s. 47** of the **Offences Against the Person Act 1861** seems the most likely here.

Minor bruising and grazes would most likely constitute actual bodily harm contrary to **s. 47** of the **Offences Against the Person Act 1861**: see *R v Miller* **[1954] 2 QB 282**. Grazing would not amount to a wound unless the definition in *C v Eisenhower* was satisfied. As indicated earlier the *mens rea* for **s. 47** would be intention or subjective recklessness. Provided Karen intended to assault Gaye it does not matter that she might not have foreseen the actual bodily harm that actually transpired; see *R v Savage; R v Parmenter*.

Karen may raise the defence of self-defence in respect of Gaye. Karen is entitled to use reasonable force to protect herself. The question will be whether or not the force she used was reasonable in the circumstances; see **s. 76** of the **Criminal Justice and Immigration Act 2008**.[7] Karen cannot avail herself of the fact that she misjudged the amount of force required due to her being intoxicated.

As to Gaye's possible liability, she makes no physical contact with Karen, hence the only possible charge could be in relation to 'narrow' assault based on her threats. The problem for the prosecution would be in establishing that Karen actually apprehended any immediate physical harm. She may not have been perturbed by Gaye's threats. Gaye would need to have the *mens rea* for assault.

Gaye could rely on self-defence (i.e. reasonable force used in defence of another), on the basis that she was acting to protect Mike, but the court may be reluctant to permit this where the evidence is that she was the aggressor in the incident. Alternatively she could invoke the statutory defence under **s. 3** of the **Criminal Law Act 1967**— using reasonable force to prevent the commission of a criminal offence. Section 76 of the **2008 Act** applies equally to the common law and the statutory defence under **s. 3** of the **1967 Act** regarding how the court should approach the question of whether or not the force used was reasonable. Assuming Gaye did believe the facts were such as to warrant her acting in self-defence, **s. 76(7)** provides that the court dealing with the issue should have regard to the fact that she may not have been able to weigh to a nicety the exact measure of any necessary action; and that her evidence of having only done what she honestly and instinctively thought was necessary for a legitimate purpose constitutes strong evidence that only reasonable action was taken by her for that purpose.

In breaking Karen's teeth Mike may have caused actual bodily harm contrary to **s. 47** of the **Offences Against the Person Act 1861**. He appears to have caused the harm with the necessary *mens rea*—i.e. he was at least aware of the risk of harm: see *R v Savage; R v Parmenter*. The obvious defence would be self-defence at common law—considered previously. The issue to note here is that Mike is mistaken—there is in fact no need for him to defend himself. Following *Beckford v R* **[1987] 3 WLR 611,** and now **s. 76(3)** of the **2008 Act**, Mike will be judged on the facts as he honestly believed them to be—hence if he honestly believed he was about to be attacked again by Karen he could use force that would have been reasonable to defend himself in such circumstances. In conclusion, therefore, we may say that Karen can be convicted of **section 20, s. 47 Offences Against the Person Act 1861** and a common assault, and that she may use the defences of self-defence and consent. She may argue that intoxication has affected the *mens rea* of these offences, but is unlikely to succeed as these are offences of basic intent.

LOOKING FOR EXTRA MARKS?

- The way in which you deal with defences in a question like this will determine whether you gain a high mark—in issues such as intoxication and self-defence it is crucial to understand the rules, but then apply them properly to the facts. For example, in discussing intoxication, you will need to consider whether this is a crime of basic or specific intent—it would be easy to ignore this issue.

- The rules on specific and basic intent usually apply but better answers will refer to academic views on this issue, and the fact that the rules do not always hold true—see for example *Heard* [2008] QB 43, in which intentional touching on a sexual offence charge was held to be a crime of basic intent.

QUESTION | 2

Critically assess the position taken in English criminal law in respect of consent to the deliberate infliction of harm and participation in activities carrying a risk of serious harm.

CAUTION!

- As English criminal law is not codified, there is no statute that sets out the law's aims and functions, so it is necessary to consider case law, Law Commission reports, and the views of commentators. In this answer, attempt to cover all aspects of this issue, as the question is not simply an invitation to write all you know about *R v Brown* **[1993] 2 All ER 75**.

- Make sure you refer back to the question and offer some critical comment throughout.

DIAGRAM ANSWER PLAN

Start by discussing the general aims of the criminal law and the development of the defence of consent.

⬇

Discussion of the decision in *R v Brown*.

⬇

Discussion of Lord Templeman's rationale for his decision—especially the 'cult of violence' argument. Other cases which do not seem to be consistent with this argument.

⬇

A discussion of law and morality and the role of judges with respect to these—the balance between autonomy and the public interest.

⬇

R v Dica and informed consent. Discussion of the Law Commission's proposals.

⬇

Conclusion with reference to the question.

SUGGESTED ANSWER

There will never be complete agreement as to the correct aims and functions of the criminal law and, in the absence of a criminal code setting out a rationale containing fundamental principles, this issue will remain a topic of debate. This is especially true of acts inflicting violence. Questions can be raised on the role of the courts in matters of private morality. The defence of consent reveals several incongruities. Smith and Hogan refer to the lack of a strong moral foundation for this defence.

A successful plea of consent will provide a complete defence to a non-fatal offence. In addition to protecting the public from harmful activity, we also expect the criminal law to respect individual liberties and autonomy. It is this conflict between individual freedoms and collective interests which was one of the major issues in *R v Brown* [1993] 2 All ER 75.

[1] This case is key to an understanding of the public policy arguments surrounding the defence of consent.

In *Brown*, a group of middle-aged men willingly participated in sado-masochistic activities that involved the deliberate infliction of wounds.[1] The men were charged with various offences including assault occasioning actual bodily harm (**Offences Against the Person Act 1861, s. 47**) and malicious wounding (**Offences Against the Person Act 1861, s. 20**) and pleaded guilty when the trial judge ruled against their defence of consent. The Court of Appeal upheld their conviction but certified the following point of law of general public importance: 'Where A wounds or assaults B occasioning him actual bodily harm in the course of a sado-masochistic encounter, does the prosecution have to prove lack of consent on the part of B before they can establish A's guilt under **s. 20** or **s. 47 of the Offences Against the Person Act 1861**?'. The House of Lords answered this question in the negative and dismissed the appeal. Lord Templeman, who gave the majority judgment, decided the issue using a mixture of precedent and public policy. He stated that consent is not a general defence where actual bodily harm or wounding has been caused. There are exceptions to this rule, and violence intentionally inflicted will not be a criminal offence if it occurs in the course of a lawful activity, such as contact sports, surgical operations, rough horseplay, or tattooing.

The question for the House therefore was whether or not sado-masochistic behaviour as occurred in *Brown* could be regarded as positively beneficial, or as falling within the domain of private activities that were of no concern to the state provided vulnerable persons were not being exploited.

Lord Templeman concluded that the criminal law had to provide sufficient safeguards against exploitation and corruption of others, particularly those who are young; weak in body or mind; inexperienced; or in a state of special physical, official, or economic dependence. He referred to three reasons leading to the conclusion that sado-masochistic behaviour was not in the public interest:

a   It glorified the cult of violence ('pleasure derived from the infliction of pain is an evil thing').

b   It increased the risk of AIDS and the spread of other sexually transmitted diseases.

c   It could lead to the corruption of youth.

Lord Templeman concluded: 'I am not prepared to invent a defence of consent for sado-masochistic encounters which breed and glorify cruelty and result in offences under **s. 47** and **s. 20 of the Act of 1861.**'

The minority (Lords Mustill and Slynn) interpreted the relevant cases (*R v Coney* (1882) 8 QBD 534; *R v Donovan* [1934] 2 KB 498; and *Attorney-General's Reference (No 6 of 1980)* [1981] QB 715) and the public interest requirements differently.[2] Lord Mustill decided that the decks were clear for the House to tackle completely anew the question of whether the public interest required **s. 47** to be interpreted as penalising the conduct in question.

In relating the majority decision to aims and functions, many questions arise. First, in ascertaining public interest, how far should the Law Lords take into account society's morals? This involves reference to the Hart–Devlin debate (see Lord Devlin, *The Enforcement of Morals*) as to whether conduct should be criminalised simply because it is a moral wrong, and whether the criminal law should simply reflect society's moral standards or try to improve them. This is virtually impossible to answer briefly, but it is submitted that if it is not morally right to encourage deliberate injury through sado-masochistic activity, the majority decision does not conflict with this objective.[3] If the majority had not declared it unlawful, their decision could have been interpreted as condoning or even encouraging such activities.

[3] You can put forward personal opinions in an essay, but try to link them to a legal issue. If your opinion is logically developed from analysis, you may get some credit for originality of approach.

Secondly, was the House of Lords' decision in *Brown* creating new law, or was it giving effect to the will of Parliament expressed in the **1861 Act**? The application of the defence of consent is probably correct as there has traditionally been a reluctance to extend its boundaries, partially because of the difficulties in deciding whether consent was freely given by a victim capable of understanding the nature of the act.

Thirdly, was this a situation where respect for individual freedom should have been outweighed by the need to protect society from such conduct? The participants were middle-aged men who were in control of the activities, but the Law Lords considered that because of the risk of future, younger, inexperienced participants, the accused's individual liberty had to be sacrificed. The confusion in this area was compounded by the Court of Appeal in *R v Wilson* [1996] 3 WLR 125, where the defendant had his conviction for actual bodily harm contrary to **s. 47** of the **1861 Act** quashed. He had agreed to his wife's request that he should brand his initials on her buttocks with a hot knife. The court took the view that the husband's activities could be regarded as coming within the tattooing exception, and that, in any event, as explained by Russell LJ:

it is not in the public interest that activities such as the appellant's in this appeal should amount to criminal behaviour. Consensual activity between husband and wife, in the privacy of the matrimonial home, is not, in our judgement, normally a proper matter for criminal investigation, let alone criminal prosecution.

In *Wilson*, therefore, individual autonomy overrode the public morality argument, whereas in *Brown*, the deciding factor was protection of the public. Both decisions were based to some extent on the concept of public policy.

The law distinguishes between situations where a victim consents to inevitable and deliberate harm, and those where the victim consents to the risk of harm. As outlined earlier, consent to inevitable harm can only operate as a defence within certain limits dictated by public policy. Hence deliberate harm of a minor nature can be incurred without criminal liability as this falls within the permissible scope of individual autonomy. More serious deliberate harm may be permitted if it is in the course of justifiable surgical interference. Many other activities, however, carry only the risk of harm, for example engagement in sports, or dangerous exhibitions, such as where a member of the audience volunteers to stand in front of a knife thrower's target as part of a show. The audience member is not consenting to being stabbed; indeed it is doubtful any such consent would be recognised as valid. What he or she is consenting to is the risk of harm, as the stunt cannot be conducted without some risk.

It follows that if consent to risk of harm is to be a more general defence than consent to inevitable harm, issues will arise as to the extent to which the victim's consent has to be fully informed. In *R v Konzani* [2005] EWCA Crim 706, the Court of Appeal held that the doctrine of informed consent should form part of the criminal law, hence the fact that a woman consented to sexual intercourse with a man, unaware that he was HIV+, did not mean that she consented to the risk that she might herself become HIV+.

[4]If you can give practical examples illustrating your point, you will clarify your arguments.

Applying this to the knife thrower example earlier in this section, the volunteer from the audience assumes the knife thrower is a professional who can perform the stunt without causing harm. If in fact the knife thrower is an amateur who has never successfully performed the stunt it would be difficult to argue that the volunteer had genuinely consented to the risk of harm, should the stunt go wrong.[4] Were the knife thrower to reveal this fact before asking for a volunteer, then anyone volunteering would do so with the necessary knowledge, although this might still throw up the question of whether any adult should be permitted to run such risks just for the sake of public entertainment.

As Lord Woolf CJ explained in *R v Barnes* [2004] EWCA Crim 3246, participants in sports certainly consent to the risk of quite serious harm—the more competitive the sport and the more it involves physical contact, the higher the level of risk. Rugby union is probably a good example of this. Players can suffer horrific injuries resulting in permanent paralysis but it does not mean a criminal prosecution must follow. Such injuries are a foreseeable risk arising from participation, even where they result from action that is in breach of the rules. What players do not consent to is the risk of deliberate harm being caused outside the normal run of play—such incidents can and have led to criminal prosecutions as the defence of consent does not extend that far.

[5]Do try to sum up your arguments and make direct reference to the question set.

In conclusion it can be said that the contours of the defence of consent, whether to the deliberate infliction of harm or the risk of harm being caused, are tolerably clear.[5] Where the law gets into difficulties, and runs the risk of looking both ridiculous and partial, is where it strays from a utilitarian approach based on 'greater good' and attempts to moralise on what consenting adults should do in private.

LOOKING FOR EXTRA MARKS?

■ Where you are attempting an essay type question that requires you to adopt a position be prepared to put your own views forward provided they are logically developed from your analysis. You are more likely to get credit for some originality of approach. For example, there have been two very detailed Law Commission reports on this subject—reference to these shows that you have read more widely than the leading case.

QUESTION | 3

Femi is driving his car through central London. At a point where the road narrows from two lanes down to one, a car driven by Roy cuts in front of Femi's car. Femi is infuriated. As the traffic is at a standstill Femi gets out of his car, pulls open Roy's car door, and shouts abuse at him. Roy is very frightened by this. Louise, a passenger in Roy's car, gets out to remonstrate with Femi, whereupon Femi head-butts her. Louise is wearing steel-rimmed glasses and, as a result of this attack, both she and Femi suffer deep cuts to their foreheads, the frame of the glasses having caused the lacerations. Chiquitta, an elderly woman, sees this disturbance and tries to intervene. Femi pushes her away, causing Chiquitta to lose her balance and fall heavily. Chiquitta suffers a fractured hip and receives hospital treatment for several months afterwards. Louise becomes increasingly ill in the weeks following the attack, and tests reveal that she has become HIV+. Subsequent tests prove that she contracted the condition from Femi who, it transpires, is a drug addict. As a result of sharing needles, he became HIV+ some months prior to his attack on Louise.

Advise the Crown Prosecution Service as to the criminal liability of Femi.

CAUTION!

■ Although you are told that Femi is a drug addict there is no evidence that he acts under the influence of drugs at the time of the assaults outlined in the question. In a question such as this, therefore, you should not consider the defence of intoxication in any depth.

■ Distinguish carefully between the *actus reus* and the *mens rea* of these different offences.

◯ DIAGRAM ANSWER PLAN

Identify the issues	■ Offences Against the Person and common law assault. ■ The issue of psychological harm.
Relevant law	■ **Sections 18 and s. 20 of the Offences Against the Person** **Act 1861**, paying particular attention to *mens rea*. Femi's attack on Roy.
Apply the law	■ Louise becoming HIV+—liability for grievous bodily harm.
Conclude	■ Conclusion on these facts.

SUGGESTED ANSWER

[1] It is immaterial that no physical contact has been made.

The facts state that Femi shouted abuse at Roy, frightening him. Femi may have incurred liability for common assault. The *actus reus* requires proof that Roy apprehended immediate physical violence.[1] The events will be viewed from the perspective of the victim, not the reasonable person: see *Smith v Chief Supt Woking Police Station* (1983) 76 Cr App R 234. It is possible to commit a 'narrow' assault by words alone. The authority for this is the House of Lords' decision in *R v Burstow; R v Ireland* [1998] AC 147. Overturning earlier decisions such as *R v Meade & Belt* (1823) 1 Lew CC 184, Lord Steyn described the proposition that a gesture may amount to an assault but that words can never suffice as unrealistic and indefensible. The *mens rea* for assault is intention to cause the victim to apprehend immediate physical harm, or recklessness as to whether the victim apprehends such harm: see *R v Savage; R v Parmenter* [1992] **1 AC 699**. The recklessness is subjective—Femi must at least be aware of the risk that Roy will fear immediate physical violence. It is submitted that Femi could be guilty of common assault on these facts and should be charged under **s. 39** of the **Criminal Justice Act 1988**; see further *DPP v Little; DPP v Taylor* [1992] **1 QB 645**.[2]

[2]Make sure you draw a mini conclusion after each point has been established.

Reference to Roy being very frightened raises the possibility that Roy may have suffered some psychological harm as a result of the abuse from Femi. Both *R v Chan-Fook* [1994] **2 All ER 552** and *R v Burstow; R v Ireland*, make it clear that psychological disturbance can amount to actual bodily harm, or even grievous bodily harm, provided there is medical evidence to substantiate this. Merely being upset will not suffice. As Lord Steyn explained, in *R v Burstow; R v Ireland*: '. . . neuroses must be distinguished from simple states of fear, or problems in coping with everyday life. Where the line is to be drawn must be a matter of psychiatric judgment.' If Roy's fright amounts to actual bodily harm Femi could be charged under **s. 47** of the **Offences Against the Person Act 1861** with assault occasioning actual bodily harm. The assault is apparent, as explained earlier. It would be for the prosecution to establish that this assault caused the actual bodily harm. The *mens rea* would be as for common assault—outlined earlier. It is not necessary to prove that Femi foresaw the risk of actual bodily harm: see further *R v Savage; R v Parmenter*.[3]

[3]This *mens rea* issue is quite subtle and must be explained carefully.

Femi then head-butts Louise, causing her to suffer deep cuts to her forehead because of the contact with the frame of her glasses. The harm done could amount to grievous bodily harm if the lacerations are categorised as 'serious harm': see *R v Saunders* [1985] **Crim LR 230**. Femi could therefore be charged with an offence under **s. 18** of the **Offences Against the Person Act 1861**. The difficulty with a **s. 18** charge would be proof of the necessary intent. Did Femi intend grievous bodily harm? The prosecution would have to prove that it was either his purpose to do some grievous bodily harm, or that in attacking Louise he foresaw such harm as at least virtually certain—thus permitting a jury to infer intent, as per *R v Woollin* [1998] **4 All ER 103**.

The more likely charge is under **s. 20** of the **Offences Against the Person Act 1861**. The lacerations would clearly amount to 'wounding'—see *C v Eisenhower* [1983] **3 WLR 537**. There has been a break in the surface of the skin.[4] The *mens rea* requires proof that Femi acted maliciously. On the basis of *R v Mowatt* [1967] **3 All ER 47**, the prosecution must prove that Femi foresaw that some physical harm to some person, albeit of a minor character, might result

[4]Apply the law to the facts. Here, do not confuse 'wounding' with grievous bodily harm.

from his actions. This direction was subsequently endorsed by the House of Lords in *R v Savage; R v Parmenter* **[1992] 1 AC 699.** On the facts there appears to be little doubt that the *mens rea* for **s. 20** will be established. There is overwhelming evidence that Femi foresaw at least some physical harm being caused to Louise. The fact that he may not have foreseen lacerations being caused by contact with the frame of her glasses is neither here nor there.[5]

[5] Again, a proper explanation of the difficult *mens rea* issue.

It should be noted that, if the lacerations are seen as amounting to grievous bodily harm, as discussed earlier, Femi might also be guilty of maliciously inflicting grievous bodily harm contrary to **s. 20** of the 1861 Act. Femi could also be charged with criminal damage in relation to the spectacles worn by Louise, provided he was aware of the risk that property might be damaged: see the decision of the House of Lords in *R v G* **[2003] 4 All ER 765,** where a subjective approach to establishing recklessness was confirmed as being correct.

Can Femi incur further liability in respect of Louise becoming HIV+? The condition itself would undoubtedly amount to grievous bodily harm—see previously. The most straightforward charge would be under **s. 18** of the **1861 Act.** The prosecution would have to prove that Femi caused grievous bodily harm (evident) and intended to do so. The complication would be the *mens rea.* There is no evidence that Femi knew he was HIV+, although it might be tempting to infer this from his having shared needles.[6]

[6] This issue has been discussed in *R v Dica* and *R v Konzani.*

As an alternative the prosecution might consider liability under **s. 23** of the **Offences Against the Person Act 1861. Section 23** requires proof that Femi unlawfully and maliciously administered to Louise any poison or other destructive or noxious thing, so as thereby to endanger her life, or inflict grievous bodily harm on her. It is submitted that the term 'administration' is liberally interpreted. The AIDS virus could be the 'noxious substance'. Causing Louise to become HIV+ would amount to endangering her life. Again the problem would be whether or not Femi was aware of his condition. If not there could be difficulties in establishing that he foresaw the risk of the harm specified in **s. 23,** assuming the courts apply *R v Mowatt.*

✚ LOOKING FOR EXTRA MARKS?

- With regard to the contraction of HIV, a discussion of *R v Dica* **[2004]** and *R v Konzani* **[2005] EWCA Crim 706** on informed consent will add value to your discussion here.

- Note that you need some knowledge of the poisoning offences as well as the GBH/ABH offences.

Ahmed, a builder, throws a small piece of concrete out of a third floor window. It narrowly misses Janet, an elderly lady who is walking in the busy street below. She manages to dodge out of the way but it falls into a pushchair. The baby, Annabel, needs treatment for minor bruises. Dave, who works opposite, sees what has happened and goes into the building with Janet to complain. He sees Ahmed and says he will 'sort him out'. Ahmed is not threatened by this, and tells Dave to mind his own business. He throws a cardboard box over towards Dave. It misses Dave but hits Janet on the shoulder. She is bruised and faints from the shock. Unknown to Ahmed, Janet has a heart condition. Dave grabs Ahmed by the shoulders and flings him on the floor. He then spits at him. Ahmed slips and falls down a lift shaft and suffers a broken arm.

In his spare time, Dave plays amateur rugby. During a friendly match, he tackles Ollie, who badly bruises his face when he falls over due to the tackle. As the tackle was illegal, the referee gives the point to Ollie's team. At the end of the match, Dave whispers to Ollie that they will get him back. Ollie reaches into his pocket for his phone. Thinking he is reaching for a weapon, Dave lunges at him, catching his ring on Ollie's face. Ollie is badly cut. That evening, Ahmed receives a text message from Dave insulting Ahmed's religion. Ahmed starts feeling very emotional and is scared to go to work as a result of receiving this message.

When she returns home, Janet suffers heart palpitations and spends several weeks in hospital. She is traumatised by the events and is unable to sleep. She is receiving treatment from her doctor. There is medical evidence to show that Dave had been drinking heavily before he played the rugby match that day.

Discuss the criminal liability of Ahmed and Dave for the non-fatal offences contained in this question.

CAUTION!

- Make sure you deal with one defendant at a time, even if chronologically other defendants appear first.

- Be careful with the *mens rea* of the statutory assaults—remember that with the *mens rea* of **s. 47** and **s. 20**, the defendant does not have to intend or be reckless as to the full *actus reus*.

DIAGRAM ANSWER PLAN

Identify the issues	■ Indirect battery, **s. 47**, **s. 20**, self-defence, consent.
Relevant law	■ A discussion of the direct/indirect rule, an explanation of the *mens rea* in these offences, the parameters of self-defence and consent, psychiatric harm as part of the definition of actual bodily harm, causation.
Apply the law	■ Actual bodily harm satisfied as medically treated, *mens rea*, consent outside the rules of the game (*R v Barnes*, *R v Donovan*). *Mens rea* of s. 47 and s. 20 (*R v Mowatt*).
Conclude	■ Conclusion on the **Offences Against the Person Act** offences committed and their relevant defences.

 SUGGESTED ANSWER

A number of non-fatal offences have been committed in this scenario. Ahmed may have committed a common law battery when he throws the concrete out of the window. It hits Annabel, the baby, who sustains minor bruises.[1] A battery is defined as an application of unlawful force to the victim (***Collins v Wilcock* [1984] 3 All ER 374**). It is committed if the defendant intentionally or recklessly inflicts that harm. It can be committed directly or indirectly, so the fact that it was not directed at anyone in particular may not matter. It may be argued by the defence that Ahmed did not hit Annabel (or anyone) directly. This will not matter as the battery can be carried out via an object. In ***Fagan* [1968] 3 All ER 442**, the defendant committed a battery by placing his car on the victim's foot and leaving it there. The question, regarding *mens rea*, will be whether Ahmed was reckless when he threw the concrete. Given that it is a busy street, we can say that Ahmed was aware of the possibility of harm.[2]

When he throws the cardboard box towards Dave, and it hits Janet instead, he has again committed an indirect battery. In ***Haystead v CC of Derbyshire* [2000] 3 All ER 890**, the accused hit a woman who was holding a baby, causing her to drop the baby. In this instance, the battery may be extended to a charge under **s. 47 of the Offences Against the Person Act 1861**. This provides:

[1] In questions on offences against the person, start with the harm caused. This will lead you to the correct offence.

[2] Recklessness, as always in the criminal law, must be assessed subjectively (*R v G* [2004] 1 AC 1034).

whosoever shall be convicted upon an indictment of any assault occasioning actual bodily harm shall be guilty of an offence.

Actual bodily harm has been defined as 'any hurt or injury which is calculated to interfere with the health or comfort of the victim' (*R v Donovan* [1934] 2 KB 498). Fainting and bruising clearly falls into this category.[3] She also suffers heart palpitations and has to spend time in hospital, and is receiving treatment for sleeplessness. Furthermore, the sleeplessness, for which Janet is receiving treatment from her doctor, may fall into the category of psychiatric harm. In *R v Ireland* [1998] AC 147 the House of Lords held that psychological injuries could be included in the definition of actual bodily harm, but only if they were medically recognised conditions. Mere fear, panic, or distress would not be included (*R v Chan-Fook* [1994] 1 WLR 689). Janet's sleeplessness would appear to fall into this category.[4]

Section 47 of the Act requires that the defendant 'occasions' the actual bodily harm. This means causation. Ahmed may argue that he did not cause this result and did not know of her condition. These conditions all fall into this category. The thin skull rule will apply here—Ahmed must take Janet as he finds her, meaning that any peculiarities, whether these be physical or social attributes, make no difference to his liability for her injuries—*R v Blaue* [1975] 1 WLR 11.[5] The prosecution will have to show that the result, i.e. the sleeplessness, was a direct cause of the events in question.

Ahmed may try to argue that he did not intend to hurt anyone by throwing a cardboard box. However, the *mens rea* for this section is an intention or recklessness as to the initial assault or battery, not as to the resulting harm. As he probably intended at least a battery when he threw the box, he will be guilty of an offence under this section.

Dave's threat to Ahmed to 'sort him out' will probably not be a common assault, as Ahmed is not threatened by it. An assault is defined as an act which causes the victim to apprehend imminent unlawful force. When he spits at him, however, he has committed a battery. A battery requires proof of unlawful physical force, but not apprehension. As this action appears to be intentional, it satisfies the requirements of this common law offence. When Dave flings Ahmed on the floor, causing him to fall down the lift shaft, he has committed a **s. 20** offence, at least. Section 20 provides that where a defendant intentionally or recklessly wounds or unlawfully inflicts grievous bodily harm, he is guilty of this offence.

A broken arm can be interpreted as grievous bodily harm[6] which is 'really serious' harm—see *DPP v Smith* [1961] AC 290. Deliberately flinging him on the floor may be proof of an intent to cause this and therefore proof of a **s. 18** offence, but this may be more difficult to prove. Dave may not have anticipated that flinging Dave on the floor

---

[3] Make sure you explain exactly which injury is actual bodily harm.

[4] This is quite a fine point so make sure you explain how this works in this scenario (it does so because Janet is being treated by her doctor).

[5] You don't need to quote verbatim from the case. Note how the *ratio* of the case has been applied to the facts here.

[6] Note that in the *actus reus* of **s. 20** you need to choose between wounding and grievous bodily harm.

would result in him sustaining a broken arm, but this will be irrelevant as long as he was aware of the possibility of his sustaining at least some physical harm (*R v Savage*; *R v Parmenter* [1992] 1 AC 699.[7] Dave need not have *mens rea* in respect of the actual injury caused.

[7] *Mens rea* is a subtle point here so make sure it is explained well.

Dave's offences towards Ollie will be considered next.

In terms of the tackle, he may have committed an offence under **s. 47** of the **Offences Against the Person Act 1861**. The tackle is a common law battery, which is defined as the application of unlawful physical force. The bad bruising on Ollie's face was occasioned or caused by Dave's actions. Bruising interferes with Ollie's health or comfort and therefore may fall into the category of actual bodily harm—*R v Donovan* [1934] 2 KB 498. The *mens rea* is simply that Dave intended to cause the initial assault or battery—this is evident in this context.

Dave may want to argue that the common law defence of consent applies because Ollie has agreed to play rugby. In principle, a victim cannot consent, validly, to physical harm if it amounts to actual bodily harm or worse unless the activity comes within a policy based exception. Sports are such an exception. In *R v Barnes* [2004] **EWCA Crim 3246**, Lord Woolf CJ observed that if the defendant's actions are within the rules and practice of the game and do not go beyond it, that will be an indication that what has happened was not criminal. Here, the tackle was illegal, so the defence may not be valid.

The cut to Ollie's face is a wound. A wound consists of the breaking of both layers of the skin—see *C v Eisenhower* (1984) 78 Cr App R 48. This could be a **s. 18** or a **s. 20** offence—depending on the *mens rea*. Dave may not have anticipated that he would wound Ollie, perhaps intending only to cause a battery. However, he may be reckless as to the causing of at least some harm. The *mens rea* for **s. 20** requires that the defendant foresees the possibility of some physical harm[8]—see *R v Mowatt* [1968] in which Lord Diplock said the following:

[8] Be careful with the *mens rea* requirement for this offence. It is not necessary that the defendant intended the full gravity of the statutory definition.

it is quite unnecessary that he accused should have foreseen that his unlawful act might cause physical harm of the gravity described in the section i.e. a wound or other physical injury. It is enough that he should have foreseen that some physical harm to some person, albeit of a minor character, might result.

It would appear that **s. 20** is the more appropriate charge.

Dave may try to argue that he is acting in self-defence and that he made a genuine mistake when Ollie reached in his pocket for his mobile phone. Section 76 of the **Criminal Justice and Immigration Act 2008** can apply here.[9] The force used by Dave must be reasonable. This is to be decided according to the facts as the defendant believed them to be. This is a subjective test. In *Williams (Gladstone)* [1987]

[9] The common law is now entrenched in the Act.

3 All ER 411, the defendant thought he had witnessed an assault by a police officer—D then assaulted the officer. An honest mistake will mean that the defendant is judged on the facts as he saw them. This is supported in **s. 76 (4)(b)** which states that as long as the defendant genuinely held that belief, he is entitled to rely on it if it is mistaken, as long as the mistake was a reasonable one to have made.

However, the court may see this differently as Dave has been drinking. For reasons of public policy, the availability of the defence may be restricted. **Section 76(5)** provides that **s. 76(4)** does not entitle the defendant to rely on any mistaken belief attributable to intoxication. In these circumstances it is unlikely that Dave will be able to benefit from this defence and will be charged as explained earlier.[10]

[10] It is useful to have a conclusion on the likely offence to be charged.

The text message containing a racial slur can be an assault occasioning actual bodily harm. The difficulty may be in establishing whether Ahmed's reluctance to go out is 'actual bodily harm' for the purposes of the legislation. In *R v Chan Fook* **[1994] 2 All ER 552**, mere emotional distress was not enough to constitute actual bodily harm. The prosecution will have to show that Ahmed apprehended an imminent use of force. Since we do not know what the message says we cannot say for certain that it did; however it stops Ahmed from going to work and we know that he is frightened. This may be sufficient. Whether this is an assault or an assault occasioning actual bodily harm, the racial element must be considered. Under the provisions of the **Crime and Disorder Act 1998**, a person who commits an assault or battery or an offence under **s. 47** or **s. 20** of the **Offences Against the Person Act 1861**, where that offence is racially or religiously motivated, may receive a more severe penalty for the commission of the offence.

LOOKING FOR EXTRA MARKS?

- Note that a battery can take many forms—direct and indirect.
- The religious and/or racial aggravation point can be easily missed. This is a procedural issue—but an important one nonetheless as it will have an impact on sentencing.

QUESTION | 5

The Offences Against the Person Act 1861 is unfit for purpose and in desperate need of reform.

Discuss this statement in relation to the statutory assaults.

CAUTION!

- The question directs you to a discussion of the statutory assaults, therefore you should not consider the common law.
- This is a typical essay question in which you are asked to evaluate the law. You should try to come to a conclusion on whether you agree or disagree with the statement. In other words, do not write everything you know about the area, but try to focus on the need for reform.

DIAGRAM ANSWER PLAN

Brief explanation of the areas to be covered: the statutory assaults in the **Offences Against the Person Act 1861**.

▼

Problems of statutory interpretation.

▼

Problems in outcome and sentencing.

▼

Proposals for reform.

▼

Conclusion.

A SUGGESTED ANSWER

The **Offences Against the Person Act 1861** covers, *inter alia*, the statutory assaults of actual bodily harm, grievous bodily harm, and grievous bodily harm with intent. It also covers the administration of a noxious substance. **Section 47** builds on the definitions of assault and battery in the common law and creates an offence of an assault (or battery) occasioning actual bodily harm. **Section 20** is malicious wounding or inflicting grievous bodily harm, and **s. 18** is intentional wounding or causing grievous bodily harm. This essay will focus on these areas and identify areas which are in need of reform. It will evaluate the need for this reform, and consider specific proposals.[1]

[1]Start by setting out the parameters of the relevant law, and explaining the scope of the essay.

One of the problems with any legislation is that the courts do not always interpret the meaning of words as Parliament intended. This is true of the **1861 Act**, whose language can be described as archaic. Modern interpretations of the concepts are sometimes contradictory.

[2] In a problematic area of law, it is a good idea to include some academic commentary.

Professor Ashworth has referred to the Act as being 'expressed in language which is difficult to convey to juries'.[2] Jonathan Herring holds that 'it is remarkable that the law on assaults is based on an Act which is 150 years old'. The courts have often had to stretch the meaning of the statutory language to fit the demands of modern society. It can be argued as a direct consequence of this interpretation, that the meaning of the statute is too widely interpreted. For example, it now includes the concept of 'biological grievous bodily harm'. Terms such as 'wounding' cover a broad range of circumstances, from a minor cut to a serious wound. This dates from a time when wounding was very serious, and could be life threatening, so it was important to reflect this in the seriousness of offences. The terms 'inflict', 'cause', and 'occasion' in **ss. 20, 18,** and **47** respectively seem to have the same meaning. After the decisions in *R v Burstow* **[1998] AC 147** and *R v Dica* **[2004] EWCA Crim 1103**, it can be confirmed that

[3] *R v Clarence* overruled *R v Dica* on this point.

these mean the same thing. The case of *Clarence* **(1888) 22 QBD 23** had established that inflict had a narrower meaning than cause and a direct assault was required.[3] There is a need for statutory clarification on this point.

The language is confusing, nonetheless. These different words to describe causation have caused the courts problems and lead to confusion. On the other hand, it can be said that these terms are justifiable. The inclusion of the word 'wound' is important due to the number of injuries caused by knife wounds, for instance, and the means by which the wound is caused (in **s. 20** with or without any weapon or instrument, and in **s. 18** 'by any means whatsoever') seems indistinguishable in these two sections.

The meaning of actual bodily harm and of grievous bodily harm has been extended, through case law, to include the meaning of psy-

[4] In a discursive essay like this, there will be more than one point of view. Acknowledge this by explaining the contrast.

chiatric harm. This was probably not envisaged by the legislators. On the one hand this may be seen as a reason for reform of the original legislation and a justifiable need in modern society; on the other that judges have gone beyond the meaning of the language in the statute.[4] This is a constitutional argument of whether judges, in interpreting legislation, are acting outside their powers. Meanwhile, certain meanings such as assault, which have a very specific meaning at common law, are not defined in the Act at all.

Furthermore, it can be argued that the definition of **s. 47** should not require proof of a battery or an assault, but proof of actual bodily harm.

Some of these interpretations are criticised on the grounds that they can be unfair to defendants.

[5] Arguably, this extends the scope of the Act and of this area of law.

The inclusion of 'biological grievous bodily harm' might mean that defendants can be convicted of a serious criminal offence for not being aware of their own sexual health, for example.[5] This is because the **s. 20** offence can be proven on the basis of recklessness, not intention. In *R v Dica* **[2004] QB 1257**, the defendant, knowing he was HIV+, had consensual sex with two women who were subsequently found to have the disease. He was charged with offences under **s. 20** on the basis that he had recklessly transmitted the disease to the women when they were unaware. Whilst this undoubtedly solved an issue of interpretation in the Act (consent to sex is not of itself to be regarded as consent to the risk of disease), it means that a defendant who does not intentionally transmit such a disease is guilty of an offence.

Stalking is now criminalised in s2A and s4A of the **Protections from Harassment Act 2007** as amended by the **Protection of Freedoms Act 2012**.

The sentencing of the offences under **ss. 20, 18,** and **47** of the Act is not logical. Section 20 has a much more serious *actus reus* (that of wounding or causing grievous bodily harm), and requires that the defendant foresaw actual harm, rather than a mere assault or battery). They both have the same maximum sentences, however. This appears to be contrary to the central importance given to *mens rea* in the criminal justice system and to proportionality (the punishment should fit the crime).[6]

[6] Often, public policy considerations play a role in the development of the law—you should acknowledge this in this type of essay.

The disparity in *mens rea* in certain sections of the Act is a further problematic issue. It might be argued that in **ss. 20** and **47** the defendant can be found guilty of an offence even where he did not have the *mens rea* for the full offence. It may be regarded as wrong to consider a defendant guilty of a criminal offence when he did not have the *mens rea* for committing that offence. In other words, if the defendant did not foresee the *actus reus* of the crime, he should not be found guilty of it.[7] *Mens rea* has central importance elsewhere in the criminal law. This is a point made by Ashworth. John Gardner disagrees with this contention, on the grounds that this 'correspondence' principle has never been a central tenet of English law. It is important that every *actus reus* is accompanied by *mens rea*, but it does not have to be of equivalent gravity:

[7] This is one of the most controversial aspects of the legislation (and the one which students find most difficult!). Make sure you express it clearly.

> the guilty act must therefore be attended by a guilty mind in line with 'actus non facit reum nisi mens rea'. What need not be attended by any mens rea are the consequences and circumstances, the risk of which one bears because one committed the original crime.

Proposed reforms were laid out in The Criminal Law Revision Committee's *Legislating the Criminal Code: Offences Against the Person and General Principles* and followed by a draft bill by the government, modelled on the 1993 report.

This bill set out a much more coherent structure of offences. In particular, it deals with the correspondence principle set out earlier, and recognises that a person ought only to be found guilty of an offence which he intended. The language has been substantially improved. Herring describes the language used in the bill as 'simple and readily comprehensible'. In November 2015, the Law Commission published a consultation paper recommending that these proposals be enacted. It also recommends the enactment of an offence of threats to kill and aggravated assaults. Although there are some differences in these two sets of recommendations, it is submitted that to enact these proposals would deal with many of the issues of clarity and unfairness on which the current law can be criticised.[8]

[8]A comment on your analysis of any proposals for reform is a good way to end the essay.

LOOKING FOR EXTRA MARKS?

- Try to give specific examples of unclear wording in the Act.
- Providing your own commentary on possible reform is likely to impress the examiner, as it will provide evidence that you have not only gone beyond the basic law, but have really thought about the issues raised.

TAKING THINGS FURTHER

- Bamforth, N., 'Sado-masochism and Consent' [1994] Crim LR 661.
  *This article suggests that sado-masochism and violence do not need to be equated as they were in the majority judgment in **R v Brown**.*

- Home Office Consultation Paper (1998) Violence: Reforming the Offences Against the Person Act 1861, London, Home Office
  Proposes more rational scheme of offences concentrating on the anomalies in mens rea.

- Law Commission Scoping Consultation Paper No. 217 (2014)
  This paper identifies incomplete and unresolved areas of the law on non-fatal offences and invites submissions for final consultation. It proposes adoption of the Home Office proposals.

- Loveless, J. and Derry, C., 'R v Dica [2004]' 38 (3) International Journal of Legal Education 'The Law Teacher' 287.
  This article discusses the problems of consent and recklessness in the offence of 'biological' grievous bodily harm.

- Murphy, P., 'Flogging Live Complainants and Dead Horses; We May No Longer Need to Be in Bondage to Brown' [2011] Crim LR 758.
  *Along with Bamforth's article (earlier), this article suggests that opinion may be shifting away from the majority view in **R v Brown**.*

■ Weait, M., 'Knowledge, Autonomy and Consent: R v Konzani' [2005] Crim LR 763.

This article examines the case law and the role of the criminal law in regulating the transmission of sexually transmitted diseases.

Online Resource Centre   www.oxfordtextbooks.co.uk/orc/qanda/

Go online for extra essay and problem questions, a glossary of key terms, online versions of all the answer plans and audio commentary on how selected ones were put together, and a range of podcasts which include advice on exam and coursework technique and advice for other assessment methods.

Sexual Offences

5

In order to answer questions on this topic, you will need an understanding of the following:

● the effect of the **Sexual Offences Act 2003, ss. 1–3** including the effect of the evidential provisions as to consent under **ss. 75** and **s. 76**

● the concept of reasonable belief under the **Sexual Offences Act 2003**

● the distinction between consent and submission

● the definition of consent under **s. 74**

● an outline knowledge of other sexual offences, including those involving children

KEY DEBATES

Debate; reform of sexual offences

Sexual offences have been the subject of a major overhaul. Convictions for these crimes have historically been very low. The **Sexual Offences Act 2003** sought to remedy this situation. In doing so, it created a new definition of rape, and shifted the responsibility for obtaining consent to the defendant in certain circumstances. It also created new offences including sexual assault and assault by penetration, recognising that these attacks can be just as traumatic for a victim as rape. Some problems remain, however, including the degree to which a victim may be said to have consented where she is intoxicated. Furthermore, putting the onus of obtaining consent on to the defendant raises wider issues of the presumption of innocence and the importance of the burden of proof in a criminal trial.

Joe, Tim, and Mike go out one night intending to meet some girls and have sexual intercourse. They meet Sue, Helen, and Jane in a local wine bar. Tim tells Jane that he is the famous footballer, Tim Jenkins, whom Jane has always admired. He tells her that he wants to start a relationship with her, and will take her to see him play. None of this is true. After two hours, the women decide to go home but invite the men back to their house for a cup of tea. Tim and Jane go into her room and have sexual intercourse. Joe and Helen started kissing on the sofa while Mike and Sue were chatting in the kitchen. While Helen was not looking, Joe slipped a sedative into her tea. Helen became very drowsy and Joe carried her into the bedroom, where he had sex with her. Sue walked back into the lounge and saw a packet of pills on the table. She guessed what had happened and told Mike to leave. Mike refused and told Sue she had better not start or she would get what was coming to her. He took a knife from his pocket and placed it on the sideboard. Sue was extremely frightened and allowed Mike to have sex with her. After the men had left, Sue called the police. Joe and Mike said that they had honestly believed that the girls had consented to sex. Jane discovers that she has contracted herpes, a sexually transmitted disease.

Discuss the liability of Joe, Tim, and Mike under s. 1 of the Sexual Offences Act 2003.

CAUTION!

- Do not be tempted to allow your own views of the defendant's behaviour interfere with your legal advice.
- When dealing with the evidential presumption under **s. 75**, remember that it does not necessarily mean that the victim has or has not consented.

DIAGRAM ANSWER PLAN

Identify the issues	■ Identify the legal issues—rape (section **s. 1** of the **Sexual Offences Act 2003**), submission and consent *R v Olugboja* and **s. 74**. ■ Evidential presumptions as to consent under **ss. 75 (2)(a)** and the conclusive presumption in **s. 76**. ■ **s. 20** of the **Offences Against the Person Act 1861**—reckless transmission of a sexually transmitted disease.
Relevant law	■ Start with the AR and MR—the sexual intercourse, the meaning of consent and the defendant's belief in consent. Then explain the AR and MR of the offence of reckless GBH under s. 20 OAPA 1861. The concept of reckless transmission in *R v Dica*.
Apply the law	■ The meaning of recklessness in the context of biological grievous bodily harm. ■ The court's presumptions as to consent.
Conclude	■ What offences are they guilty of? Conclude.

SUGGESTED ANSWER

This question raises issues of the offence of rape, including the evidential presumptions as to consent in the **Sexual Offences Act 2003** and the reckless infliction of grievous bodily harm under **s. 20** of the **Offences Against the Person Act 1861**.

With regard to Joe, the crime here is rape. Under **s. 1(1)** of the **Sexual Offences Act 2003**, rape is committed when a person (A) intentionally penetrates the vagina, anus, or mouth of another person with his penis, B does not consent to the penetration, and A does not reasonably believe that B consents. The problem question here is clear that sexual intercourse has taken place, therefore the key fact in issue is that of consent.

Sexual intercourse has taken place here, so the *actus reus* element is satisfied. In terms of the *mens rea* for the offence of rape the prosecution must show that the defendant intended to have sexual intercourse and that he did not reasonably believe that the victim was consenting. In other words, where the defendant claims he believed that the victim was consenting, if such a belief is proved to be unreasonable, the jury should convict. This is the case even where the belief is held honestly.[1] In deciding whether the defendant's belief was unreasonable, the jury should have regard to all the circumstances, including any steps the defendant could reasonably have been expected to take to ascertain whether the victim consented (**s. 1(2)** of the **Sexual Offences Act 2003**). This provision places an onus on the defendant to ascertain whether or not there is consent in situations where there might be doubt. In certain carefully defined circumstances, the Act provides for certain evidential presumptions to be raised against consent. These include a situation where the victim may be in fear and a situation in which the victim is not acting in full capacity due to ingesting a substance. If it is proved that the defendant did the relevant act and one of the circumstances existed at the time it will be presumed that the complainant did not consent to the act, and the defendant did not reasonably believe that the complainant consented unless the defendant adduces sufficient evidence to raise an issue to the contrary.

Section 76 allows the court to presume, conclusively, that consent was not valid in circumstances of fraud.

The prosecution needs to prove the absence of consent beyond reasonable doubt as part of the *actus reus* of the offence. The Act contains the definition of consent in **s. 74**: 'a person consents if he agrees by choice, and has the freedom and capacity to make that choice'. The section makes it clear that one will not be consenting unless there is agreement by choice, freely entered into, by a person with capacity. In *R v Bree* the issue of capacity was raised in terms of a complainant's ability to give consent under the influence of alcohol. The key question here was whether the complainant had the capacity to decide whether to engage in sexual activity.

Helen's capacity may well be diminished by alcohol, but the facts do not elaborate on this. The better approach for the prosecution here would be to consider the evidential presumption in **s. 75**.[2] **Section 75** states that if the *actus reus* of the act is proven and that one of the specified circumstances applies then the complainant is to be taken not to have consented to the relevant act unless sufficient evidence is adduced to raise an issue as to whether he consented, and the defendant is to be taken not to have reasonably believed that the complainant consented unless sufficient evidence is adduced to raise an issue as to whether he reasonably believed it. Furthermore, **s. 75(2)(f)** states that one of these circumstances is as follows:

> any person had administered to or caused to be taken by the complainant, without the complainant's consent, a substance which, having regard to when it was administered or taken, was capable of causing or enabling the complainant to be stupefied or overpowered at the time of the relevant act.

[1] The **Sexual Offences Act** reverses the previous common law position—see *DPP v Morgan* on this point—on the concept of reasonable belief.

[2] Note—**ss. 75** and **76** work alongside **s. 1** to enable the prosecution to show that in certain circumstances, the defendant could not have believed in consent.

Joe slips a sedative into Helen's drink and then proceeds to have sexual intercourse with her. It can safely be said therefore that if Helen drank the tea with the sedative in it, the court will presume that Helen was not able to give her consent in these circumstances. It will be difficult for Joe to adduce any evidence to the contrary, and he has, therefore, committed both the *actus reus* and *mens rea* of rape.

Mike's threat to Sue, followed by sexual intercourse which appears to be consensual, will be examined next. The *actus reus* is satisfied, and again the key issue here is whether the consent given by Sue can be said to be valid. If it is not, Mike will also be guilty of rape. In relation to consent, it can be said that Sue has not truly consented, but instead has submitted to sexual intercourse. The common law tenet that there is a clear distinction between consent and submission as reviewed in *R v Olugboja* (1982) is now an integral component of **s. 74**.[3] Dunn LJ *obiter* stated that the jury should be directed to concentrate on the state of mind of the victim having regard to all the relevant circumstances.

Alternatively, the court will presume, again under **s. 75**, that consent was not obtained, as the victim was in fear. **Section 75(2)(a)** states a rebuttable presumption applies in circumstance in which the following circumstances apply:

any person was, at the time of the relevant act or immediately before it began, using violence against the complainant or causing the complainant to fear that immediate violence would be used against him.

The fact that Sue is very frightened by the threats made to her by Mike suggests that this presumption could be raised. Furthermore, as Mike places a knife on the sideboard, the threat of violence is clear. The court will therefore presume that no consent was obtained in these circumstances.

The fact that the boys' claim that they thought they had obtained consent will fail due to the provisions above. Furthermore, the old defence of 'honest mistake' or the 'young man's defence' is eradicated in the new Act. Under the pre-**Sexual Offences Act 2003** law, ***DPP v Morgan*** [1975] 2 All ER 347 would have required Joe and Mike to be judged on the facts as they honestly believed them to be.[4] Under the 2003 Act the onus instead is on the men to obtain the girls' consent.

They may want to argue that they were intoxicated and therefore unable to form the sufficient *mens rea* for rape and that they were so drunk that they mistakenly, but reasonably, had a belief in consent. This is highly unlikely to succeed as Joe gave Helen a sedative and also went out for the night with the intention of having sexual

[3] The old distinction between submission and consent, therefore, is no longer tenable.

[4] This was the case even if it was unreasonable to make this mistake. The decision was heavily criticised, and the idea of reasonable belief now effectively entrenches this reversal into statute.

intercourse: neither of these facts appear to support a case that he was even concerned with Helen's consent.

[5] Effectively, rape is a crime of negligence, so it cannot be said to be a crime of specific intent.

Although it is still uncertain, it is likely that rape will be classified as a crime of basic intent.[5] Following *DPP v Majewski*, the defendant was not able to argue that his attack on a police officer lacked sufficient *mens rea* because of intoxication. The House of Lords held that the defendant's recklessness in taking drugs rendered his behaviour uncontrolled and unpredictable and was in itself a sufficient substitute for the *mens rea* of the offence. Likewise, Joe's voluntary consumption of alcohol, even if excessive, is unlikely to succeed as a defence or negate a charge of rape.

Tim may also be guilty of rape under **s. 1** of the **Sexual Offences Act 2003**. Sexual intercourse, again, has taken place so the question will be whether the consent given by Jane is valid consent. Tim has lied to Jane about his intentions. The presumption under **s. 76** will be brought into play here as the prosecution seeks to establish that Tim did not reasonably believe in Jane's consent. Under **s. 76** the jury will be entitled to presume (and Tim will not be able to rebut this) that Jane was not consenting if the prosecution can prove that, in order to have sexual intercourse with her, he intentionally deceived her as to the nature or purpose of what he was doing, or that he induced her to have sexual intercourse by impersonating a person known personally to her. As Jane does not know the footballer personally, the latter is unlikely. It is also unlikely that Jane is deceived as to the purpose or nature of the activity.

LOOKING FOR EXTRA MARKS?

- Sexual offences questions require advanced fact management skills—do ensure you relate each fact to the particular part of the provision.
- Some facts may be left deliberately open—concentrate on how certain issues will be put to the jury.

QUESTION | 2

Discuss the extent to which the **Sexual Offences Act 2003** is an improvement on previous law.

CAUTION!

- As with all essays, ensure you add some value through critical comment and reference to the question.

- Do not become drawn into discussion of social issues. The conviction rate was an important driver for the changes in the law, but you should concentrate on legal definitions and analysis within the **Sexual Offences Act**.

 DIAGRAM ANSWER PLAN

> Outline the current law in the **Sexual Offences Act 2003** and the legislation it was designed to replace. Consider the Law Commission's proposals for reform.

▼

> Widenng of the scope of the *actus reus* of rape.

▼

> The meaning of consent and issues. **Sections 75 and 76.** The previous common law. Consent and submission.

▼

> Intoxciation and consent. Fraud as to the nature and purpose of the Act.

▼

> Conclusion on the uncertainties described above.

 SUGGESTED ANSWER

The **Sexual Offences Act 2003** was enacted in response to the well-known problems of obtaining convictions for rape and sexual assault.

[1]Reference to the background to the legislation demonstrates that you can put the law in context and have researched the problems.

It was the result of a review and subsequent consultation paper by the Home Office (Setting the Boundaries: Reforming the Law on Sexual Offences vol 1, 2000; and Protecting the Public, Cm 5668, 2002).[1] In these reports the previous law on rape was described as inconsistent and piecemeal. This essay will attempt to evaluate to what extent the **2003 Act** has been successful in replacing it.[2]

[2]Explain what you intend to achieve.

The Act swept away the **Sexual Offences Act 1956** to create, *inter alia*, a revised offence of rape, and new offences of sexual assault and assault by penetration. A revised approach to consent in relation to sexual offences was also introduced.

In relation to rape, a new definition was created. The offence of rape is defined in **s. 1** of the **Sexual Offences Act 2003**:

[3] Provide a brief definition of the law in question.

A person commits rape if (a) he intentionally penetrates the vagina, anus or mouth of another person (B) with his penis, (b) B does not consent to the penetration, and (c) B does not reasonably believe that B consents.[3]

Thus, the physical definition of rape has changed to include other parts of the body.

Section 1 of the Sexual Offences Act has widened the scope of rape beyond sexual intercourse to include penile penetration of other body orifices on the grounds that such penetration is as degrading, demeaning, and damaging as sexual intercourse (HO, Setting the Boundaries 2000). Sexual intercourse was also a concept which implied completion of the act, whereas case law, such as *R v Katamaiki* **[1985] AC 147**, had held that it was a continuing act and that consent could be withdrawn at any time before completion. This is, indeed, now specifically recognised by **s. 79(2)** of the **Sexual Offences Act 2003** which states that penetration is a continuing act from entry to withdrawal.

In relation to *mens rea*, the key issue is consent and the standard of reasonable belief. Consent is further defined in **s. 74** of the Act. This provides the following definition: 'a person consents of he agrees by choice, and has the freedom and capacity to make that choice'.

It is important to note that the offence requires that the complainant agrees and the onus is on the defendant to ascertain that agreement. Consent embraces consent to both the nature and purpose of the act. One of the reasons for defining consent in such terms was to draw a distinction between consent and submission (*R v Olugboja* **(1981) 73 Cr App R 344**).[4]

[4] This shows the relationship between the new legislation and the previous common law.

The concept of submission and consent has also been improved by the Act. The law was previously covered in the common law by the case of *R v Olugboja*, in which the judge had directed the jury that although the complainant had not struggled, and no threats had been made to her, it was open to the jury to consider that she had submitted rather than consented to the intercourse. Dunn LJ stated that full regard was to be had to the state of mind prior to the act. Furthermore, a full direction was required:

they should be directed that consent or the absence of it is to be given its ordinary meaning, and if need be, by way of example that there is a difference between consent and submission: every consent involves a submission, but it by no means follows that a mere submission involves consent.

The last *mens rea* requirement is that the defendant must reasonably believe that A consents. This is an objective test. However, Temkin and

Ashworth argue that the contextualisation of requiring the defendant to ascertain consent has the effect of watering down the objective nature of the test.

Furthermore, in certain circumstances the court will presume that the defendant has not obtained consent. This presumption can be rebutted in certain circumstances, but not in others. Thus, **s. 75** proscribes certain circumstances in which lack of consent will be presumed, provided the act of sexual intercourse has taken place.[5] These circumstances include putting the complainant in fear, where the complainant has a physical or mental disability, or where the victim has become stupefied due to the administration of a substance. The Act also provides an irrebuttable presumption whereby the court will conclusively find that there has been no consent (**s. 76**). This provision applies in circumstances of fraud, such as intentional impersonation and inducement.

These provisions replace the common law rules with regard to fraudulent consent. One example of this is the decision in *R v Williams* **[1923] 1 KB 340** in which a singing teacher told the victim that he needed to make an air passage to assist in her breathing and to help her to sing better.[6]

A further change which the **Sexual Offences Act 2003** has made to the previous law is the impact on the decision in *DPP v Morgan* **[1975] 2 All ER 347**. This controversial decision required the defendant to be judged on the facts as he believed them to be. The requirement in the **2003 Act** for the defendant to ascertain whether the victim has consented effectively removes this decision. The concept of reasonable belief has not been extensively interpreted by the courts. However, the decision in *R v Whitta* **[2006] EWCA Crim 2626** seems to suggest that the provision may be interpreted quite widely.

One of the difficulties arising from the Act is that of the intoxicated victim.[7] In *R v Bree* **[2007] EWCA Crim 256**, the Court of Appeal observed that if, through drink, a complainant in a rape case temporarily loses her capacity to choose whether or not to have intercourse, she is not consenting. On the other hand, if she has voluntarily consumed even substantial quantities of alcohol, but nevertheless remains capable of choosing whether or not to have intercourse, and in drink agrees to do so, the defendant would not be guilty of rape. Hence it will be a fine question of fact for the jury.

It has been suggested that far from improving the conviction rate, the Act will instead lead to a large number of appeals due to its definitional complexity (HL Debs, Col 860, 13 February 2003).

It could be argued that placing the onus on the defendant to effectively prove that consent was obtained unfairly removes the presumption of innocence from the defendant in the criminal trial.

[5] Ensure that you understand how an evidential presumption works. In the case of **s. 75**, it is rebuttable—meaning that the defendant can raise evidence against it. **Section 76** provides for an irrebuttable presumption, which is conclusive (no argument can be brought in rebuttal).

[6] Another example of the entrenchment of the common law.

[7] The key issue here is that of capacity.

[8] Conclude by summarising the arguments.

In conclusion, whilst the **Sexual Offences Act 2003** has sought to provide clarity in the law it may have made the law more difficult for juries to understand, thereby increasing the risk of appeals. It might be argued that placing the onus of proof on the defendant in a criminal trial shifts the burden of proof from the prosecution to the defence, thereby undermining the presumption of innocence.[8]

Lastly, whilst the law has entrenched some common law decisions into statute, and has reversed the effect of some problematic areas such as **DPP v Morgan**, the problem of the intoxicated victim is not dealt with in the Act.

LOOKING FOR EXTRA MARKS?

■ A discussion of the issue of submission and consent and the issue of intoxication will demonstrate that you have thought critically about this legislation and its effectiveness.

QUESTION | 3

Answer both parts (a) and (b).

(a) Steve is having a coffee with his friends Dave and Barry. They discuss women's attitudes to sex and Dave expresses the view that all women really mean 'yes' when they say 'no' to sexual intercourse. Steve invites Dave and Barry back to his house where Linda, Steve's wife, is asleep. Steve tells Barry that Linda loves to have sex with men other than her husband, but also likes to pretend that she is being raped. Steve reassures Barry that any resistance on the part of Linda will be part of her 'play-acting'. Dave visits the bathroom and, in error, enters the bedroom where Linda is asleep in bed. He goes into her bedroom and starts to have sexual intercourse with Linda who is still asleep. On waking, Linda tries to fight Dave off but he continues to have sex with her.

Linda runs downstairs in distress. Barry takes this as his cue to have sexual intercourse with her on the sofa in the living room. Linda begs Barry to leave her alone but he persists. Steve stands by watching the events unfold.

Discuss the criminal liability of Dave and Barry.

(b) One evening Rory walks past Lizzie's house and notices that the front door is not fully closed. He pushes the door open and has a look around inside the house. He discovers Lizzie asleep in her bed. Without waking Lizzie he pulls her bedclothes aside and raises her nightclothes enabling him to see her naked body.

The next day Rory, seeking to impress, tells his friend Kasra how he went out on a blind date the previous evening with Lizzie. He tells Kasra that the evening culminated in them having sexual intercourse at her house. Rory concludes by telling Kasra that Lizzie is 'always dead keen for it'.

The following day Kasra visits Lizzie's house posing as a double-glazing salesman. Lizzie agrees to let Kasra in so that he can give her an estimate. Whilst they are in her bedroom Kasra suggests that she might like to have sex with him there and then. Lizzie is shocked and frightened but she remains calm, suggesting that Kasra gets himself ready whilst she visits the bathroom. Lizzie leaves the bedroom intending to call the police. Kasra, encouraged by her response, runs after Lizzie and, pushing her onto the hallway floor, proceeds to have sexual intercourse with her, despite her protestations that he should stop. Once Kasra leaves, Lizzie calls the police.

Advise the Crown Prosecution Service as to the criminal liability of Rory and Kasra. Do not consider Rory's liability as an accomplice to Kasra, or any potential liability Rory may have under Part 2 of the Serious Crime Act 2007.

CAUTION!

- Do not be tempted to allow your own views of the defendant's behaviour interfere with your legal advice.

- Note the rubric to part (a) does not require consideration of Steve's liability, hence the answer does not cover issues relating to his accessorial liability. Similarly there is an injunction against considering Roy's accessorial liability in part (b). Examiners will attach such limitation where necessary to keep the candidate's task within reasonable bounds, given the time constraints imposed by the examination format, or the word limits imposed on coursework.

DIAGRAM ANSWER PLAN

Identify the issues	■ The issues raised by this question are the offences in **sections 1, 3,** and **4 Sexual Offences Act 2003**. *Actus reus* of rape. ■ *Mens rea* of rape—consent. ■ Sections 3 & 4 of the **Sexual Offences Act 2003**. ■ Evidential presumptions as to consent under **ss. 75(2)(a)** and **s. 76**.
Relevant law	■ Outline the relevant law: statutory, general principles, and case law, in particular the evidential provisions as to consent and the concept of reasonable belief. ■ Trespass with intent to commit a sexual offence
Apply the law	■ Application of the law to the facts. Does **s. 75** raise evidential presumptions? How will they apply?
Conclude	■ What offences are they guilty of?

SUGGESTED ANSWER

Part (a)

On the given facts it is likely that Dave would be convicted of rape contrary to **s. 1** of the **Sexual Offences Act 2003**. In terms of *actus reus* the prosecution would first have to prove that Dave had penetrated the vagina, anus, or mouth of another person with his penis.[1] The fact that he started to have sexual intercourse with Linda would appear to satisfy this. The prosecution would have to establish that, at some time during the penetration, Dave had the necessary *mens rea*. The second element of *actus reus* to be established is that Linda did not consent to the penetration. The issue of consent is now governed by the rather complex provisions of **ss. 74–76** of the **2003 Act**.

Under **s. 76** the jury will be entitled to conclusively presume[2] that Linda was not consenting if the prosecution can prove that, in order to have sexual intercourse with Linda, he intentionally deceived her as to the nature or purpose of what he was doing, or that he induced her to consent to sexual intercourse by impersonating a person known personally to her. There is no evidence to support either assertion.

[1] Begin by identifying the issues and setting out the relevant law—here, in relation to *actus reus*.

[2] No argument can be brought in rebuttal.

[3] This presumption is rebuttable—
if the defendant can raise evidence
that, in fact, the victim consented to
the relevant act, the *mens rea* may
not be made out.

The prosecution may be able to rely on **s. 75**, which goes on to establish certain presumptions as to consent.[3] Where the defendant has:

(i) committed the *actus reus* of rape and;

(ii) the complainant was asleep at the time of the penetration,

(iii) the defendant knew that this was the case

the complainant will be taken not to have consented to the sexual intercourse unless sufficient evidence is adduced to raise an issue as to whether the complainant consented. This effectively places Dave under a burden to provide evidence that Linda was consenting even though she was asleep—on the facts there would appear to be no such evidence.

[4] In other words, the court would revert to the main part of **s. 1**.

In the event that the absence of consent cannot be resolved by reliance on **s. 75**, **s. 74** provides that a person consents if she agrees by choice, and has the freedom and capacity to make that choice.[4] A person who is asleep does not have the capacity to make decisions.

Turning to *mens rea*, Dave's penetration of Linda is clearly intentional, hence the only live issue will be as to whether or not he reasonably believed that Linda was consenting.

Under **s. 75** of the **2003 Act** the jury can *presume* that Dave did not reasonably believe that Linda consented to the relevant act, unless sufficient evidence is adduced by Dave to raise an issue as to whether he reasonably believed Linda was consenting. If **s. 75** does not lead the jury to a conclusion that Dave had the necessary *mens rea*, they would be directed that, in any event, **s. 1(2)** of the **2003 Act** provides that whether or not a belief is reasonable is to be determined having regard to all the circumstances, including any steps the defendant took to ascertain whether the complainant was consenting. There is no evidence of Dave having taken such steps, hence he will be guilty of raping Linda.

Barry's situation is very similar, except that Linda was clearly conscious at the time of the sexual intercourse. Again the prosecution would have to prove that Barry penetrated the vagina, anus, or mouth of Linda with his penis, and that at the time she was not consenting. Given that the preconditions for the application of **s. 76** of the **2003 Act** are not apparent on the facts, the starting point again is **s. 75**. Under **s. 75**, if it can be proved that:

(i) Barry had sexual intercourse with Linda;

(ii) Barry was, immediately before the sexual intercourse, using violence against Linda, or causing her to fear that immediate violence would be used against her; and

(iii) Barry knew that those circumstances existed,

Linda will be presumed not to have consented to the sexual intercourse unless sufficient evidence is adduced to raise an issue as to

[5] This is, of course, an objective test.

whether she consented. The problem here for the prosecution is the absence of any direct evidence that Barry used force on Linda, although if she did not want sexual intercourse with him it may be implied that he would have had to physically overpower her for this to have happened.[5] If **s. 75** cannot be relied upon to establish the absence of consent, the prosecution will turn to **s. 74** which provides that Linda consents if she agrees to the sexual intercourse by choice, and has the freedom and capacity to make that choice. The facts indicate that there was no free choice on her part.

As outlined earlier in relation to Dave's liability, the absence of any reasonable belief by Barry as to whether or not Linda was consenting could be resolved under **s. 75** if it can be shown that, immediately before the sexual intercourse, Barry was using violence against Linda, or causing her to fear that immediate violence would be used against her; and he knew that those circumstances existed. If **s. 75**

[6] Ensure that you answer the question directly by analysing the facts of the problem set.

does not, of itself, dispose of the *mens rea* issue, the issue of whether Barry's belief in Linda's consent was reasonable is to be determined having regard to all the circumstances,[6] including any steps Barry took to ascertain whether the complainant was consenting. Under the pre-**Sexual Offences Act 2003** law, *DPP v Morgan*

[7] This position is now reversed by the Act, and included in the concept of reasonable belief.

[1975] 2 All ER 347 would have required Barry to be judged on the facts as he honestly believed them to be.[7] Hence he could have relied on Steve's assurances as to Linda's consent. Under the 2003 Act the onus instead is on Barry to obtain Linda's consent. On the one hand

[8] You can incorporate prosecution and defence arguments into your discussion in this way.

Barry will contend that he acted on Steve's reassurances. On the other hand the prosecution will argue that the **2003 Act** requires the jury to have regard to the steps taken by Barry to ask Linda if she was consenting.[8] The test is now objective, but the reassurances by Steve may be seen as making Barry's assumptions as to consent reasonable.

Part (b)

When Rory enters Lizzie's house he does so as a trespasser as he has no permission to be there. Where he subsequently pulls her bedclothes aside and raises her nightclothes to see her naked body, he probably does commit an offence contrary to **s. 4** of the **Sexual Offences Act 2003**—causing a person to engage in sexual activity without consent. The prosecution would have to prove that the activity was 'sexual' in nature. For these purposes 'sexual activity' is defined by

[9] Define each element of the definition.

s. 78 as penetration, touching or any other activity that, whatever its circumstances or any person's purpose in relation to it, a reasonable person would consider of a sexual nature.[9] Alternatively it can be penetration, touching, or any other activity that, because of its nature, may be sexual and, because of its circumstances or the purpose of any person in relation to it (or both), is sexual. The test is clearly objective, although the court can take into account the defendant's purpose.

That Lizzie was not consenting to the activity is presumed from the fact that she was asleep and the fact that Rory was aware of this. In terms of *mens rea*, Rory's actions are intentional in lifting the nightclothes. There is no need to prove that he was aware that the actions were sexual. Given the facts there appears to be no basis on which he could argue that he reasonably believed Lizzie to be consenting.

The facts also raise the possibility of a charge of sexual assault contrary to **s. 3** of the **2003 Act**. This provides that a person commits an offence if he intentionally touches another person, the touching is sexual, the complainant does not consent to the touching, and the defendant does not reasonably believe that the complainant consents. There is no evidence that Rory actually touches Lizzie, although he may have done so 'through' her nightclothes. Note that in *R v H* **[2005] All ER (D) 16 (Feb)**, it was held that where a person was wearing clothing, touching of that clothing constituted 'touching' for the purposes of the offence contrary to **s. 3** of the **2003 Act**. If this technicality can be overcome, a **s. 3** charge is possible.[10]

[10]Note that you need to deal with each issue specified in the Act. Here the term 'touching' is construed quite widely.

Assuming the *actus reus* is made out, the prosecution must prove the absence of any reasonable belief that the victim was consenting. Again regard would be had to **s. 75(2(d)** of the 2003 Act—as Lizzie was asleep the jury would be able to presume that there was no reasonable belief on Rory's part that she was consenting. Beyond **s. 75**, whether Rory's belief in Lizzie's consent is reasonable is to be determined having regard to all the circumstances, including any steps he took to ascertain whether she was consenting. On the facts the *mens rea* seems evident.

Does Kasra commit rape when he has sexual intercourse with Lizzie? The facts make it quite clear that the *actus reus* of the offence under **s. 1** of the **2003 Act** is made out. Kasra commits the act of penile penetration in respect of Lizzie and she was not consenting. If necessary resort could be had to **s. 75** of the **2003 Act**:

(i) Kasra had sexual intercourse with Lizzie;

(ii) Kasra was, immediately before the sexual intercourse, using violence against Lizzie, or causing her to fear that immediate violence would be used against her; and

(iii) Kasra knew that those circumstances existed.

On this basis the jury could presume Lizzie was not consenting unless Kasra can raise evidence to rebut the assumption.

[11]See the discussion earlier on *DPP v Morgan*.

The problem area for the prosecution will be *mens rea*. Kasra will contend that he honestly believed Lizzie was consenting.[11] The absence of any reasonable belief on the part of Kasra as to whether or not Lizzie was consenting could be resolved under **s. 75** if it can be shown that Kasra was using violence against Lizzie and he knew that those circumstances existed. Kasra will rely upon the fact that he did ask Lizzie if she would like to have sex. As a ploy to buy time to telephone the police she gave him the impression that she would be willing. All of this is evidence that Kasra will rely on to contend that a reasonable person would have thought Lizzie was consenting, and that he checked to make sure that she was.

LOOKING FOR EXTRA MARKS?

■ Proper fact management and careful application of the statutory provisions will help you here. In particular, don't forget that the common law adds to concepts such as 'touching'.

■ Don't forget to explain the effect of the presumptions.

QUESTION | 4

Jake, an artist, is a member of a cult which has persuaded him that women always want sex and that when they say 'no' they really mean 'yes'. The cult's mission is to encourage its members to 'give sexual pleasure to women'. Jake decides that to be faithful to the cult's mission he should have sex with Anna, his long-standing friend. Anna has always made it clear that they will never be more than good friends, but Jake now believes that she does not mean this. He goes to her bedroom where she is asleep. He climbs into bed and has sexual intercourse with her. She only vaguely recalls this incident the next morning.

The following week Jake meets Fiona in a bar. While they are chatting she tells him that she suffers from migraine headaches. Jake tells her that he is a faith healer with mystical powers and can cure such headaches through the medium of sexual contact. Fiona is doubtful but thinks it is worth a try and they go to her house where they have sexual intercourse.

Jake is then invited to the cult leader's house for dinner, where he meets Debbie, the leader's 16-year-old daughter. Jake and Debbie go out into the garden for a walk and, when out of view of the house, Jake asks Debbie to perform oral sex on him. Debbie does not want to, but has been taught by her father never to deny a man sexual pleasure and so she agrees to Jake's request.

Assess the criminal liability, if any, of Jake.

CAUTION!

■ Do not allow your own personal view of the offences lead you to a certain conclusion— stick to the law.

■ The structure of the sexual offences can be quite tricky. Deal with the questions in the usual way, explaining *actus reus*, then *mens rea*. *Mens rea* is based on reasonable belief, which is an objective test.

DIAGRAM ANSWER PLAN

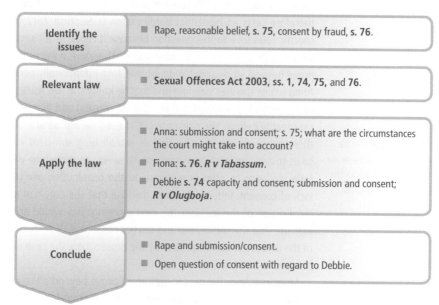

Identify the issues	■ Rape, reasonable belief, **s. 75**, consent by fraud, **s. 76**.
Relevant law	■ Sexual Offences Act 2003, ss. **1**, **74**, **75**, and **76**.
Apply the law	■ Anna: submission and consent; **s. 75**; what are the circumstances the court might take into account? ■ Fiona: **s. 76**. *R v Tabassum*. ■ Debbie **s. 74** capacity and consent; submission and consent; *R v Olugboja*.
Conclude	■ Rape and submission/consent. ■ Open question of consent with regard to Debbie.

SUGGESTED ANSWER

[1] Set out all the requirements for the *actus reus*, but focus on the fact in issue.

[2] The Sexual Offences Act encapsulates much of the previous common law, therefore it is a good idea to refer to it.

Jake has sexual intercourse with Anna. The central issue on the facts, however, is the question of consent.[1] In order to satisfy the *actus reus* of rape the prosecution must prove beyond all reasonable doubt that the complainant did not consent to penile penetration. Some assistance is provided in the Sexual Offences Act as to the legal definition of consent. Section 74 states that: 'a person consents if he agrees by choice, and has the freedom and capacity to make that choice'. The purpose of defining consent in such terms was to draw a distinction between consent and submission (*R v Olugboja* [1982] QB 320).[2] Therefore, a person will not consent to penetration unless there was agreement to the act, with the freedom to consent or refuse and the capacity to make such a choice. Previous common law cases stated that it was not necessary for the complainant to dissent. Therefore, sexual intercourse with a sleeping woman could never be construed as consensual on the sole basis that she had not dissented. The prosecution must prove lack of consent. In order to provide some clarification for juries, **s. 75(2)(a)–(f)** set out six circumstances in which an evidential presumption regarding consent will arise. If the facts of a case fall within any of these circumstances, it will be presumed that the complainant did not consent to penetration and that D did not reasonably believe in consent unless he can adduce sufficient evidence to raise an issue as to both consent and reasonable belief. **Section 75** therefore casts an evidential burden upon D. **Section 75(2)(d)** is of specific relevance to this question because it concerns a complainant who is 'asleep or otherwise unconscious'. Therefore, if the prosecution prove beyond all reasonable doubt that Jake intentionally penetrated Anna whilst she was sleeping and that he knew she was asleep, it will be evidentially presumed that she did not consent and that he did not reasonably believe she consented. However, he will be able to rebut these presumptions by adducing or establishing sufficient evidence so as to raise an issue as to consent.[3] It seems as though he will have little evidence to offer in response to the prosecution allegation of lack of consent. Indeed, the facts disclose that she only had a vague recollection of the incident the next morning. This would appear to indicate that she was asleep and did not consent. If these two aspects of the *actus reus* can be proved by the prosecution, the case will then proceed to *mens rea*.

Mens rea: here the prosecution must prove beyond all reasonable doubt that the penetration was intentional and that Jake did not reasonably believe in consent. Proof of the former is rarely a problem and would seem to be irrefutable here. The latter is by far the more difficult aspect of *mens rea*. Whereas the former law on rape required intention or recklessness as to lack of consent on D's part, the new law requires a straightforward lack of reasonable belief. This is an objective test but **s. 1(2)** provides that: 'whether a belief is reasonable is to be determined having regard to all the circumstances, including any steps A (D) has taken to ascertain whether B consents'. The test is therefore objective but also takes into account 'all the circumstances' and efforts D has made to obtain the complainant's consent. The circumstances are that Jake and Anna have been long-standing good friends and that Anna has not previously indicated that she would consent to sexual relations with Jake.[4] If one accepts the question at face value, and Anna is asleep when Jake penetrates her, having taken no steps to ascertain her consent, the jury should decide in the light of all the facts and circumstances that Jake could not reasonably believe that Anna was consenting. However, the jury will also need to take into account Jake's committed belief that all women who say 'no' to sex really mean 'yes' and that this was the result of cult membership the mission of which is to 'give sexual pleasure to women'. There can be no doubt that this is an unreasonable belief on his part and is unlikely to alter the jury's view that he lacked a reasonable belief in consent. If he should choose to defend himself on the basis of a mistaken belief in consent, his mistake needs to be both honest and

[3] **Section 75** is an evidential presumption. This means that the defendant can bring evidence to the contrary. This is not the case for the conclusive presumption in **s. 76**.

[4] Be sure that you consider the circumstances in the problem.

[5]Prior to this, the defendant could make an honest mistake, even if it was unreasonable.

reasonable. This is a reversal of the *Morgan* test of honest mistaken belief previously applying to sexual offences.[5] Clearly, he has not made a reasonable mistake in relation to Anna's consent.

Jake's offence against Fiona: again, the relevant offence is rape as defined in **s. 1(1)** of the **Sexual Offences Act 2003** set out earlier. Given that sexual intercourse has again taken place, it is clear that the prosecution will be able to prove beyond all reasonable doubt the *actus reus* element of penetration and the *mens rea* element that penetration was intentional. The *actus reus* issue which arises here is that of consent and whether Fiona's consent has been induced by fraud.

It might appear that Fiona has consented to sexual intercourse with Jake and that no offence has been committed. However, looking at the consent provisions in **ss. 74–76** of the **Sexual Offences Act 2003**, it can be seen that the prosecution may be able to prove a lack of consent on her part by reference to **s. 76** which concerns consent induced by fraud. **Section 76** states that if it is proved that D did the relevant act (i.e. performed intentional penetration) and that any of the circumstances specified in subsection (2) existed, it is to be conclusively presumed that: (a) the complainant did not consent to the relevant act; and (b) that D did not believe that the complainant consented to the relevant act. If successful, the prosecution will prove that any consent given by Fiona to the physical act of intercourse was undermined by Jake's fraud and was therefore ineffec-

[6]The defendant has no opportunity to bring extra evidence in these circumstances.

tive. It will be conclusively presumed that the complainant did not consent and that he knew this to be so.[6] He will therefore be guilty of rape. The subsection (2) circumstances are that: (a) D intentionally deceived the complainant as to the nature or purpose of the relevant act; and (b) that D intentionally induced the complainant to consent to the relevant act by impersonating a person known personally to the complainant. It does not appear from the facts as though (b) applies because although Jake has assumed what must be presumed to be false attributes or qualifications, he has not impersonated any-

[7]Again, this is an example of the common law being entrenched in statute.

one that Fiona knows. This part of **s. 76** is aimed at impersonation of a husband or boyfriend (*R v Elbekkay* **[1995] Crim LR 163**).[7] However, by professing mystical healing powers and the ability to cure headaches by sexual contact, Jake may fall foul of **s. 76(2)(a)**: fraud as to nature or purpose. Previous common law cases indicate that by 'nature', **s. 76** is aimed at fraud as to the 'sexual' nature of the act. Fraud as to the nature of the act means deceiving the victim as to the sexual nature of the act; see *R v Clarence* **(1888) 22 QBD 23** and *R v Flattery* **(1877) 2 QBD 410**, where sexual intercourse was falsely represented as a surgical operation, and *R v Williams* **[1923] 1 KB 340**, where it was falsely represented by a singing teacher as a breathing technique. **Section 76** now entrenches these common law rules into statutory form. Jake is falsely and intentionally claiming that sexual contact may mystically offer a medical remedy for the very headaches from which Fiona suffers. It would also be possible to view this as a fraud as to his purpose. *R v Tabassum* [2000] **2 Cr App R 328**, held that fraud as to a 'quality' of the act would negate consent. The victims consented to being touched for medical and no other purposes. Section 76(2)(a) reflects *Tabassum* through the use of 'purpose' in place of 'quality'. If it was Jake's purpose to have sexual intercourse with Fiona for his own purposes of sexual gratification as opposed to her purpose of medical cure for headaches, then he has intentionally deceived her as to his purpose. Consequently, it will be conclusively presumed that she did not consent to sexual intercourse and that he did not reasonably believe that she did. No further enquiry into Jake's *mens rea* is necessary and he will therefore be guilty of rape.

Jake's offence against Debbie: the relevant offence here is rape contrary to **s. 1(1) of the Sexual Offences Act 2003**. Jake will have committed rape if he intentionally penetrated Debbie's mouth without consent and he had no reasonable belief in consent. The issue for the prosecution in relation to the *actus reus* will be whether she consented or not. **Section 74** provides that 'a person consents if he agrees by choice, and has the freedom and capacity to make that choice'.

[8] Capacity is a crucial part of **s. 74**.

Although Debbie is 16, she is legally above the age of consent and there is therefore no issue regarding her capacity on age grounds.[8] However, does she lack freedom or choice to consent? Debbie appears to have been inculcated by her father not to deny men sexual pleasure, in other words, to agree to sexual activity even when she may not want to. This is a denial of her personal autonomy (i.e. choice or freedom), not to mention a highly dangerous state of mind to induce in one so young. Her father's coercion may therefore induce her to submit to sexual activity without real consent. There is a difference between submission and consent as explained in *Olugboja* above. It is clear from her point of view that she does not wish to have oral sex with Jake. However, she agrees to his request so as not to disobey her father. Whereas in reality she has probably submitted, it is likely that her agreement, albeit reluctant, will be seen legally as consent. It is not possible to say with certainty therefore that the *actus reus* of rape has been satisfied.

Regarding *mens rea*, Jake's penetration was intentional and he is likely to have a belief in consent in view of Debbie's agreement. Whether his belief could be said to be both honest and reasonable as required by **s. 1(c)** in view of the circumstances and his own misguided beliefs is an open question.[9]

[9] Note that sometimes, you will not come to a definite conclusion. This does not matter as long as you have argued well.

LOOKING FOR EXTRA MARKS?

■ In this type of question it is tempting to say that the presumptions apply without looking at them in detail. Think about these carefully—a good answer will apply s. 75 to the facts and consider what evidence could be brought in rebuttal.

■ The circumstances in which consent will be negated are rare in fraud cases. It is important, however, to distinguish between consent as to purpose and consent as to the nature of the Act.

TAKING THINGS FURTHER

■ Gross, H., 'Rape, Moralism and Human Rights' [2007] Crim LR 220.
This article argues that a wider definition of rape is undesirable as the criminal law must be carefully defined.

■ Herring, J., 'Human Rights and Rape: a Reply to Hyman Gross' [2007] Crim LR 228.
Herring's response to the comments made by Gross.

■ Herring J, 'Mistaken Sex' [2005] Crim LR 511–18.
Herring examines the idea that traditionally the onus for establishing lack of consent was placed on the victim and that sexual autonomy and mistaken consent are inextricably linked. A better, more precise definition is required.

■ Home Office, Setting the Boundaries: Reforming the Law on Sexual Offences (2000).
Proposals for reform leading to the enactment of the Sexual Offences Act 2003.

■ Lacey, N., 'Beset by Boundaries: The Home Office Review of Sex Offences' [2001] Crim LR 3.
This is a critical analysis of the Home Office report.

■ Selfe, D., 'The Meaning of Consent under the Sexual Offences Act 2003' [2008] 178 Criminal Lawyer 3–5.
*This article discusses the conclusive evidential presumptions under **s. 76** and whether it replaces the common law.*

■ Temkin, J. and Ashworth, A., 'Rape, Sexual Assaults and the Problem of Consent' [2004] Crim LR 328.
*This article assesses the effectiveness of the **Sexual Offences Act 2003**, particularly with regard to consent.*

Online Resource Centre www.oxfordtextbooks.co.uk/orc/qanda/

Go online for extra essay and problem questions, a glossary of key terms, online versions of all the answer plans and audio commentary on how selected ones were put together, and a range of podcasts which include advice on exam and coursework technique and advice for other assessment methods.

6 Property Offences

In order to answer questions on this topic, you will need an understanding of the following:

- **section 1** of the **Theft Act 1968**, including the concept of appropriation, *inter vivos* gifts, and consent
- dishonesty using **s. 2** of the **Theft Act 1968** and the common law test in *R v Ghosh* [1982] 1 QB 1053
- fraud under the **Fraud Act 2006**
- robbery under **s. 8** of the **Theft Act 2006**
- burglary and aggravated burglary under **s. 9** and **s. 10**
- making off without payment under **s. 3** of the **Theft Act 1978**
- criminal damage under the **Criminal Damage Act 1971**
- blackmail under **s. 21** of the **Theft Act 1968** and handling stolen goods under s. 21 and s. 22 Theft Act 1968

KEY DEBATES

Debate: defining appropriation and dishonesty

The law of property offences is vast, and contained in a number of different pieces of legislation. In theft the courts have struggled with the concept of appropriation, holding, controversially, in *Hinks* [2001] 2 AC 241 that a defendant has appropriated property even where the victim consents to him taking it. *Shute* [2002] **Crim LR 445** is in favour of this decision, but Simester and

▶

Sullivan criticise the law's emphasis on the protection of proprietary interests at the expense of individuals, even when there is no harm to society. Dishonesty is a key concept in both theft and fraud, but again, this has been criticised as being too vague. It is jury-dependent, and thus unreliable. On the concept of dishonesty, Griew argues that it is impossible to reach a common standard of dishonesty and that the *Ghosh* test may lead to longer and more complex trials.

QUESTION | 1

Frank is staying with Hattie for the weekend. Hattie, who works on Saturdays, called Frank from work on Saturday morning and told him to take £10 from her purse to pay the window cleaner. Frank had seen a suit in the window of his favourite clothes shop which he really liked. However he had already spent all of his salary that month. In addition to the £10 for the window cleaner, he took two £50 notes out of her purse, intending to tell Hattie later that he would pay her back from next month's salary. He also took Hattie's Oyster travelcard which had been prepaid to the value of £10.

He returned to the shop and bought the suit, which cost £49. Frank handed over the two £50 notes and received three £20 notes in exchange. When Frank realised that he had received too much change, he was delighted and treated himself to lunch in a restaurant, being careful that no one saw him leave the shop. He left the £10 as a tip for the waitress, who was very pretty. After his lunch he did not feel like walking home, so he took the bus, using £2.00 from the Oyster travelcard.

Just before he got home, he saw some flowers growing on the side of the road outside his neighbour's garden and picked five to give to Hattie. At home he did not say anything to Hattie, but replaced the Oyster travelcard.

Frank said later that he didn't think that she would mind if he took the money and the travelcard as they were sharing a flat.

Discuss Frank's liability under the Theft Act 1968.

CAUTION!

- You need to make sure you have dealt with each element of theft, in order to secure a conviction. It is best not to dwell too long on one issue as there are several incidents to cover.

- Take care not to spend too long on issues of fact that are really in the province of the jury.

- **Sections 5(3)** and **5(4)** can raise tricky issues about when property passes.

DIAGRAM ANSWER PLAN

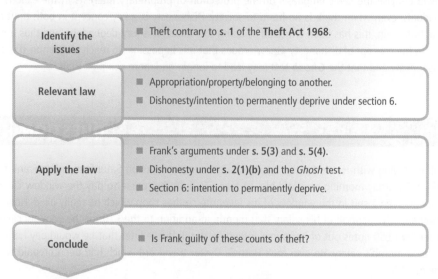

Identify the issues	■ Theft contrary to **s. 1** of the **Theft Act 1968**.
Relevant law	■ Appropriation/property/belonging to another. ■ Dishonesty/intention to permanently deprive under section 6.
Apply the law	■ Frank's arguments under **s. 5(3)** and **s. 5(4)**. ■ Dishonesty under **s. 2(1)(b)** and the *Ghosh* test. ■ Section 6: intention to permanently deprive.
Conclude	■ Is Frank guilty of these counts of theft?

SUGGESTED ANSWER

[1]Start with a definition of the relevant statutory provision.

In taking Hattie's wallet from the table, Frank may have committed theft contrary to **s. 1** of the **Theft Act 1968**. Theft is defined as the dishonest appropriation of property belonging to another with an intention to permanently deprive that other of it.[1] Appropriation is defined under **s. 3** as an assumption of the rights of ownership. Simply by taking the money, Frank has assumed one of Hattie's rights in the property. The money is property (**s. 4(1)** of the **Theft Act 1968**), and it belongs to another.

[2]These are technically 'defences' rather than a definition of dishonesty. If none of these apply, or if they do not work, consult the common law test in *Ghosh*.

Frank may try to argue that he is not dishonest because if Hattie had been there, she might have lent or given him the money to buy the suit as they shared a flat. Section 2(1) sets out that one is not to be regarded as being dishonest if the act was committed with any one of three beliefs: (a) belief in a legal right to the property; (b) belief that the owner would consent; and (c) a belief that the owner could not be found by taking reasonable steps.[2] Frank will not be dishonest if he honestly believes that Hattie would have consented. This seems to be a large amount of money for such a belief. He could argue, following ***R v Ghosh*** [1982], that even though his conduct appeared dishonest according to the standards of most people, he did not think that most people would find him to be dishonest. His assertion that he did not think that Hattie would mind is further evidence of this belief.

The prosecution must also prove that Frank intended to permanently deprive Hattie of the property. Given that he states that he intends to return the money, the court will not treat this as a straightforward deprivation, but instead will invoke **s. 6** of the **Theft Act 1968**.[3] Frank can be regarded as having the intention of permanently depriving Hattie of the money if it was his intention to treat the thing as his own regardless of the other's rights. This is the case here. Keeping the money until his next pay date indicates an intention to treat the money as his own regardless of Hattie's rights. The money is clearly 'property' under **s. 4(1)** and it belongs to another. With regard to the travelcard, he might argue that he simply borrowed it. **Section 6** provides that if the borrowing is for a period and in circumstances making it equivalent to an outright taking or disposal, then this will also be an intention to permanently deprive the owner of the property. In *R v Lloyd* **[1985] QB 829**, the Court of Appeal held that there would be a sufficient intent to deprive if the accused in the course of borrowing changed the property so that all its 'goodness and virtue' was diminished. The Oyster card can be used again, but the money on it has been used, and Hattie is prevented from using the credit on it.[4]

When Frank receives too much change he may argue that the property does not belong to the shop, but to him, given that he now has possession of it. **Section 5(1)** of the **Theft Act 1968** provides that where the defendant gets property by mistake and is under an obligation to return it he has an obligation to make restoration. The obligation to restore the property must be a legal one. This was inserted into the Theft Act to deal with the problem raised in the old law of larceny that a defendant could not be convicted for keeping excess wages paid to him by mistake.[5] The other requirements of theft will also need to be satisfied. As he has noticed the mistake and has gone on to spend the money, he appears to be dishonest. According to *R v Ghosh*, a defendant is dishonest if he would be dishonest according to the standards of reasonable and honest people. If this is the case then the defendant must be asked whether he realised that he was being dishonest by those standards. As he is concerned to check that no one is watching him, this condition is satisfied.

The £10 destined for the window cleaner is also property. Frank may try to argue that it is not property belonging to another because it is in his possession. Under **s. 5(3)** where the property is received by the defendant on account of another and the defendant is under an obligation to the defendant to deal with the property in a particular way, then the property is to be regarded as belonging to another. Whether there is an obligation is a matter of law. There is not automatically an obligation. For example in *R v Hall* **[1973] QB 126**

---

[3] Be careful with this: resort should only be had to **s. 6(1)** and **6(2)** in cases of difficulty where the defendant needs to be deemed to have an intention to permanently deprive. Avoid a common mistake that candidates make—there is usually no need to prove that the owner was permanently deprived.

[4] Remember to apply this complicated section to the facts.

[5] An obligation must be shown for this section to operate.

because the prosecution had been unable to prove an obligation, the Court of Appeal quashed the conviction of a travel agent who had failed to use his client's deposit to book his holiday. In the context of the other events here, Frank may well be regarded as being sufficiently dishonest to secure a conviction. In *Davidge v Bunnett* **[1984] Crim LR 296,** the defendant was held to be under an obligation to her fellow occupants of the property from whom she had collected money to pay an electricity bill—she stole the money when she used it to buy presents.

[6]Where you cannot prove one of the elements of theft, you do not need to discuss the other elements.

Taking the roses will not be regarded as theft as the roses are not property under **s. 4(1).**[6] It is not possible to 'steal' fruit, flowers, or foliage growing wild on any land unless this is done for reward or sale or other commercial purpose. As he picks a few flowers to give to Hattie, he does not do so for reward or for sale. These are not 'property' for the purposes of the Act.

LOOKING FOR EXTRA MARKS?

■ Careful fact management and application of the law is crucial in a question like this. Time management is also crucial in exams. You can deal with obvious issues fairly quickly, enabling you to concentrate on the more difficult problem areas.

QUESTION 2

Saul and Tim go out one night looking for houses to break into. They see a ground floor window open where Jen is working. Jen waves to Tim and beckons him in, thinking that it is her brother, Jason. Tim climbs in and Saul follows. When Jen realises her mistake she screams and tries to run away. Tim punches her, and ties her to a chair, while Saul goes upstairs and helps himself to Jen's jewellery. On the way out, Tim grabs a knife which is on the kitchen table.

Saul and Tim visit an off licence. While Andy, the assistant, is not looking, Tim takes some cans of beer from a shelf and puts them in his bag. Andy notices, and Tim points the knife at him. Andy is frightened and retreats. They leave the shop with the beer.

They then visit Saul's grandfather, Cyril. At Cyril's house, they both help themselves to some chocolates on the sideboard and Saul takes a £20 note from Cyril's wallet.

Jen, a hospital administrator, is traumatised by her attack. The following week, she uses her brother's credit card to buy £1000 worth of consumer goods without his knowledge and agrees to put a patient at the top of the operation waiting list in return for £500.

Saul says that he didn't think his grandfather would mind if he took the money and the chocolates.

Advise the Crown Prosecution Service on any criminal liability arising from these facts. Do not discuss accessorial liability.

CAUTION!

- There is quite a lot of overlap between the different property offences of theft, robbery, burglary, and fraud. It is best to deal with them separately as the questions can be highly technical.

- Don't forget about the issue of continuing appropriation in robbery.

DIAGRAM ANSWER PLAN

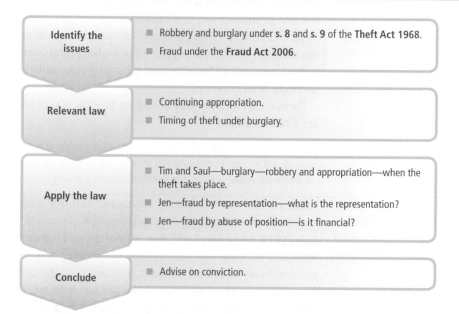

| Identify the issues | ■ Robbery and burglary under **s. 8** and **s. 9** of the **Theft Act 1968**.
■ Fraud under the **Fraud Act 2006**. |

| Relevant law | ■ Continuing appropriation.
■ Timing of theft under burglary. |

| Apply the law | ■ Tim and Saul—burglary—robbery and appropriation—when the theft takes place.
■ Jen—fraud by representation—what is the representation?
■ Jen—fraud by abuse of position—is it financial? |

| Conclude | ■ Advise on conviction. |

SUGGESTED ANSWER

This question raises issues of robbery, burglary, and theft offences. When Saul and Tim enter Jen's property they may have committed burglary. This is defined under **s. 9** of the **Theft Act 1968** and the relevant part in this case is **s. 9(1)(a)**, whereby a person is guilty of burglary if he enters any building or part of a building as a trespasser with intent to commit an offence as defined in **s. 9(2)**.[1] This includes stealing or attempting to steal anything therein. They intend to look for houses to break into, so this is the appropriate section. It is not necessary to prove that they actually steal. They may state that they were not trespassing as Jen invited them in. In *R v Collins* **[1972] 2 All ER 1105**, the defendant, wearing only his socks, climbed a ladder and was perched on a bedroom window sill. The 18-year-old girl inside assumed that her boyfriend had returned for a nocturnal

[1] The difference between the two types of burglary is dependent on the moment the intent is formed.

visit, invited him in and they had sexual intercourse. The defendant was convicted of burglary under **s. 9 (1)(a)**—at the time burglary of this type included the intent to rape. Although the Court of Appeal quashed this because the trial judge had not properly directed the jury on the need for *mens rea* as to presence as a trespasser, later cases show that the defendant's entry must be effective, not just substantial. Jen's mistake would seem to negate any argument that the men are not trespassing.[2] Furthermore, it has been held that the defendant will be trespassing if he enters in excess of any permission he might otherwise have. In *Jones and Smith* **[1976] 3 All ER 54** the two defendants entered the house belonging to Smith's father with the intention of stealing, and their convictions for burglary were upheld.

This seems to imply that any person entering a building with an intention to exceed the terms of any express or implied permission to do so must be trespassing.[3] The *actus reus* of burglary along with the *mens rea* seems to be made out.

The men may also be guilty of robbery. **Section 8(1)** of the **Theft Act 1968** states that:

A person is guilty of robbery if he steals, and immediately before or at the time of doing so, and in order to do so, he uses force on any person or puts or seeks to put any person in fear of being then and there subjected to force.

Robbery is essentially a form of aggravated theft. The prosecution must show that there has been an appropriation of property.[4] In *R v Hale* **[1978] 68 Cr App R 415**, two defendants went to their victim's house and while one was upstairs stealing a jewellery box, the other was downstairs restraining the victim. The Court of Appeal upheld the conviction for robbery even though the box had been appropriated before any force was used against the victim. The theft was regarded as a continuing event, and the jury could conclude that it was still in progress as the victim was being tied up. The facts of this question are almost identical.

A further count of robbery may be charged in relation to the events in the shop. The key difference between theft and robbery is that force or fear of force is used. The force or threat of force must be used in order to steal and before or at the time of stealing.[5] As the threat with the knife seems to take place after the theft of the beer, the elements of robbery will not be made out. The elements of theft will need to be satisfied. Theft is a dishonest appropriation of property with an intention to permanently deprive the other of it.

Are the men guilty of burglary at Cyril's house? As discussed earlier, they may be regarded as having trespassed under the principle in *Jones and Smith* (discussed earlier). They have clearly appropriated the money and the chocolates. Therefore, they have committed burglary under **s. 9(1)(b)**.[6]

---

[2] It is now settled that entry must be effective.

[3] The key here is not the permission to enter, but the defendant's behaviour once on the property.

[4] This does not have quite the same meaning as in theft—in robbery there may be a question of whether the appropriation is continuing or not.

[5] The timing is all important here.

[6] This type of burglary requires an actual theft to have taken place.

Jen may have committed fraud by representation and fraud by an abuse of position under **ss. 2** and **4 of the Fraud Act 2006**. On the assumption that her brother does not consent to the use of the credit card, using the card to buy £1,000 of goods would appear to constitute an offence under **s. 2** of the **Fraud Act 2006**. The *actus reus* of this offence consists of a false representation (**s. 2(1)**) which is untrue or misleading, and can be express or implied. Representation means any representation as to fact or to law, and can be express or implied (**s. 2(4)**). Jen will have made an implied false representation to the cashier when she paid for the goods that she had the credit card company's authority to pay for the goods. The *mens rea* of fraud is the dishonest making of a false representation (**s. 2(1)(a)**), knowledge that the representation is untrue or misleading, and an intention by that misrepresentation to make a gain or cause a loss to another or to expose another to a risk of loss. This is defined in terms of money. The fact that the store will not lose financially because the payment is guaranteed by the card company is irrelevant. Dishonesty is a key issue in fraud, and is defined according to the principles in the *Ghosh* test.

Alternatively, Jen may have committed fraud by abuse of position under **s. 4** of the **Fraud Act 2006**. A person will commit this offence if he occupies a position in which he is expected to safeguard or not to act against the financial interests of another person (**s. 4(1)**). He must dishonestly abuse that position and intend to make a gain or cause a loss to another. An employment situation has been held to fall into this section. In *R v Gale* **[2008] 1 All ER 230** a defendant was found guilty under this section when he falsified customs documents to show that he had inspected goods, when he had not. The court said that it was essential that employees trusted to do things of this nature showed a high level of trust and probity. Whether Jen would fall into this category is debatable, but when demand for operation waiting lists is high, it might be argued that a high level of probity is required to ensure that the correct procedures are followed.

LOOKING FOR EXTRA MARKS?

- Proper fact management is required in these questions, when a number of different offences may have been committed.

- Make sure that you do not forget the dishonesty issue in fraud. An operative deception is no longer necessary. This means that there is no need to prove that the victim acted on the deception.

Critically assess the tests for dishonesty and appropriation in the law of theft.

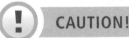

CAUTION!

- This question straddles civil law and criminal law.
- Be sure not to simply describe the two concepts under the Act and at common law—you need to add critical value.

DIAGRAM ANSWER PLAN

Outline the law—how are these two concepts defined under the **Theft Act 1968** and at common law?

▼

Section 3 appropriation; appropriation and consent—problems of intervivos gifts.

▼

Section 2 dishonesty providing only a defence—*R v Ghosh*.

▼

Problems in *R v Ghosh*.

▼

Conclusion.

SUGGESTED ANSWER

Section 1(1) of the **Theft Act 1968** defines theft in the following terms: a person who dishonestly appropriates property belonging to another with the intention of permanently depriving that other of the property. The terms 'appropriation' and dishonesty have been debated widely and have proven to be controversial and, to some extent, uncertain.

[1]Start with a definition of appropriation under the Act.

Appropriation is defined under **s. 3(1)** as any assumption of the rights of an owner.[1] This is wider than mere taking, and can include selling, giving away, or destroying. Following the *obiter dictum* of Lord Roskill in ***R v Morris*** [1983] **3 All ER 28**8, it would appear that any assumption of a (single) right of an owner can amount to an appropriation. One debatable issue arises when the alleged victim of theft has supposedly given consent to the defendant. If the victim has genuinely given consent then why should the criminal courts intervene?[2] In *R v Hinks* [2000] **4 All ER 833** the appellant befriended P, a 53-year-old man of limited intelligence. P had inherited money that was deposited in a building society account. Over a period of time the appellant persuaded P to transfer sums totalling £60,000 from the building society account to her own account. She was charged with the theft of this money and made a submission of no case to answer on the basis that the monies had been gifts from P. This submission was rejected and the defendant found guilty of theft. The House of Lords held that a defendant could appropriate property notwithstanding that this was a valid gift and that the donor had consented to his receiving it. Effectively this decision means that a defendant can be guilty of theft even though under civil law he is the lawful owner of the property because he is the recipient of the valid gift.[3]

A further controversy in relation to appropriation is the issue of when an appropriation occurs. In *R v Atakpu* [1993] **3 WLR 812** Ward J attempted to clarify the matter by explaining that theft can occur in an instant by a single appropriation but it can also involve several appropriations before the transaction is complete. This is a matter for the jury to decide on the facts of each case.

The issue of dishonesty has caused the courts some problems. The first port of call in deciding dishonesty is to consult the partial definition of dishonesty in **s. 2** of the **Theft Act 1968.** The Act does not define theft but rather provides three scenarios in which the defendant will not be regarded as dishonest.[4] **Section 2(1)(a)** provides, firstly, that where the defendant appropriates the property in the belief that he has in law the right to deprive the other of it, he is not to be regarded as dishonest. This might apply, for example, where the defendant thought that the victim owed him money, and is sometimes referred to as the 'claim of right' defence. Secondly, where the defendant appropriates the property in the belief that he would have the other's consent if the other knew of the appropriation and the circumstances of it, he will not be regarded as dishonest. Thirdly, the defendant will not be regarded as dishonest if he appropriates the property in the belief that the person to whom the property belongs cannot be discovered by taking reasonable steps.

Where the **s. 2** situations do not apply the courts will fall back on the common law direction relating to dishonesty which is contained in *R v Ghosh* [1982] **QB 1053.** This will be a question of fact for the jury:

a Whether according to the standards of ordinary, reasonable and honest people what was done was dishonest. If it was not

[2] Identifying the problem—what if the victim consents?

[3] Add critical value—what problems are created in this decision?

[4] It is crucial to remember that this is a *mens rea* issue. It does not matter, for example in **s. 2(1)(c)** whether reasonable steps to find the owner are actually taken.

dishonest by those standards, that is the end of the matter and the prosecution fails. If it was dishonest by those standards, then the jury must consider

b Whether the defendant himself must have realised that what he was doing was by those standards dishonest.

This seems to be aiming to 'carve a path' between a purely subjective approach where the belief of the defendant would be all important and a purely objective approach where the latter is ignored and the standard of the reasonable man is invoked, no matter what the defendant believed.

The problem with leaving this decision in the hands of the jury is that it is very difficult for a jury of 12 to reach a decision on what is honest when their opinions may be very diverse. This is especially true in situations in which a defendant thinks that he is 'doing the right thing'. A defendant who takes £50 from his employer's cash register intending to replace it may be regarded as dishonest by one jury, but gain sympathy (and acquittal) from another.[5]

[5] Try to give practical examples where you can—this adds critical value to your answer.

In a seminal article, Edward Griew argues that the *Ghosh* test will lead to more trials and longer trials. He also refers to the 'fiction of community norms'. The test assumes that reasonable people, sitting on a jury, will all think in the same way, but in fact the behaviour that people find to be dishonest varies hugely. Furthermore, juries may find it difficult to apply the tests in situations they have no experience of themselves such as fraud trials.

[6] Try to refer back to the question set. This will remind the reader that you are thinking about the question, and are staying relevant.

The two pivotal concepts of appropriation and dishonesty are controversial and may lead to inconsistent decision making. It is submitted that a better statutory definition may avoid these problems.[6]

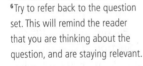

➕ LOOKING FOR EXTRA MARKS?

■ Refer to academic opinion in essay questions. Griew, for example, argues that the *Ghosh* test in dishonesty creates too many problems for juries and leads to inconsistent verdicts.

■ In the case of *R v Hinks* [2000] 4 All ER 833, think about the wider implications of the decision, on both criminal law and civil law. It seems remarkable that the House of Lords has confirmed the approach set out in the case.

Martina contacts Andrew for a quotation to renovate a bathroom at her house, having searched on the internet and seen a page stating, 'Andrew Holter Bathrooms—use the best. Experience, reasonable prices and quality workmanship guaranteed.' Andrew has just set up his own business after leaving college with a diploma in marketing. He tells her the materials will cost £15,000 which he requires in advance as this is a trade requirement. This is untrue.

Martina agrees to hire him to renovate her bathroom. Andrew goes to the local DIY store to buy the materials which cost him £5,000. Knowing he has insufficient credit on his credit card, he uses his father's credit card for which he knows the PIN number. Before entering the store, he is approached and asked if he would like his van cleaned for which he must pay £5 when he leaves the store. He agrees. When he leaves the store, he sees that his van had been washed but he drives off without paying.

When he returns to Martina's house to start work, she is just leaving. She tells him that she has left some money on the kitchen table to pay the window cleaner. When the window cleaner calls later that morning, Andrew tells him Martina did not leave any money for him. Andrew then uses the money to buy his lunch. Three weeks after completing the building job, the shower stops working and the plasterwork starts to crumble. Martina has to have it rebuilt.

Andrew's neighbour, Vince, has been observing and following Andrew and threatens to post details all over his website and call the police if he does not pay him £10,000. As he is secretly in love with Martina, he plans to give this to her as compensation for the money she has lost and therefore be in her favour.

Discuss the liability, if any, of Andrew and Vince.

CAUTION!

- This question covers a number of property offences, so deal with them all in turn. There will be overlap between the offences, so be careful and don't worry about repetition. This might particularly apply to theft and making off without payment.

- When discussing fraud, avoid a common error and ensure you give due weight to the *mens rea*.

DIAGRAM ANSWER PLAN

Identify the issues	▪ Fraud under the **Fraud Act 2006**. ▪ Theft under the **Theft Act 1968**. ▪ Making off without payment under **s. 3** of the **Theft Act 1978**.
Relevant law	▪ **s. 2** of the **Fraud Act 2006**—concept of representation. ▪ *Mens rea*—is he dishonest? ▪ **s. 11** of the **Fraud Act 2006**—obtaining services dishonestly. ▪ Making off without payment—**s. 3**—payment on the spot?
Apply the law	▪ Has he committed a **s. 4** fraud offence? ▪ Discussion of 'position'.
Conclude	▪ Advise on the basis of the above discussion.

SUGGESTED ANSWER

Andrew may be found guilty of fraud under the **Fraud Act 2006**. He may also be guilty of theft under the **Theft Act 1968** and of making off without payment under the **Theft Act 1978**.

The advertisement placed on the internet seems to imply that he has experience in building work whereas he has in fact left college with a diploma in marketing. This statement is untrue. **Section 2** of the **Fraud Act 2006** states that a fraud by false representation has occurred where the defendant makes a false representation. A representation means any representation as to fact or law, including a representation as to the state of mind of the person making it or any other person (**s. 2(3)**). The advertisement falls into this category, especially as the subsequent work was shown to be unsatisfactory (the shower has stopped working and the plasterwork starts to crumble).[1] Furthermore his assertion that the materials would cost £15,000 when they cost a third of this amounts to a false representation, especially when viewed in the context of the poor workmanship.

The *mens rea* of this offence of fraud is defined as the dishonest making of a false representation. Dishonesty here is defined following *Ghosh* **[1982] 2 All ER 689**. This will be a question of fact for the jury:

[1] Apply the law to the facts from the outset.

a Whether according to the standards of ordinary, reasonable, and honest people what was done was dishonest. If it was not dishonest by those standards, that is the end of the matter and the prosecution fails. If it was dishonest by those standards, then the jury must consider

b Whether the defendant himself must have realised that what he was doing was by those standards dishonest.

[2] Do not dwell too long on matters that are for the jury to decide.

It seems unlikely that the jury would regard Andrew as an honest bathroom renovator. This aspect of the *mens rea* would appear to be satisfied.[2]

The work is clearly carried out with a view to gain (**s. 2(b)** and **s. 5 of the Fraud Act 2006**).

A further offence under **s. 2** of the **Fraud Act 2006** may have arisen when he uses his father's credit card. Under **s. 2(4)** a repre-

[3] This aspect of the common law has now been entrenched into the Act.

sentation can be express or implied. Here, Andrew makes an implied false representation to the cashier that he has the credit card company's authority to use the card and is within the credit limit (*Lambie* **[1981] 1 All ER 332**.[3] The *mens rea* requirements of dishonesty and intention to make a gain appear to be met here: Andrew knows what he is doing when he uses the credit card. Furthermore, **s. 2(5)** states that a representation is regarded as having been made if it submitted to any system or device designed to receive, convey, or respond to communications (with or without human intervention). The fact that a human being is not deceived is irrelevant, although the situation would have been somewhat different in the previous law of deception. In re *London and Globe Finance Corp.* **[1903] 1 Ch 728**, deception was defined as inducing a man to believe that a thing is true which is false, and which the person practising the deceit knows or believes to be false.

[4] In this situation, there are several offences you could choose from. The best thing to do is to work through the technical requirements of each.

Andrew then drives off without paying.[4] He may be guilty of an offence under the **Fraud Act 2006**. He may have committed **s. 2** of the **Fraud Act 2006**. By agreeing to pay, he has made a representation which he knows to be false. **Section 11** states that a person is guilty of an offence if he obtains services dishonestly, knowing that the service is made available on the basis that payment is required, and with an intention either not to pay or to pay in full. He may also be guilty of **s. 3** of the **Theft Act 1978**, which refers to making off without payment. This section applies where a person, knowing that payment on the spot (for goods supplied or services done) is required

[5] Don't forget to apply the law to the facts.

or expected, dishonestly makes off without paying. The fact that he knows he has insufficient credit probably indicates that he does not intend to pay and has no intention of ever paying.[5]

Andrew may also have committed theft under **s. 1** of the **Theft Act 1968**. He may argue that he has not appropriated property 'belonging to another' but the principle in ***Turner (No 2)* [1971] 55 Cr App R 336** will mean that he may be regarded as having done so. **Section 5** states:

property shall be regarded as belonging to any person having possession or control of it, or having any proprietary interest.

In the case, the defendant was convicted of the theft of his car because at the time he drove it away the garage had lawful control of it and had a proprietary interest in it (the debt owed by the owner to the garage). When Andrew drives his van away, he is doing something similar.

The *mens rea* of the fraud offences and of the theft offence must now be dealt with. Is Andrew dishonest? The ***Ghosh*** test will apply. Whilst ordinary and reasonable people might believe Andrew to be dishonest, there is no evidence on which to assert that he believed himself to be honest according to the standards of reasonable people.[6]

With regard to theft, the prosecution must prove that Andrew intended to permanently deprive.

With regard to the money left for the window cleaner, Andrew may be found guilty of theft contrary to **s. 1** of the **Theft Act 1968**. There is a dishonest appropriation of property belonging to another with an intent to permanently deprive. Andrew may try to argue that the property does not belong to another. According to **s. 5(3)** of the **Theft Act 1968**, he will be regarded as having taken property belonging to another if he has a legal obligation to retain this money and deal with it in a particular way.[7]

Furthermore, this may constitute a fraud by abuse of position contrary to **s. 4 of the Fraud Act 2006** or fraud by misrepresentation contrary to **s. 2** of the **Fraud Act 2006**—when he uses the money to pay for his sandwich he represents that the money belongs to him.

Vince may be guilty of blackmail contrary to **s. 21** of the **Theft Act 1968**. There needs to be a 'demand', which there clearly is, here. A reasonable person would realise that a demand is being made (***R v Collister and Warhurst* (1955) 39 Cr App R 100**). There is also clearly a 'menace' here. On the basis of ***R v Clear* [1968] QB 670**, the threat is such as would influence the mind of an ordinary person of normal stability and courage so as to make them accede unwillingly to the demand. Vince's threat is made with a view to gain. Although Vince's motives are to impress Martina, he intends to gain £10,000 to give to her. Under **s. 34 (2)(a)(i)** gain and loss are to be construed as extending only to a gain or loss in money.

[6] Be careful with this aspect of the *Ghosh* test—it does not ask simply whether the defendant thought he was being dishonest but whether he thought other people would think he was so.

[7] This must be a legal obligation.

The prosecution would also have to prove that the demand was unwarranted. A demand with menaces is made in the belief that there are reasonable grounds for making the demand and that the use of the menaces are a proper means of reinforcing the demand. These conditions would seem to be satisfied here as Vince believes that Martina is at an unfair advantage.

LOOKING FOR EXTRA MARKS?

■ You may find that in questions on property offences issues such as dishonesty are repeated several times. There is nothing wrong with 'referring above', in the context of the same question. This should enable you to get to grips with trickier areas and give them due weight.

■ There is some overlap in the fraud offences as the initial offence is drafted widely, so you should consider all possibilities.

QUESTION | 5

Susan owns and runs a convenience store. Martina opens up a rival business in the same shopping precinct. Susan enters Martina's shop and, for fun, swaps price labels on two boxes of chocolates so that a £10 box is now priced at £2, and a £2 box is now priced at £10.

Stephen enters Martina's shop and, unaware of Susan's actions, selects the box of chocolates now (wrongly) priced at £2, knowing full well that it should be priced at £10. Stephen takes the box of chocolates to the counter and buys it for £2. The cashier, Gavin, does not realise that the item is wrongly priced.

Natasha goes to the delicatessen counter in Martina's shop and asks Joanne, the assistant, for six spicy sausages. The sausages cost 50p each. Joanne selects eight spicy sausages by mistake and wraps them up for Natasha. Joanne writes on the bag that it contains six sausages. Aware of Joanne's mistake, Natasha takes the bag to the counter where Gavin, unaware that the bag contains eight, not six, sausages, charges her £3.

Advise the Crown Prosecution Service of any criminal liability arising from these facts.

CAUTION!

■ Make sure you do not fall into the trap of assuming that a defendant must have committed an offence. You should be prepared to advise that the prosecution may not, in some situations, be able to establish criminal liability for some incidents, especially where dishonesty is an issue.

■ This question looks simple as the facts involving each defendant are quite similar. Consequently you will need to work through the elements of each offence of theft and fraud systematically.

DIAGRAM ANSWER PLAN

Identify the issues	■ Theft, fraud, burglary, and making off without payment.
Relevant law	■ **Section 1** of the **Theft Act 1968** especially appropriation and the dishonesty 'defences'; dishonesty in *R v Ghosh*. ■ **The Fraud Act 2006, ss. 1, 2,** and **3**. ■ **Section 9(1)(a)** and **s. 9(1)(b)** of the **Theft Act 1968**. ■ The **Theft Act 1978, s. 3**.
Apply the law	■ Whether appropriation has taken place (switching labels) and whether there is dishonesty using the *Ghosh* test. ■ Can fraud be said to have been committed given the gain/loss rule? ■ Effect of *R v Hinks*.
Conclude	■ Theft and possible fraud given the above discussion; payment as required or expected according to **s. 3** of the **Theft Act 1978**.

SUGGESTED ANSWER

When Susan enters Martina's shop and swaps price labels on two boxes of chocolates so that a £10 box is now priced at £2, and a £2 box is now priced at £10, she may have committed the offence of theft contrary to **s. 1(1)** of the **Theft Act 1968**. The two boxes of chocolates are clearly property (see **s. 4(1)**), and can be regarded as belonging to another as against Susan—see **s. 5(1)** of the **1968 Act**. Swapping the price labels over would be regarded as an appropriation of property belonging to another. On the basis of **s. 3(1)** an appropriation is any assumption of the rights of the owner. In *R v Morris* [1983] 3 All ER 288, this was interpreted as any assumption of any right of the owner. Swapping labels is effectively an assumption of the owner's right.[1] The live issue is dishonesty.[2] As this was a practical joke it is unlikely that Susan can 'escape' under **s. 2(1)(a)–(c)** of the **1968 Act**. Therefore, the issue of dishonesty will be a question of fact for the jury, directed in accordance with *R v Ghosh* [1982] QB 1053:

a whether according to the ordinary standards of reasonable and honest people what was done was dishonest. If it was not dishonest by those standards, that is the end of the matter and the

[1] Note here that the legal issue has been applied to the facts.

[2] In a criminal trial, several facts may be agreed. Facts which must still be argued are 'live' issues. Therefore, you can concentrate on these issues in a problem question, briefly mentioning the issues.

prosecution fails. If it was dishonest by those standards, then the jury must consider

b whether the defendant himself must have realized that what he was doing was by those standards dishonest.[3]

It is hard to tell how a jury might regard Susan's actions. As the value involved is small, and given that there is no direct personal gain for her, a jury might be reluctant to conclude that she was dishonest. In addition, Susan has no actual intention to permanently deprive. The issue is whether she can be deemed to have had this intent by virtue of **s. 6(1)** of the **Theft Act 1968**.[4] Is it a situation where it was her intention to treat the property as her own to dispose of regardless of the other's rights? It could be argued that switching labels is evidence of her treating it as her own to dispose of, as she is creating the risk that someone might buy the goods at an undervalue.

[4] The point is that the court may regard her as having this intent, even if she does not have it on the face of it.

There are two other possible offences to consider. The first is fraud by false representation contrary to **s. 2** of the **Fraud Act 2006**. The offence requires proof that Susan dishonestly made a false representation, and intended by that representation to make a gain for herself or another,[5] or to cause loss to another or to expose another to a risk of loss. Switching price labels would constitute the false representation (**s. 2(3)**). Susan is representing the selling price to be something other than the correct amount—this satisfies **s. 2(2)**, which provides that a representation is false if it is untrue or misleading. Obviously the wrong price label is likely to mislead. As to *mens rea*, the prosecution will have to prove three elements. First that Susan intended, by making the representation, to make a gain for herself or another, or intended to cause loss to another or to expose another to a risk of loss. The facts indicate that Susan swaps the price labels 'for fun'. Against this is the fact that she has a financial interest in Martina's business not doing well, and this may lead the jury to infer an intent to cause Martina loss. The second element of *mens rea* is that Susan must be shown to have known that the representation as to price was or might have been untrue or misleading. Her knowledge that the label indicated the wrong price is evident from the facts. Thirdly it must be proved that Susan was dishonest.[6] Again the jury would be asked to consider her actions in the light of a *R v Ghosh* [1982] QB 1053 direction.

[5] Note that an actual gain need not be made

[6] Don't forget the dishonesty element in fraud. It isn't defined in the Act, so you need to use this test.

If she had the intention to swap labels before entering the store, and if this could be equated with an intention to steal, she might be charged with burglary contrary to **s. 9(1)(a)** of the **Theft Act 1968**. By entering intending to switch labels, even as a joke, she would be trespassing as *per R v Jones and Smith* [1976] 3 All ER 54.[7] Similarly if she does commit theft in swapping labels she could be guilty of burglary under **s. 9(1)(b)** of the **1968 Act**.

[7] Trespass is a wide concept, and includes permission.

At the time Stephen selects the box of chocolates it is property belonging to another—see **s. 4(1)** and **s. 5(1)** of the **Theft Act 1968**. Does he commit an offence of fraud by false representation contrary to **s. 2** of the **Fraud Act 2006** when he offers to buy the chocolates for £2? The prosecution will argue that he is presenting himself as an honest shopper who believes £2 to be the correct price, and perhaps rely on **s. 2(3)** of the **2006 Act**, which provides that a representation can include a representation as to the state of mind of the person making the representation. Even if this was the case, *mens rea* would have to be established and a jury might not regard his attempt to buy the chocolates at less than the normal selling price to be dishonest.

Section 3 of the **Fraud Act 2006** creates the offence of fraud by failing to disclose information. Liability would arise if it could be shown that Stephen dishonestly failed to disclose information that he was under a legal duty to disclose, and that he intended to make a gain for himself thereby. Stephen knew that the chocolates were mispriced, but there is serious doubt as to whether he was under any legal duty to disclose this fact.[8]

[8]This would have to be a legal duty by contract or similar.

Turning to his possible liability for theft, did he appropriate the chocolates when he selected the box? As explained earlier, any assumption of the rights of the owner will suffice. Further, appropriation can be conduct to which the owner consents—see *Lawrence v Metropolitan Police Commissioner* [1970] 3 All ER 933 and *R v Gomez* [1993] 1 All ER 1. The *actus reus* of theft is therefore made out when Stephen selects the chocolates. Was he dishonest? Stephen will rely on **s. 2(1)(a)** of the **1968 Act**, contending that he appropriated the property in the belief that he had, in law, the right to deprive the store of it. Again, if the **s. 2(1)(a)** argument does not succeed, directed as *per R v Ghosh* the jury might not consider his actions as dishonest.[9] The prosecution might seek to rely on the House of Lords' decision in *R v Hinks* [2000] 4 All ER 833, in which a majority of their Lordships held that a defendant could commit theft even where he acquired a valid title to property under a valid *inter vivos* transfer.[10] In other words a defendant can steal property whilst becoming the owner of it. On this basis it could be argued that, notwithstanding that Stephen becomes the owner of the chocolates when he buys them, he nevertheless appropriates property belonging to another. The prosecution would still have the difficulties outlined earlier in relation to dishonesty, however.

[9]At times, you will need to consider both these tests, if the outcome is not clear.

[10]Set out the ratio of the case, then explain what it means in practical terms.

If fraud and theft charges fail, the prosecution might fall back on a charge of making off without payment, contrary to **s. 3** of the **Theft Act 1978**. The offence requires proof that Stephen dishonestly made off without having paid as required or expected, that he knew payment was expected from him, and that he had intent to avoid

[11] Conclude by applying the law to the facts.

payment of the amount due. The obvious problem is that he will argue that he did pay as required and expected—he paid the amount requested by the cashier. [11]

Does Natasha steal the sausages when she first takes possession of them? The sausages are property—see **s. 4(1)**. Does property pass to her at the deli counter? Possibly not as she has not yet paid—hence she appropriates by taking them. Does she have *mens rea* at this point? As to dishonesty see **s. 2(1)(a)–(c)** and *R v Ghosh*. She may believe that it is her good luck that she has been given the extra sausages and that she has the legal right to keep them (see **s. 2(1)(a)**). She has intention to permanently deprive. If property in the sausages does pass to Natasha at the deli counter, notwithstanding that she has not paid, **s. 5(4)** of the **Theft Act 1968** (property got by mistake), cannot operate to prevent property passing here as she is not under

[12] There is no need to go into detail here as it does not apply.

any legal obligation to make restoration of the sausages. Section 5(4) does not create the legal obligation to make restoration, it applies if there is, in civil law, a legal obligation to make restoration. [12]

Natasha may have committed a fraud offence at the checkout. She knows the bag is wrongly labelled but says nothing. The prosecution may argue that her conduct amounted to an implied representation that she believed the bag to be correctly marked-up—see *DPP v Ray* **[1974] AC 370** (an authority on the pre-**Fraud Act 2006** law, but still persuasive on this point). If her conduct can amount to a representation it is clearly untrue or misleading. As the **s. 2** offence does not require anything more by way of *actus reus*, liability would therefore hinge upon proof of *mens rea*. Natasha knows the price on the bag is too low—hence the jury would have to determine whether or not her actions were dishonest following a direction in accordance with *R v Ghosh*. Some jurors might be minded to think that the mistake by the assistant is Natasha's good luck and that she ought to be allowed to benefit by it, especially as she did not induce it.

As with Stephen's liability considered earlier, it is hard to see how there could be liability under **s. 3** of the **Fraud Act 2006** (fraud by failing to disclose information), the issue again being the absence of

[13] This is an important distinction.

any legal (as opposed to moral) duty [13] on the part of Natasha to point out the shop assistant's error.

On a similar basis to Stephen, Natasha could be charged with making off without payment contrary to **s. 3** of the **1978 Act**, and could also be charged with theft if *R v Hinks* was relied upon by the prosecution. In each of these offences dishonesty might still prove the stumbling block for reasons outlined earlier.

LOOKING FOR EXTRA MARKS?

- One of the problems with theft and fraud offences is the overlap between them, and also the dividing line between civil and criminal law. A good discussion of *R v Hinks* in this question will add quality to your answer as the point is not immediately obvious.

- An ability to focus on the 'live' issues for discussion will ensure that you stay relevant throughout the answer.

QUESTION | 6

Brian and Helen are neighbours. Brian agrees to keep an eye on Helen's house whilst she is away on holiday and she gives him a key to gain access. Whilst she is away, Brian goes into Helen's house to check that all is well. He thinks he might have a look around while he is there to see if there is anything worth taking. He helps himself to a £20 note he finds on the sideboard as he had lent Helen £15 earlier that year and she had forgotten to pay him back. As he leaves he notices that the milkman has left two pints of milk on the doorstep. Brian takes them home. That night, as he is lying in bed, Brian realises that he may have forgotten to shut Helen's door properly, but decides not to worry about it until the following day. At 4 a.m. Charlie enters Helen's house through the un-locked front door and steals her DVD player. The next day Brian checks the house and notices that the DVD player has gone. He does not report this to the police and leaves the house securely locked up. On her return Helen calls on Brian before visiting her house. She gives him a £50 gift voucher saying it is to make up for the money she owes him and to thank him for keeping her house safe. Brian says nothing about the DVD player or the £20 note. The next day, Charlie goes into a shop selling DVDs. As he wants some to play in his new DVD player, he puts several in his pocket. He is spotted by a security guard, Steve, and runs from the shop. On his way out, Steve confronts Charlie, who grabs his coat, forcing him to fall. Steve's wallet falls on the floor. Charlie takes £20 out of the wallet and runs out of the shop with the money and the DVDs.

Advise the Crown Prosecution Service as to the criminal liability of Brian and Charlie under the Theft Act 1968.

CAUTION!

- This question raises a number of different property offences so ensure you deal with them separately, technically, and carefully.

- Remember not to jump to conclusions on issues such as trespass; this is a fluid concept.

DIAGRAM ANSWER PLAN

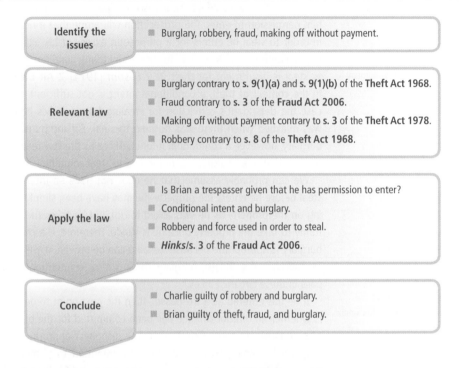

Identify the issues
- Burglary, robbery, fraud, making off without payment.

Relevant law
- Burglary contrary to **s. 9(1)(a)** and **s. 9(1)(b)** of the **Theft Act 1968**.
- Fraud contrary to **s. 3** of the **Fraud Act 2006**.
- Making off without payment contrary to **s. 3** of the **Theft Act 1978**.
- Robbery contrary to **s. 8** of the **Theft Act 1968**.

Apply the law
- Is Brian a trespasser given that he has permission to enter?
- Conditional intent and burglary.
- Robbery and force used in order to steal.
- *Hinks*/s. 3 of the **Fraud Act 2006**.

Conclude
- Charlie guilty of robbery and burglary.
- Brian guilty of theft, fraud, and burglary.

SUGGESTED ANSWER

This question raises issues of burglary, theft, and fraud. The first question is whether Brian has committed burglary when he enters the house. Burglary may be committed in two ways. Under **s. 9(1)(a)** a person is guilty of burglary if he enters any building or part of a building as a trespasser with intent to steal, inflict grievous bodily harm on any person therein, or commit criminal damage. Under **s. 9(1)(b)** a person is guilty of burglary if, having entered as a trespasser, he steals or inflicts grievous bodily harm on any person therein or attempts to commit any of these offences.[1] For burglary under **s. 9(1)(a)** the ulterior offences do not need to be committed, but there must be proof beyond any reasonable doubt of an intention to commit them. Under **s. 9(1)(b)** it must be proved that the defendant has committed one of the offences stated in the statute.

The first element to prove is entry. Brian has entered the property with a key. The question is whether he can be considered to be a trespasser even though he has Helen's permission to enter. In *R v Jones and Smith* **[1976] 3 All ER 54**, the court found that the defendants had entered as trespassers despite their previous permission, as

[1] It's a good idea to start with a definition of the offence. This gives you a ready-made structure.

they had entered for purposes beyond the scope of the consent given. Here, Brian will argue that he did not intend to steal when he entered, and that he could not be a trespasser because Helen had given him permission to enter. The prosecution will argue that if he enters in order to steal he enters for a purpose in excess of his express or implied permission. Brian may further argue that a conditional intent to steal is insufficient for theft (*R v Easom* **[1971] 2 All ER 945**.[2] In the context of theft, a conditional intent is not sufficient. In that case the defendant's conviction for stealing from a lady's handbag was quashed when there was nothing to steal. For the purposes of burglary, however, a conditional intent suffices as the law recognises the fact that most burglars do not intend to steal something specific.

² Note the different application of the rule for theft and for burglary.

We can probably assume that he does not have an intention to steal before he enters the property (he may have been simply checking on the property as he was asked to do), but he takes the opportunity to take the property once he is inside. Therefore, if a charge of burglary is appropriate because trespass can be proven, it will be the second type of **s. 9(1)(b)** burglary. There is also an intention to trespass in these circumstances.[3]

³ Note that the *mens rea* for these offences is twofold—the intention (or recklessness) to commit the offence; and an intention to commit the ulterior offence.

If he has entered as a trespasser, then the next point to deal with is whether an ulterior offence has been committed for the purposes of **s. 9(1)(b)**. He takes £20. Theft is the dishonest appropriation of property belonging to another with the intention to permanently deprive the owner of it (**s. 1** of the **Theft Act 1968**). By removing the money from the sideboard he has assumed one of Helen's rights (**s. 3(1)**); the money is property (**s. 4(1)**) and it belongs to Helen (**s. 5(1)**). The live issue here is dishonesty. The facts here suggest that Brian will argue that he was entitled to take the money. Dishonesty is not defined under the **Theft Act 1968** but **s. 2(1)** sets out that a defendant is not to be regarded as being dishonest if the act was committed with any of the following beliefs: (a) belief in a legal right to the property; (b) a belief that the owner would consent; (c) a belief that the owner could not be traced by taking reasonable steps. In any of these situations, it is the defendant's personal belief which counts, even if this is unreasonable.[4] Does Brian genuinely believe that he has a legal right to the property? There is a debt here, but whether this argument works will depend on the jury. It might be reasonable to ask why Brian did not simply ask Helen for the money as they were neighbours! The **s. 2** argument may be more persuasive with regard to the milk. He may wish to argue that if Helen had realised that she had forgotten to cancel the milk, she may have given Brian permission to take it. It will have gone off by the time she gets home, so will be of no further use to her. He has appropriated it, it is property and it belongs to another.[5]

⁴ Note that this is a subjective test.

⁵ Don't forget to deal with all the elements of theft for each incident.

When Helen returns, he accepts the £50 voucher from Helen. Two potential issues arise here. The prosecution might seek to rely on the House of Lords' decision in *R v Hinks* **[2000] 4 All ER 833**, in which a majority of their Lordships held that a defendant could commit theft even where he acquired a valid title to property under a valid *inter vivos* transfer.[6] In other words a defendant can steal property whilst becoming the owner of it. The next question is whether he was dishonest in accepting the gift of the £50 voucher. The jury may well conclude that he is, taking the facts as a whole.

Secondly he may have committed fraud by failing to disclose. **Section 3** of the **Fraud Act 2006** creates the offence of fraud by failing to disclose information. Liability would arise if it could be shown that Brian dishonestly failed to disclose information that he was under a legal duty to disclose, and that he intended to make a gain for himself thereby. The question is whether any legal duty to disclose the information arises, rather than a moral duty. In addition, the prosecution must prove dishonesty. As the Fraud Act does not provide a definition of dishonesty the court will follow the *R v Ghosh* principles, discussed earlier. Would most people consider that failing to mention what has happened to be dishonest? If so, then the court will move on to the subjective test, which is to ask whether the defendant realised, by those standards, that he was being dishonest.[7] As he chooses not to reveal what has happened it seems clear that Brian realised that he was doing something that most people would disapprove of.

Charlie may be charged with burglary contrary to **s. 9(1)(a)** of the **Theft Act 1968**. He has entered the building without permission— therefore he is a trespasser. Whilst in the building, he steals the DVD player. He commits theft, the ulterior offence, by appropriating property belonging to another with an intention to permanently deprive Helen of the player. Charlie may also be liable for **s. 3** of the **Theft Act 1978**. The offence requires proof that Charlie dishonestly made off without having paid as required or expected, that he knew payment was expected of him, and that he had intent to avoid payment of the amount due.

The elements of theft and burglary are made out in relation to the DVDs in the shop. As no force is used at this point, a charge of robbery is not appropriate. With regard to the money taken from Steve, however, a robbery charge may be appropriate. The last charge is robbery contrary to **s. 8** of the **Theft Act 1968**. Robbery is defined as follows:

A person commits robbery if he steals, and immediately before or at the time of doing so, he uses force on any person or puts or seeks to put any person in fear of force.

Theft is therefore an essential element of robbery, and the element of timing is crucial. The next element to consider is whether force was

---

[6] Set out the *ratio* of the case, then explain what it means in practical terms.

[7] Do be careful with this test. The subjective test does not involve asking the defendant whether he thought his actions were dishonest.

used and whether it was used in order to steal. The force need not be directed at a person, but can be directed to clothing. As Charlie grabbed Steve by the jacket, there is evidence of his using force on Steve prior to stealing. The offence of robbery may be made out.

LOOKING FOR EXTRA MARKS?

- The issue of making off without payment will be spotted by stronger students and is an alternative.
- Dishonesty is not defined in the Fraud Act so the *Ghosh* test will need to be applied carefully.

QUESTION | 7

To what extent has the **Fraud Act 2006** improved the law?

CAUTION!

- Be careful that you do not stray into explanations which are overly descriptive. By all means explain the effect of the old and the new law, but keep this brief and concentrate on the flaws and criticisms.
- As there is still relatively little case law on this area, you will have to be specific on the statutory provisions.

DIAGRAM ANSWER PLAN

> Explanation of the introduction of the **Fraud Act 2006** and its key provisions.

▼

> Explanation of the previous law.

▼

> Causation and deception.

▼

> Dishonesty.

▼

Overlap.

▼

Width of the provisions, especially abuse of position and a failure to disclose.

▼

Conclusion—despite the criticisms, the Act has simplified and consolidated the law.

SUGGESTED ANSWER

The **Fraud Act 2006** was designed to replace many of the discrepancies and inconsistencies in the previous law of deception. These were spread over diverse provisions in the **Theft Acts 1968** and **1978**, and often related to very specific circumstances. Often, there was overlap with other property offences. The Act abolishes the deception offences in the **Theft Acts 1968** and **1978**, namely obtaining property by deception (**s. 15** of the **Theft Act 1968**); obtaining a money transfer by deception (**s. 15A** of the **Theft Act 1968**); obtaining pecuniary advantage by deception (**s. 16** of the **Theft Act 1968**); obtaining services by deception (**s. 1** of the **Theft Act 1978**); and evasion of liability by deception (**s. 2** of the **Theft Act 1978**).

[1] In discussing any piece of legislation, it is a good idea to think about the rationale for it.

Apart from the piecemeal nature of the previous law, there was a feeling that the existing legislation was not adequate to cope with increasingly complicated commercial fraud cases, or the internet age.[1] One of the problems surrounding this type of offence was the length, cost, and complexity of fraud trials. It might be argued that juries lack the specialist knowledge to deal with this type of complexity. Herring notes:

there are especial difficulties for jurors who have the task of determining the boundary between the hard nosed business person, the exciting entrepreneur and the dishonest criminal.

The problems of the previous law referred to above were well known, and acknowledged by Griew in his seminal work, *The Law of Theft*:

No one wanting to construct a rational, efficient law of criminal fraud would choose to start from the present position. The law . . . is in a very untidy and unsatisfactory condition. The various offences are not so framed and related to each other as to cover, in a clearly organised way and without doubt or strained interpretation, the range of conduct with which the law should be able to deal.

A more modern law of fraud was needed in order to cope with these complexities and to bring the law up to date. Furthermore, the aim was to substantially simplify the law of fraud, thereby assisting juries in assessing guilt.

This essay will briefly outline the changes brought about by the Act, and identify some of the key criticisms of it, before drawing a conclusion in order to answer the question set.²

The **Fraud Act 2006** was designed to replace the complexities in the previous law of deception and creates an overarching offence of fraud. The Act received Royal Assent on 8 November 2006. It was based mainly on the recommendations in the Law Commission's *Report on Fraud* (Cm 5560) in 2002 and a Home Office consultation in May 2004 entitled *Fraud Law Reform*. It is worth noting that the Fraud Bill was remarkably well-received in Parliament. For example, on the Second Reading in the House of Lords, Lord Lloyd of Berwick said:

My Lords, it seems to me that this is one of the best Bills to have come out of the Home Office for many a long year [*Official Report, House of Lords,* 22 June 2005; Vol. 672, c. 1664].

It certainly had an ambitious remit:

The Fraud Bill is a small Bill [16 sections and 3 Schedules] but it is intended to do a big job. It aims to deliver an effective legal structure for tackling the growing threat posed by fraud. Fraud affects us all. It causes long-term damage to UK businesses, wrecks ordinary lives by destroying jobs, savings and pensions, and hits the pockets of every citizen of this country. An effective framework for tackling fraud is therefore crucial to citizens as well as to the economy. The Government's strategy is threefold:

- first, to modernise the law;
- secondly, to improve the investigation of fraud; and
- thirdly, to ensure that the prosecution and court procedures are efficient and effective.

Section 1 creates a general offence of fraud. **Section 2** creates an offence of fraud by false representation; **section 3** creates an offence of fraud by a failure to disclose; and **section 4** creates an offence of fraud by abuse of a financial position.³ **Section 11** of the **Fraud Act 2006** creates an offence of obtaining services dishonestly. **Section 2** in particular would include, for example, the offence of 'phishing' in which claims are made on the internet, but it will also include the inclusion of false information on a mortgage or insurance premium application form, for example. The offence is triable either way, with the penalties on summary conviction reflecting the new sentencing regime (including imprisonment for a term not exceeding 12 months) or following conviction on indictment, to imprisonment for a term not exceeding 10 years and/or a fine.

The sections have various points in common. The *mens rea* of the Act requires, firstly, that the defendant is dishonest. This is not defined in the Act and the common law test for dishonesty in *R v Ghosh* has been adopted. Secondly, it is necessary that the defendant has a 'view' to gain or to cause a loss to another. In addition there must be an intent to falsely represent, to fail to disclose, or to abuse a financial position. These definitions, of themselves, provide a sharp contrast to the previous legislation on deception where actual loss to the victim needed to be proved. There is no need to prove a causal link between the false representation and any loss caused to the victim. This simplifies matters for the prosecution and creates a more general offence. This made it difficult to prosecute anyone who 'deceived' a machine, for example. The Law Commission noted:

> a machine has no mind, so it cannot believe a proposition to be true or false, and therefore cannot be deceived. A person who dishonestly obtains a benefit by giving false information to a computer or machine is not guilty of any deception offence.

[4] In this essay, you can identify some of the things which have worked with the new Act, before moving on to the criticisms.

On this, undoubtedly the **Fraud Act 2006** has made the prosecution's job easier.[4]

On the other hand, a significant criticism of the Act is its width. David Ormerod argues that the offences of fraud does nothing more than to criminalise lying and is no more than an inchoate offence. He argues that **s. 2** of the Act is overly broad, requiring as it does that the defendant makes a false representation. Ormerod states:

[5] By including some of the recognised critics of the Act, you are showing the examiner that you have not only studied the law, but that you have read around the topic.

> should lying be a sufficient basis for criminal liability? What is the wrong which the defendant performs which warrants the criminal sanction?[5]

Ormerod further argues that the broadness of the Act means that there is no distinction between the fraudster who causes millions of pounds' worth of loss and the fraudster who does not. It is difficult to deal with sentencing of the offence if there is no distinction in terms of loss caused.

This uncertainty applies to the **s. 2** offence of fraud by false representation, but also to fraud by a failure to disclose or fraud by an abuse of position. In the case of the former, the offence was said to be necessary to cater for a situation in which the victim may be ignorant of a loss, or where, according to the previous law, the effect of the deception would have had to be proven.

A further argument that the law is drafted too widely is acknowledged by Jennifer Collins. Whilst Herring argues that the offence is potentially very wide (it can include for example employees making an unlawful profit from their position), Collins argues that because there is a moral reason for including it (avoiding disloyalty) its inclusion is justified:

> disloyalty is criminalised because it has a corrosive effect on an important basic value held by society . . . the importance of trust relationships.

The Law Commission made it clear that:

⁶This definition was not translated into the Act itself, possibly leading to a lack of clarity.

> The necessary relationship will be present between trustee and beneficiary, director and company, professional person and client, agent and principal, employee and employer, or between partners. It may arise otherwise, for example within a family, or in the context of voluntary work, or in any context where the parties are not at arm's length.⁶

This has now been confirmed in case law. In *R v Gale* **[2008] EWCA 1344** an office manager for DHL was convicted of this offence when he signed documentation stating that he could vouch for the contents of the cargo. In fact this contained an illegal substance in the USA (khat). The court said that the defendant was in a position of trust as he could be exploited by those wanting to commit criminal offences. Similarly, in *R v Woods* **[2011] EWCA Crim 1305**, a deputy manager of a betting shop changed a customer's bet from £1 to £100, enabling her to collect £990 whilst giving the customer £10. It wasn't clear whether there was an abuse of position, but the court said that an employment situation was included. Ormerod holds that the range of defendants included in this offence is too wide.

Furthermore, the requirement for dishonesty is open to potential criticism. The definition of dishonesty can vary from defendant to defendant. The test has been criticised on the basis of its circularity; see Edward Griew, 'The Objections to Feely and Ghosh'. A person who does not genuinely believe he is being dishonest according to ordinary standards, as opposed to his own value, is entitled to the defence.

⁷A comparison to other property offences shows that you understand the law in context.

It is important to note that the **s. 2** defences do not apply to the offence of fraud in the same way as they do to theft.⁷

In a similar way, the requirement for an intention to gain or cause loss is defined, broadly, in monetary terms. It also includes temporary deprivation, which neither theft nor the previous law of deception did.

Finally, it may be argued that there is substantial overlap in the different sections of the Act. A failure to disclose may also include a false representation or an abuse of position. It might be argued that this problem can be resolved with sensible prosecuting, but not all defendants will be confident to trust in this approach.

In conclusion, whilst the **Fraud Act 2006** has simplified the law and dealt with the piecemeal approach of the previous law of deception, it can be criticised on the basis of the width of its application, leading to uncertainty and possibly, therefore, unfairness.

LOOKING FOR EXTRA MARKS?

▪ In a question like this, try to include some of the rationale behind the Act. Here, for example, we have included Law Commission Reports and Explanatory Notes to the Act.

▪ A key concept in all of the property offences is dishonesty. This is largely defined at common law. It helps if you can explain and critique the problems this might create (such as overlap with existing offences or a circular definition).

TAKING THINGS FURTHER

▪ Collins, J., 'Fraud by Abuse of Position: Theorising s 4 of the Fraud Act 2006' [2011] Crim LR 513–22.

▪ Griew, E., 'Dishonesty: The Objections to Feely and Ghosh' [1985] Crim LR 341.

*This is a discussion of the subjective and objective tests in the **Ghosh** direction as to dishonesty and argues that the test leads to inconsistent verdicts and is difficult for juries to use.*

▪ Ormerod, D., 'The Fraud Act 2006—Criminalising Lying?' [2007] Crim LR 193.

*This article provides an assessment of the **Fraud Act 2006** and argues that its key concepts are drafted too widely.*

▪ Shute, S., 'Appropriation and the Law of Theft' [2002] Crim LR 445.

*This article provides an assessment of disagreements that **R v Hinks** is the wrong decision in cases where the owner has consented to the appropriation.*

▪ Smith, J.C., 'R v Hinks: a Case Commentary' [2001] Crim LR 162.

*This article criticises the decision in **R v Hinks** on the grounds that not even a civil right in property has been violated.*

▪ Withey, C., 'Comment—The Fraud Act 2006—Some Early Observations & Comparisons with the Former Law' (2007) 70 Journal of Criminal Law 220.

This is an assessment of whether the new provisions under the Fraud Act 2006 are an improvement on the previous law of deception.

Online Resource Centre   www.oxfordtextbooks.co.uk/orc/qanda/

Go online for extra essay and problem questions, a glossary of key terms, online versions of all the answer plans and audio commentary on how selected ones were put together, and a range of podcasts which include advice on exam and coursework technique and advice for other assessment methods.

7 Defences

ARE YOU READY?

In order to answer questions on this topic, you will need an understanding of the following:

- the test for insanity in the *M'Naghten* Rules 1843
- the rules on automatism
- the rules on voluntary and involuntary intoxication
- duress and necessity
- self-defence
- the defence of consent

KEY DEBATES

Debate: the 'defence' of necessity

It has been doubted whether there is any defence of necessity at all in English law. *Dudley and Stephens* [1884] is often cited in this context. However, in *Re A* [2000] not only did the Court of Appeal agree that the defence exists, but two of the judgments suggested that it could be extended to the crime of murder, albeit in very limited circumstances. The defence would be available where the act is needed to avoid inevitable evil, no more is done than would be reasonably necessary for the purpose to be achieved, and the evil inflicted is not disproportionate to the evil avoided. Gardner has argued that to require judges to make an assessment of the lesser of two evils is an impossible task. The answer, suggests Gardner, is to frame the necessity of choice in terms of human rights (for example the right to life under **Article 2** of the **European Convention on Human Rights**).

Gina took the tube to work. Whilst on the train, she started to feel dizzy. She noticed that one of the passengers, Bill, was staring at her. Gina shouted at Bill that if he did not stop staring she would kick him in the head. Bill was quite frightened by this, and got up to move. As he did so, the train moved suddenly and he fell over, hitting his head on a metal pole. Gina got up from her seat in order to get off at the next station but was accidentally jostled by Stella. Gina pushed Stella over causing bruising to Stella's arm. Gina then barged out of the train, thrusting people aside, including an old man, Tom. Bill received treatment from his doctor for concussion and depression as a result of this incident. Tom fell between the train and the platform and suffered two broken legs.

Advise the Crown Prosecution Service on Gina's criminal liability, including any defences she may have in the following alternative scenarios:

(a) Gina is diabetic and took insulin before she left for work, but forgot to eat afterwards.

(b) It comes to light that Gina has stolen things from shops in the past when she has forgotten to eat after taking insulin.

(c) Gina had forgotten to take her insulin that morning.

(d) Gina is not diabetic but had been drinking heavily that morning.

CAUTION!

- The defences are a wide topic and as such can be difficult to study systematically. This topic is a good example of how criminal law is not easily separable into separate topics, as every offence may give rise to a defence.

- The difficulty with the mental defences is that there is some considerable overlap between the different categories. You should look carefully at the facts, as certain defences may be excluded due to the type of offence committed. Here, Gina has potentially committed non-fatal offences, therefore, loss of control and diminished responsibility cannot be considered as they apply to murder only.

- Check the rubric carefully as you may not need to prove the substantive offence first.

DIAGRAM ANSWER PLAN

Identify the issues	■ The legal issues are **ss. 18, 20**, and **47** of the **Offences Against the Person Act 1861**. ■ The defences are consent and self defence. *mens rea* may be affected by intoxication.
Relevant law	■ Discuss the *actus reus/mens rea* of the offences, starting with the most serious.
Apply the law	■ Discuss which defences apply, taking care to explain each requirement. ■ *R v Barnes* criteria. ■ Duty to act.
Conclude	■ What is the effect of the defences? *Majewski* test.

SUGGESTED ANSWER

With regard to Bill, Gina may be guilty of an offence under the **Offences Against the Person Act 1861**. She has potentially committed an assault towards Bill. A common law assault can be committed contrary to **s. 39** of the **Criminal Justice Act 1988**, which does not define the offence but provides the penalty. The *actus reus* of this offence requires that the defendant causes the victim to apprehend unlawful physical violence, and the *mens rea* that s/he intended or was reckless as to whether the victim apprehended the violence[1] (**Collins v Wilcock [1984] 3 All ER 374**). This seems to be the case here. It is well established that words can be an assault and Bill suffers depression as a result of this incident. Where an assault occasions actual bodily harm, the charge may be raised to **s. 47** of the **Offences Against the Person Act 1861**. The assault requirement has been made out. As Bill is receiving medical treatment for the depression, this will be recognised as actual bodily harm, which requires an interference with the defendant's health or comfort: **R v Miller [1954] 2 QB 282**. Actual bodily harm can include psychiatric harm such as depression as long as this is medically treatable. Mere emotions such as fear, distress, and panic do not fall into this category, but as Bill is receiving treatment for his concussion and his depressed state, the court is likely to find that he has suffered actual bodily harm.[2] The

[1] The *mens rea* of this offence can be difficult to establish, but the courts tend to look at the reaction of the victim, and give this more weight.

[2] It must be medically recognisable to be counted as actual bodily harm.

mens rea of this offence requires the *mens rea* of the initial assault. The prosecution need only show that the assault or battery caused the actual bodily harm. This is the case here.

Stella's bruising is likely to fall into the same category. Gina may argue that she has not caused this directly. Section 47 of the **Offences Against the Person Act 1861** requires an assault or battery occasioning actual bodily harm. A battery is defined as an unlawful infliction of violence. The 'violence' can be direct or indirect. In *R v Martin* **[1881] 1 QBD 54** the defendant was guilty of unlawful and malicious infliction of harm when he barred the exits to a theatre, turned out the lights, and caused members of the public to panic and injure themselves. Gina pushes Stella so there is an intentional or at least reckless infliction of harm. The fact that Stella falls and bruises her arm may prompt Gina to argue that she did not anticipate the resulting harm, but proof of this is not needed.[3]

With regard to Tom, Gina may have committed an offence either under **s. 20** or **s. 18** of the **Offences Against the Person Act 1861**. The first requires proof of either wounding or grievous bodily harm. There is no break in the skin, but broken legs surely amount to grievous bodily harm. This is a 'really serious injury' (*DPP v Smith* **[1960] 3 All ER 161**), particularly in the light of Tom's age. The *mens rea* of **s. 20** is intention or recklessness as to some degree of physical harm (*R v Mowatt* **[1968] 1 QB 421**). Gina acts recklessly here by barging him out of the way with no regard to Tom. As proof of intention is required for s. 18, this charge is unlikely to succeed.

(a) The fact that she is diabetic and has forgotten to eat after taking her insulin enables her to plead automatism. The courts divide this concept into non-insane automatism (which, when successful, is a valid defence) and insane automatism (which is not). This is due to the close relationship between insanity and automatism.[4] Automatism was defined by Lord Denning in *Bratty v Attorney General for Northern Ireland* **[1963] AC 386** as:

> an act which is done by the muscles without any control by the mind such as a spasm, a reflex or a convulsion, or an act done by a person who is not conscious of what he is doing such an act done whilst suffering from concussion or sleep walking.

For automatism to succeed the court must accept that there is a total loss of control. In addition, the state of automatism must be caused by an external factor, and not an inherent state. When the condition is caused by an inherent condition, the courts will invoke the common law defence of insanity.

In the case of diabetes the courts' approach has not been consistent.

In *R v Quick* **[1973] 1 QB 910**, the defendant's conviction for assault occasioning actual bodily harm was quashed when it was accepted by

[3] The *mens rea* of this offence is quite subtle. The prosecution do not have to prove that the outcome was foreseen by the defendant, just that the defendant is intentional or reckless as to the initial assault or battery.

[4] In other words, a plea of automatism cam result in a verdict of not guilty by reason of insanity. This may not be what the defendant is trying to achieve.

the Court of Appeal that, at the time of the attack, he was in a state of hypoglycaemia produced by a combination of an insulin injection and lack of food. Lawton LJ observed that Quick's mental capacity was not caused by the diabetes itself but by his use of the insulin.

(b) This case would suggest that Gina should be able to benefit from the defence of automatism. However, Gina has previously experienced similar incidents after failing to eat after her insulin shot. In *R v Bailey* **[1983] 2 All ER 503** the court ruled that the defence would not be available in cases where the state of automatism could be regarded as 'self-induced' or where the defendant was at fault in becoming, say, hypoglycaemic.[5] The test here would be whether Gina was aware of the consequences of not eating after her shot. If she was reckless in taking the insulin and not eating this will provide the *mens rea* for offences she may commit whilst in that state. Gina may argue that she could not have foreseen that she might become violent. If the prosecution is successful in establishing this *mens rea*, then Gina will be guilty of the offence charged.

(c) On the basis of *R v Hennessy* **[1989] 1 WLR 297,** the defence of automatism would not be available to Gina on these facts. The hyperglycaemia will be regarded as having been caused by an internal factor—here an inherent condition (the diabetes). If that disease causes a malfunction of the mind that manifests itself in violence the courts will permit Gina to advance the defence of insanity. Under the *M'Naghten* Rules 1843 (*M'Naghten's Case* **(1843) 10 C & F 200**), everyone is presumed sane until the contrary is proved. However it is a defence for the accused to show that he was labouring under such defect of reason due to disease of the mind as either not to know the nature and quality of his act; or, if he did know this, not to know that what he was doing was wrong. The verdict will be not guilty by reason of insanity.

(d) The fact that Gina is intoxicated before she commits these offences allows her to argue that she did not, in fact, have the *mens rea* for them. This is a common law 'defence'. It is necessary to distinguish between crimes of specific intent and crimes of basic intent for this purpose. A further distinction is drawn between voluntary and involuntary intoxication. Crimes of specific intent may benefit from the defence; crimes of basic intent may not (*DPP v Majewski* **[1977] AC 443**). Crimes of basic intent are those for which recklessness may suffice for proof of the *mens rea;* those with basic intent are those for which actual intention is required (e.g. murder). The rationale expressed by the House of Lords in *Majewski* for denying the offence of intoxication in basic intent offences was that the drunkenness itself supplies the evidence of *mens rea* since it is a reckless course of conduct. As the offences against the person of which Gina appears to be guilty are crimes of basic intent, intoxication will not afford a defence.

[5] Effectively, this is a form of recklessness.

LOOKING FOR EXTRA MARKS?

■ The interplay between automatism and intoxication could be important here.

■ A proper explanation of the rationale of *DPP v Majewski* will help to give your answer sufficient depth.

■ Knowledge of debates in the area –such as the controversy over the issue of diabetes—will boost your mark.

QUESTION | 2

If the defence of necessity is to form a valid and consistent part of our criminal law it must, as has been universally recognised, be strictly controlled and scrupulously limited to situations that correspond to its underlying rationale per Dickson J in *Perka v The Queen* [1984] cited with approval by Lord Bingham of Cornhill in *R v Hasan* [2005].

Discuss this statement with regard to the defences of duress, duress of circumstances, and necessity.

CAUTION!

■ In addition to identifying the three defences and addressing any problems therein, it is important to address the rationale referred to in the question. To what extent are these defences 'controlled'? Are these controls logical, given the expressed reasons for limiting the defences?

DIAGRAM ANSWER PLAN

> The three defences: duress, necessity, and duress of circumstances.

▼

> Necessity as a defence to murder and its limitations.

▼

> Duress and the return to the objective test.

▼

> Duress of circumstances.

▼

Discussion of the limitations on the defences.

▼

Do the defences live up to their original rationale?

▼

Conclusion.

SUGGESTED ANSWER

[1] Set out early on what you intend to achieve in the essay. You should address the question here specifically.

The three defences will be considered in turn before assessing their effectiveness according to their rationale.[1]

An accused may plead the defence of necessity where he has acted in an unlawful and criminal way to avoid a greater danger than that created by his unlawful conduct.

It has been doubted whether any defence of necessity is recognised in English criminal law and ***R v Dudley and Stephens* [1881–5] All ER Rep 61** is often cited in this context. This case was atypical in that it dealt with murder. For many years the development of the defence of necessity (duress of circumstances) was hindered by the decision, in which two shipwrecked seamen killed and ate a cabin boy in order to survive. The court ruled that necessity could be no defence to murder and the accused were found guilty, and many commentators believed that the case was authority for the principle that necessity was not available as a general defence to other charges. It was thought that giving the defence a greater scope would 'open the floodgates' to spurious claims and that the difficulty in deciding whose life or property should be sacrificed outweighed the desirability of having the defence.

The point is further illustrated by ***Southwark London Borough Council v Williams* [1971] 2 All ER 75** in which Lord Denning said:

if hunger were once allowed to be a defence for stealing, it would open the way through which all kinds of disorder and lawlessness would pass.

[2] Case seems to widen the defence.

In ***Re A* [2000] *(Conjoined Twins: Surgical Separation)* [2000] 4 All ER 961** not only did the Court of Appeal agree that a defence of necessity exists, but two of the judgments thought that it could be used for murder, albeit in very limited circumstances.[2]

The Court of Appeal in ***Re A*** permitted a separation operation, recognising the intentional nature of the killing of the weaker twin, and that it was necessary in order to save the life of the stronger twin. This was the case as otherwise it was inevitable that both would die. Lord Brooke gave several other examples: a parachutist may be justified in kicking away a victim clinging to his legs whose parachute has failed to open if both would die when they fall; a man may be justified in pulling a victim frozen with fear from an escape ladder in a capsized ship so that others may be led to safety. In these circumstances, an 'evil' is committed so that others' lives may be saved. Necessity may be characterised as a 'choice between evils'. The defendant is making a decision that one course of action in preferable to another. In *F v West Berkshire Health Authority* **[1989] 2 All ER 545**, the action taken against the victim was considered to be in the victim's best interests and this formed a prominent part of the argument for the defence of necessity. In this case a sterilisation operation was carried out on a patient who lacked capacity to prevent the grave risk of pregnancy which could have been psychologically harmful to her.

[3] Provide some critical commentary after each point you make.

However, *Re A* seems to widen the scope of the defence, even suggesting that a general defence exists.[3] The criteria applied were as follows:

- the act is needed to avoid inevitable and irreparable evil;
- no more should be done than necessary for the purpose to be achieved;
- the evil inflicted must not be disproportionate to the evil avoided.

[4] This is the 'floodgates' argument and is closely linked to public policy arguments in the criminal law.

Although the court stressed that the case was limited to its own facts, it could be argued that this is very wide indeed. In addition, it could be said that to open up the defence of necessity in this way could open up the prospect that there might be other instances where people would try to justify their actions.[4] It might further be argued that it would not be possible to say who should be the judge of the comparative value of lives. In this way, it might be said that the defence of necessity suggested by *Re A* is wider than it has been and has lost sight of its original rationale.

[5] This is a relatively new development.

Duress of circumstances has been developed by the courts in a series of cases which initially all involved driving offences committed while under some external threat.[5] The sequence began with *R v Willer* **(1986) 83 Cr App R 225**, where D's conviction for reckless driving (as it then was) was quashed because the jury refused to allow the defence of necessity. There was evidence that the defendant may have driven onto a pavement to escape from a gang of youths threatening violence to himself and his passenger. In *R v Conway* **[1989] 3 All ER 1025** the defendant drove recklessly to escape from two men who had approached his car. There were similar results in *R v Martin* **[1989] 1 All ER 652**. The defendant's stepson was late for work. The defendant's wife, who had suicidal tendencies, threatened suicide if the defendant did not drive his stepson to work. D's conviction for driving while disqualified was quashed. In *R v Pommell* **[1995] 2 Crim LR 607** the Court of Appeal made it clear that the defence was not limited to driving offences. In *R v Baker and Wilkins* **[1997] Crim LR 497** the courts removed one of the remaining ambiguities of the defence by stating, confirming *Pommell*, that the defence is only available where the accused has acted to prevent death or injury to others.

[6] This sentence links the discussion back to the essay title.

The defence seems very close to necessity. It is, however, restricted to threats of death or serious injury whereas a general defence of necessity would simply weigh the harmful consequences sought to be avoided against the harm involved in the commission of the offence. In this sense, to avoid overuse, the limits are desirable.[6]

The defence of duress is well established and provides that the defendant may be excused from liability where he engages in otherwise criminal conduct in circumstances where his will has been overborne by threats of death or serious injury designed to compel him to commit a criminal offence. He must reasonably have believed these threats to exist and to be inescapable except by compliance. The defence will only apply where a reasonable person of ordinary firmness would have done as he did.

Duress, however, cannot be used as a defence to murder. This was confirmed by the House of Lords in *R v Howe* **[1987] AC 417**. Lord Hailsham stated:

[7] A careful quote from a case can bolster the central argument. Here, Lord Hailsham's quote demonstrates the narrow approach of the law.

I have known in my lifetime of too many acts of heroism by ordinary human beings of no more than ordinary fortitude to regard a law as either just or humane which withdraws the protection of the criminal law from the innocent victim and casts its cloak of protection on the coward and the poltroon in the name of a 'concession to human frailty'.[7]

Nonetheless on two occasions the Law Commission have recommended that duress should be available as a defence to murder, but the courts still refuse to recognise it. In *R v Gotts* **[1992] 1 All ER 832**, Lord Keith stated that: 'the complexities and anomalies involved in the whole matter of the defence of duress seem to me to be such that the issue is better left to Parliament to deal with'.

[8] Explain the law in outline.

There are two tests to be satisfied. Firstly, the defendant must have been impelled to act as he did because he was in fear of death or personal injury to himself or a member of his family. Secondly, might a sober person of reasonable firmness, sharing the characteristics of the defendant, have responded to the situation as the defendant did?[8]

There appear to be a number of uncertainties emerging from these tests. The overlap with self-defence is one. A defendant can act in self-defence to protect anyone, but in duress the scope of potential victims is limited. The threat cannot pertain to, for example, financial loss.

The decision in *R v Hasan* [2005] **UKHL 22** has substantially narrowed the availability of the defence. The threat must now be immediate. Also, it was held that if a person becomes voluntarily associated with those involved in criminal activity in a situation where he knows or ought reasonably to know that he may be the subject of compulsion by them or their associates, he cannot rely on the defence.

These restrictions seem to be driven by public policy and are not entirely convincing.

It is notable that the Law Commission have recognised that it is not fair to expect the standard of the reasonable person to be one of heroism and it should be for the jury to decide if the threat was one which the accused could reasonably expect to resist.

LOOKING FOR EXTRA MARKS?

■ Make sure you refer to some critical arguments in addition to the judgments. Here, you could refer to the Law Commission's critique of Lord Hailsham's arguments in *R v Howe*.

■ A comment comparing the old law to the new will demonstrate that you understand not just the mechanics of the defence, but also its implications. *R v Hasan* has substantially tightened the operation of the defence, notably with regard to immediacy and the defendant's voluntary association with criminals.

QUESTION | 3

James was driving on a narrow mountain road. He came to a hairpin bend where he saw Norma sitting in her parked car. Because the road was narrow he could not go back or forward, or around the car. He saw a sign by the side of the road, 'Danger—serious risk of avalanche', and noticed small rocks coming down the mountainside. Fearing an impending avalanche and believing he had no alternative, he drove into the car in front, knocking it over the mountainside. He realised that this course of action was dangerous, and it resulted in Norma (the occupant of the car) being killed and the car being badly damaged. There was in fact no avalanche.

Discuss the criminal liability (if any) of James.

CAUTION!

■ This question involves a detailed consideration of the defence of necessity/duress of circumstances. There are many uncertainties concerning the defence and this question should be attempted only by candidates confident in dealing with these issues.

■ In answering the question candidates must, however, guard against the risk of dealing only with this defence, as due consideration must be given to the ingredients of the offences with which James could be charged. Thus a full discussion of the concepts of intention and recklessness must be given in relation to murder, manslaughter, and criminal damage.

DIAGRAM ANSWER PLAN

Identify the issues	■ Murder and involuntary manslaughter—defences.
Relevant law	■ Murder and involuntary manslaughter—defences.
Apply the law	■ Discuss which defences apply, taking care to explain each requirement. The conditions and each defence. *R v Graham*.
Conclude	■ What is the effect of the defences?

SUGGESTED ANSWER

[1]Establish the key offences and defences first.

James could face charges involving unlawful homicide and criminal damage, but he may be able to raise the defence of necessity and/or duress of circumstances.[1] The most serious offence to consider is murder. James has clearly caused Norma's death in fact—but for his actions she would not have died. There is no evidence to suggest that there has been any break in the chain of causation. The *mens rea* of murder is satisfied by the prosecution proving that James intended to kill or cause grievous bodily harm (***R v Moloney* [1985] 1 All ER 1025**). This is a question of fact for the jury. Although the general rule is that intention is a word in common use, easily understood by the public, and therefore there is no need for the trial judge to embark on a detailed explanation of the concept, this case might require a further direction.

Whereas it is clear that foresight of consequence is evidence that can be used to prove intention, it is not in itself conclusive evidence. Similarly, a judge cannot direct the jury that if James foresaw the consequence and the result was a natural consequence, James intended it. The trial judge would now use the direction suggested by the House of Lords in ***R v Woollin* [1998] 4 All ER 103** that the jury would not be entitled to find the necessary intention unless they felt sure that death or serious bodily harm was a virtually certain result of D's actions (barring some unforeseen intervention), and that D had foreseen death or grievous bodily harm as virtually certain.

James could argue that although he foresaw this possible consequence, death or grievous bodily harm was not his purpose as his motive was to save himself. Although this argument succeeded in *R v Steane* [1947] **1 All ER 813**, this was not a murder case, and it is recognised that motive is not the same as intention. Motive is the reason why one acts, whereas intention is the state of mind present when the act is committed. In short, indirect intention will suffice.[2]

[2] Motive is not to be confused with intent for the purposes of *mens rea*.

If the jury decided that James lacked the *mens rea* for murder, he could still be found guilty of involuntary (constructive) manslaughter, i.e. unlawful killing without intention to kill or do grievous bodily harm. In order to establish liability for constructive manslaughter the prosecution will have to prove that James committed a dangerous criminal act that caused the victim's death. There are two possible bases for such liability here.[3] The first is in relation to his driving of the vehicle. There seems little doubt that the objective test for dangerousness (whether a reasonable and sober person would recognise that the unlawful activities D inevitably subjected P to the risk of some physical harm resulting from them) would be satisfied here. James may argue that a driving offence should not be used as the unlawful act in constructive manslaughter.

[3] You always need to be able to identify an unlawful criminal act for this type of manslaughter.

The alternative basis for constructive manslaughter could be for the prosecution to rely on offences under the **Criminal Damage Act 1971** as the basis for an unlawful act manslaughter charge. It appears that James committed criminal damage under **s. 1(1)** of the Act when he damaged Norma's car. Liability could be based on 'simple' criminal damage contrary to **s. 1(1)** of the 1971 Act, or on aggravated criminal damage contrary to **s. 1(2)**, i.e. damaging or destroying property either intending that or being reckless that the life of another would thereby be endangered.

The second ingredient of constructive manslaughter is that the act must be dangerous. It is enough that a sober and reasonable person at the scene of the unlawful act would have been aware of the possibility of some physical harm occurring as a result of James' actions.[4] Given the facts, it is submitted that the prosecution would have no difficulty in satisfying this condition.

[4] This is an objective test, although its interpretation now includes an assessment of events as the defendant would have seen them.

There has always been uncertainty as to how the *mens rea* requirement for unlawful act manslaughter should be expressed. As Lord Hope explained in *Attorney-General's Reference (No 3 of 1994)* **[1997] 3 All ER 936**, the prosecution must prove that the defendant intended to do what he did. It is not necessary to prove that he knew that his act was unlawful or dangerous. It is unnecessary to prove that he knew that his act was likely to injure the person who died as a result of it.[5] All that need be proved is that he intentionally did what he did—in practice it will suffice if James was at least reckless as to

[5] Be careful with the *mens rea* of this type of manslaughter. Any more than this and it might be confused with murder.

whether property would be damaged or destroyed; see *R v G* [2003] **4 All ER 765**.

On this basis, liability for constructive manslaughter should be made out.

It is worth noting that James could also incur liability for causing death by dangerous driving contrary to **s. 1** of the **Road Traffic Act 1991**. The fault element is 'dangerousness', and this is assessed objectively.

⁶As the defences here do not negate an element of the defence but are defences of justification or excuse, the structure of your answer is important. Start by identifying the offences and then outline the requirements for each defence.

What defences might be available to James?[6]

For many years the development of the defence of necessity (duress of circumstances) was hindered by the decision in *R v Dudley and Stephens* [1881–5] All ER Rep 61, in which two shipwrecked seamen killed and ate a cabin boy in order to survive. The court ruled that necessity could be no defence to murder and the accused were found guilty, and many commentators believed that the case was authority for the principle that necessity was not available as a general defence to other charges. It was not until the mid-1980s that the argument was renewed in a number of cases involving road traffic offences (*R v Willer* (1987) 83 Cr App R 225; *R v Conway* [1988] 3 WLR 1338; and *R v Martin* [1989] 1 All ER 652) and the related defence of duress of circumstances was developed.

If the defence is raised the prosecution retains the burden of proof, and according to the Court of Appeal in *R v Martin* (1988) 88 Cr App R 343 the jury will be directed to consider whether James acted reasonably and proportionately, in order to avoid a threat of death or serious injury. The direction should be in these terms:

a   Was James, or may he have been, impelled to act as he did because, as a result of what he reasonably believed to be the situation, he had good cause to fear that otherwise death or serious physical injury would result? If so;

b   Might a sober person of reasonable firmness, sharing the characteristics of James, have responded to that situation by acting as James did?

If both questions are answered affirmatively James should be acquitted.

Note that the test applied to the defendant's belief in the reality of the threat is objective. This could be a problem for James as, although he believed there was an impending avalanche, this was not in fact the case.[7]

⁷Apply the law to the facts.

Although in *R v Williams* [1987] 3 All ER 411 it was recognised that for the defence of self-defence, the accused should be judged on the facts as he believed them to be, and an honest but unreasonable mistake would not prevent the defence succeeding, the objective basis for compulsion defences, such as duress, was confirmed by the House of Lords in *R v Hasan* [2005] **UKHL 22**.

Assuming duress of circumstances is established according to the tests outlined here, are there policy reasons that would prevent the defence being available to James? Duress is not a defence to murder—that much is clear from *R v Howe* [1987] **1 All ER 771**. *R v Dudley and Stephens* (see earlier in this section) provides that necessity is not a defence to murder, but *R v Dudley and Stephens* is actually a case involving duress of circumstance, hence directly applicable to James' case. James would have no duress-based defence to a charge of murder. *Re A (Children) (Conjoined Twins: Surgical Separation)* [2000] **4 All ER 961**, does envisage necessity being available as a defence to murder, but the key distinguishing point is that there the Court of Appeal was concerned with a situation where the doctors causing the death of one of the conjoined twins would not have been acting to save their own lives at the expense of another.[8] James is clearly acting to save his own life at the expense of Norma's, hence *Re A (Children) (Conjoined Twins: Surgical Separation)* is not applicable.

[8] You can distinguish your case form the authorities you are using.

If James is charged with unlawful act manslaughter, duress of circumstances could be available as a defence—success will depend upon the extent to which the jury conclude that he acted as the reasonable person would have done.

LOOKING FOR EXTRA MARKS?

■ Do not apply the rules from the cases in a blanket fashion. If you can distinguish the facts of the case in question from an established legal rule, do so.

■ Make sure you know what you are expected to cover by checking your syllabus carefully.

QUESTION | 4

Albert and John attend a party where they have some non-alcoholic drinks. It is known that Albert has recently been experiencing dizzy spells and fainting fits, but he has not sought medical treatment. At the party Albert becomes dizzy and is given six Valium tablets by an unknown person in an attempt to calm him down. Very shortly after taking the tablets Albert leaves the party with John. On the way home Albert repeatedly hits John over the head with a bottle, thereby killing him.

When arrested and charged with murder, Albert says: 'I cannot remember hitting him. I must have had a blackout.'

Discuss Albert's possible defences.

CAUTION!

■ Questions on mental abnormality are quite common in examinations. They are often in essay form, but this problem does require the student to take into account the alternative reasons why Albert acted as he did. If a murder has taken place and insanity is an obvious issue, a consideration of the related defences of automatism and diminished responsibility is required.

■ The ingredients of all three defences must therefore be covered in detail with a clear demonstration of the differences between them. Sometimes voluntary intoxication must also be considered, as it is easy to link relevant facts giving rise to this issue in a question of this nature.

DIAGRAM ANSWER PLAN

Identify the issues	■ Diminished responsibility. ■ Automatism, insanity, and intoxication
Relevant law	■ **s. 2** of the **Homicide Act 1957** as amended by **s. 52** of the **Coroners and Justice Act 2009**. ■ *R v Bratty*/AC 386/*M'Naghten*/*DPP v Majewski*.
Apply the law	■ Discuss which defences apply, taking care to explain each requirement.
Conclude	■ What is the effect of the defences?

SUGGESTED ANSWER

Albert has caused the death of John in fact and in law. There is no evidence of anything that would suggest a *novus actus interveniens*. In order to support a charge of murder the prosecution will have to establish that Albert intended to kill John, or intended to do him some grievous bodily harm.[1] If Albert's evidence is plausible it may be that he will successfully defend a murder charge by relying on one of a number of defences involving a partial or complete denial of *mens rea*, such as automatism, insanity, or diminished responsibility.

Diminished responsibility is a partial defence that reduces the defendant's liability from murder to manslaughter. The defence was

[1] The first thing you should do is identify what he may be guilty of—even if that is not the conclusion.

introduced by **s. 2(1)** of the **Homicide Act 1957** but has been extensively amended by **s. 52** of the **Coroners and Justice Act 2009**. Defendants charged with murder tend to rely on diminished responsibility rather than insanity, and it has succeeded in a wide variety of circumstances, including mercy killings, crimes of passion, and killings as a result of irresistible impulse. Professor Andrew Ashworth has pointed out that in 80% of cases where it is raised the prosecution are prepared to accept the plea.

[2] The key is that the defendant must have a recognised medical condition. This is an improvement on the previous law, but also may be more narrow.

For the defence to be made out Albert will have to prove that, at the time of the killing, he was suffering from an abnormality of mental functioning arising from a medical condition.[2] The facts indicate that Albert has been suffering from some symptoms suggesting he was unwell, but the difficulty he will encounter in discharging the legal burden of proof is the fact that there appears to be no expert medical evidence to support the defence. Simply having dizzy spells will not, of itself, discharge the legal burden of proof on Albert as regards establishing the defence. Neither will the transient effect caused by the taking of Valium suffice. Voluntary acute intoxication is not, of itself, to be regarded as a recognised medical condition for the purposes of **s. 52** of the **2009 Act**; see *R v Dowds* **[2012] EWCA Crim 281**.

Even if he were able to provide the necessary expert medical evidence, Albert would have to go on to establish that this abnormality of mental functioning caused a substantial impairment in: (a) his understanding of the nature of his conduct; (b) his ability to form rational judgement; or (c) his ability to exercise self-control. The Court of Appeal has confirmed that, for the purposes of the **2009 Act**, the concept of substantial impairment should be approached in the same way as was the case under the **Homicide Act 1957**. Hence there should be evidence of more than some trivial degree of impairment but there does not have to be evidence of total impairment; see *R v Lloyd* **[1967] 1 QB 175**. Of these three the lack of understanding of the nature of his actions is likely to prove the most fruitful for Albert (note he claims to have been unaware of his actions), provided the jury is satisfied that the impairment is substantial and, further, that the abnormality of mental functioning provided an explanation for Albert's actions in the sense that it was the cause or a contributory factor in making Albert act as he did. In summary, therefore, there are grounds for this defence succeeding provided some expert medical evidence is available to establish the requirements of **s. 52**.[3]

[3] It is essentially a case of a causative link.

Prima facie, the most attractive defence to Albert is automatism, as this is a complete defence to murder and the burden of proof is on the prosecution to disprove the existence of the defence. Albert simply has to provide an evidential basis for reliance on the defence. Automatism was defined by Lord Denning in *Bratty v Attorney-General for*

Northern Ireland [1963] AC 386 as 'an act which is done by the muscles without any control by the mind such as a spasm, a reflex or a convulsion, or an act done by a person who is not conscious of what he is doing such as an act done whilst suffering from concussion or whilst sleep-walking'.

Albert will argue that he did not know what he was doing and therefore his act was involuntary. The prosecution must prove that the act was voluntary, but they are entitled to rely on the presumption that every man has sufficient mental capacity to be responsible for his act; and if the defence wishes to displace this presumption they must give some evidence from which the contrary may reasonably be inferred. Much will therefore depend on the expert medical evidence.

For automatism to succeed the court must accept that there was a total loss of control.[4] In *Attorney-General's Reference (No 2 of 1992)* [1993] 4 All ER 683, the Court of Appeal ruled that the trial judge was wrong to direct the jury that a syndrome known as 'driving without awareness' could amount to automatism. Impaired, reduced, or partial control is not enough. So the prosecution could argue that as Albert had enough control to pick up a bottle and repeatedly hit John over the head, automatism should not apply.

A second problem concerns the fact that Albert had not sought medical treatment for his condition. The prosecution could argue that the automatism was therefore self-induced and that Albert was blameworthy in not seeking treatment. Further, if Albert had taken alcohol or non-prescribed hallucinatory drugs, automatism will not succeed (*R v Lipman* [1969] 3 All ER 410)—but see later in relation to comsumption of Valium tablets. Notwithstanding these two issues, if the Valium had the effect of completely destroying Albert's self-control, and he was unaware that this would be the consequence of taking the drug, he may succeed with the defence of automatism.

Where, however, there is evidence that Albert actually suffered from some inherent medical condition that, in conjunction with the Valium, had the effect of causing him to lose his self-control, the prosecution may seek to lead evidence suggesting that insanity is a more appropriate defence. Under the *M'Naghten* Rules 1843,[5] everyone is presumed sane until the contrary is proved. However, it is a defence for the accused to show that he was labouring under such defect of reason due to disease of the mind such that either:

a   he does not know the nature and quality of his act; or

b   if he does know the nature and quality of his act, he does not know that what he was doing was wrong (in the sense of contrary to law, as opposed to morally wrong).

The trial judge must first decide if Albert was suffering from a disease of the mind, and if so, the jury will then decide if the other

[4]Set out the requirements for the defence of automatism to succeed.

[5]Set out the requirements for the defence to succeed.

ingredients of the defence have been satisfied. The judicial pro-
nouncements on insanity are certainly at variance with medical
practice, and the question of public safety is a factor that the judici-
ary obviously takes into account. In *Bratty*, Lord Denning stated
that 'any mental disorder which has manifested itself in violence
and is prone to recur is a disease of the mind' and this was reiter-
ated by Lord Diplock in *R v Sullivan*, where the House of Lords
upheld the trial judge's decision to label epilepsy 'a disease of the
mind',[6] when he stated:

[6] Essentially, this is a public policy argument.

> if the effect of a disease is to impair these facilities [of reason, memory, and
> understanding] so severely as to have either of these consequences referred to
> in the latter part of the rules, it matters not whether the aetiology of the impair-
> ment is organic, as in epilepsy, or functional, or whether the impairment itself is
> permanent or is transient and intermittent, provided that it subsisted at the time
> of the commission of the act.

Thus arteriosclerosis and violent sleepwalking have all been deemed
diseases of the mind. In the latter case the Court of Appeal held that
many people sleepwalk, but that if an accused uses violence while
sleepwalking, the condition would have to be regarded as being due
to a disease of the mind. So the accused in *R v Burgess* [1991] 2 All
ER 769, who while sleepwalking violently assaulted the victim, was
found 'not guilty by reason of insanity' as he was plainly suffering
from a defect of reason from some sort of failure of the mind causing him to act as he did without conscious motivation. The Court of
Appeal upheld the trial judge's decision to label the condition as a
disease of the mind, on the basis that it was due to an internal factor
that manifested itself in violence.

Albert may seek to rely on the common law defence of intoxication.
There is little doubt that, if his loss of awareness was caused by the
consumption of the Valium tablets, he could be regarded as having
been in a state of intoxication. Murder is a specific intent crime, hence
on the basis of *DPP v Majewski* [1976] 2 All ER 142, self-induced
intoxication can be raised as a defence. If it succeeds it will reduce
Albert's liability to manslaughter.

[7] Note that this is not strictly speaking a defence but a denial of *mens rea*.

There may be an argument that Albert might escape liability altogether on the basis of the intoxication.[7] Even in respect of basic intent
crimes such as manslaughter there must be evidence that the defendant was reckless in consuming the intoxicant. In the case of alcohol or
Class A drugs this is rarely an issue. In the case of Valium there may be
some debate as to whether Albert was aware of the risk of what side
effects there might be. *R v Hardie* [1984] 3 All ER 848 provides that
if there is evidence that the self-administration of drugs may not have
been reckless, the issue ought to be left to the jury. In short, if it was
not Albert's fault that he lost consciousness he should be acquitted.

LOOKING FOR EXTRA MARKS?

■ You need to develop a sense of the areas the examiner is going to give credit for rather than writing about everything you think may be relevant. Here, automatism is likely to be more successful—this is a good reason to plan your answer carefully.

■ Be ready to explain the role of recklessness and basic/specific intent.

QUESTION | 5

A group of friends are on a Thames Clipper cruise. One of the doors has been left open by Sam, a member of the crew, and when they are on their way, the boat starts to sink. Panic ensues, and the friends realise that the only way to escape will be to jump off. Sue and Graham run to the edge where there is a convenient place to jump. When they get there, they see that Pete is trying to climb down but is frozen with fear. Sue pushes him away. Pete drowns, and Sue and Graham manage to escape.

Graham punches his colleague, Rob, when Rob suggests that he could have done more to save Pete. Rob falls unconscious and Graham, feeling guilty, calls an ambulance. At the hospital, he is left unattended when Annie, the doctor on duty, wrongly concludes that he does not need immediate treatment. Rob dies from his injury. Graham says that he was acting out of character as he is diabetic and although he had taken his insulin injection that morning, he had not had time to eat. As a result he had been experiencing some dizzy spells. He had also had several glasses of wine the night before in order to cope with the stress of the boat accident. It transpires that this is not the first time that Graham has felt dizzy at work, but it has always passed within a few minutes, so he didn't think anything of it.

Discuss any criminal liability arising from these facts. Do not discuss inchoate offences.

CAUTION!

■ You need to work through the requirements of any potential offences before you consider which defences might apply. Do not make the mistake of discussing the defences straight away.

■ The rubric makes it clear that you should not discuss inchoate offences. Make sure you do not fall into this trap. This is the examiner's way of making sure that you do not have too much to write about.

DIAGRAM ANSWER PLAN

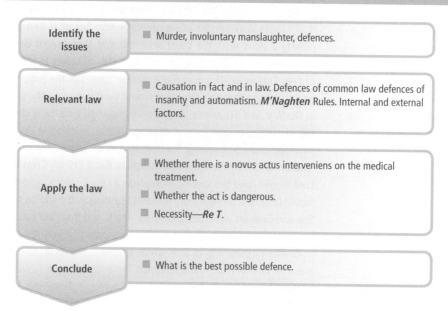

Identify the issues	■ Murder, involuntary manslaughter, defences.
Relevant law	■ Causation in fact and in law. Defences of common law defences of insanity and automatism. *M'Naghten* Rules. Internal and external factors.
Apply the law	■ Whether there is a novus actus interveniens on the medical treatment. ■ Whether the act is dangerous. ■ Necessity—*Re T*.
Conclude	■ What is the best possible defence.

SUGGESTED ANSWER

This question concerns murder, manslaughter, and the defences. Murder is defined at common law as the unlawful killing of a human being under the Queen's Peace. The *mens rea* requires that the defendant has an intent to kill or to cause grievous bodily harm. In order to establish the *actus reus*, the prosecution must show that the defendant has caused the death. Pete's death has been caused by being pushed off the ladder. Sue has not done anything to try to prevent him from falling. He would not have died if he had not been pushed (*R v White [1910] 1 QB 410*.[1] The next question is whether they are a substantial and operating cause of death. There is no evident *novus actus interveniens* here. Sue will argue that she was forced to push Pete out of the way and it was necessary to do so in order to save themselves. Where the defendant is presented with two harms and decides to avoid the greater and accept the lesser by means of committing a crime, he may have the defence of necessity. It is a complete defence, being a justification for the defendant's conduct, thereby negating any unlawfulness in the crime. The feared harm that the defendant chooses to avoid must be serious personal injury or death. Sue will argue that if she had not pushed him off she and Graham would have died themselves. Historically, necessity was not

[1] Also known as the factual causation test.

available as a defence to murder (*R v Dudley and Stephens [1884] LR 14 QBD 273*). Lord Coleridge stated 'the broad proposition that a man may save his life by killing certainly is not law in the present day'[2]. In *Re A (Children)(Conjoined Twins: Surgical Separation) [2001] 2 WLR 480*, the court accepted that there might be exceptions to the rule. This case is similar to the situation in the Herald of Free Enterprise. This was not a murder case, but the judge on appeal admitted that this situation would be different to the situation in *Dudley and Stephens*, because the man had effectively chosen to put himself in danger by not moving, so that in theory a defence of necessity could be available.[3] In *Dudley and Stephens*, the victim was 'chosen' to die, by the other defendants. In *Re: A* [1990] **Crim LR 256**, Lord Brooke gave this specific example as a case in which the defendant would be able to benefit from necessity. As long as it could be said that Sue and Graham were 'designated for death' and that Pete was impeding their escape, they will probably be able to benefit from the defence.

Graham's punching of Rob which results in his death may be the basis of unlawful act manslaughter. The problem here is causation. Graham has committed an unlawful act, which is dangerous.[4] The act is at least a battery and probably the infliction of at least actual bodily harm—a punch is likely to 'interfere with the health and comfort' of Rob. He might argue that he does not have *mens rea*, however, this is satisfied on proof of intention or recklessness as to the unlawful act. The unlawful act must be dangerous. Dangerousness is defined objectively in *R v Church* [1966] **1 QB 59**:[5]

the unlawful act must be such as all sober and reasonable people would inevitably recognize would subject the other person to at least the risk of some physical harm.

Most people would recognise that a punch like this could be dangerous. The next question is whether Graham can argue that the chain of causation was broken. Medical evidence will not generally break the chain of causation unless it is 'palpably wrong' (*R v Jordan* (1956) **40 Cr App R 152**). The cases of (*R v Smith* [1959] **2 QB 35** and (*R v Cheshire* [1991] **1 WLR 844** are likely to prevail here.[6] In the former case it was held that the defendant's act had to be a substantial and operating cause of the victim's death, and in the latter the Court of Appeal held that even though medical negligence was the immediate cause of the victim's death, it did not exclude the defendant's responsibility. It is unlikely that Annie's treatment of Rob in the hospital will break the chain of causation, even if it is negligent.

Graham will try to raise a defence on the basis of automatism on the basis of the insulin he has taken. Automatism is a plea that the link between mind and body is missing resulting in a lack of voluntary

---

[2] Note how a direct quote from the case bolsters the point.

[3] This was a key part of the *ratio* in *Dudley*. You can show the examiner how you can use your powers of legal reasoning by distinguishing the facts of our case.

[4] Clearly set out the requirements of this new offence.

[5] It is important to discuss this here. Students often forget to discuss this element of involuntary manslaughter.

[6] Note that they nearly always do, unless the facts are very similar indeed to *Jordan*.

control over one's actions. In **Bratty** Lord Denning defined the offence as 'an involuntary act done by the muscles . . . without control of the mind'. If successful, it provides a complete acquittal.[7] In order to be successful, it must be shown that the defendant experienced a complete loss of control, and that that loss of control was caused by an external factor, such as medication. Medication in respect of an underlying internal disease can provide the necessary external source. The use of insulin by a diabetic defendant, causing hypoglycaemia, would fall into this category. However, if the prosecution can show that the defendant was reckless in taking the insulin (for example by failing to eat, knowing that particular behaviour would ensue) then the defence cannot usually succeed. Whether it succeeds will depend on the type of crime with which the defendant is charged. If it is a crime of basic intent, then it likely to prevent the defence from succeeding, as there is already an element of recklessness. In this situation, we know that Graham has experienced some dizzy spells in the past after taking insulin but failing to eat. However, we do not know that these spells have resulted in violence. The result, here, is therefore uncertain.[8] As alcohol is a factor here too the court will need to consider whether this is a crime of specific or basic intent (manslaughter is a crime of basic intent as it can be established via proof of recklessness). If it is basic intent, the usual rules on intoxication will apply.

[8] Apply the law to the facts, as best you can.

Graham may be able to plead, in relation to his plea of automatism, that his emotional state triggered these events. In **Re T [1990] Crim LR 256** the defendant suffered from post-traumatic stress disorder as a consequence of being raped. Later the defendant stabbed the victim during a robbery. If the internal/external factor had been strictly applied, then automatism would not have been available, but the rape was considered to be the external factor needed for proof of the defence. The traumatic event of the boat sinking might be considered to be in this category.

If not, Graham will be considered to be insane. This will lead to a verdict of not guilty by reason of insanity with disposal ranging from indefinite detention in a mental hospital to an absolute discharge **(Criminal Procedure (Insanity and Unfitness to Plead) Act 1991 and the Domestic Violence, Crime and Victims Act 2004.** The defence is defined according to the **M'Naghten** Rules 1843[9] as a defect of reason due to a disease of the mind so as to deprive the defendant of either knowledge as to the nature and quality of his actions or knowledge that the act is legally wrong. The concept of disease of the mind is wide enough to include physical as well as mental disorders. Diabetes would fall into this category.[10] If Graham wants to raise this defence, he will have to do so on the balance of probabilities. It may be easier for him to prove automatism, as he can raise medical

[9] You can summarise the definition before applying it.

[10] As we explained earlier in **R v Quick**.

evidence (on an evidential burden only) of his condition. It is possible that Graham may (although this will be difficult/unlikely) be able to show that he was suffering from a form of post-traumatic stress as a result of the accident. Furthermore, as the incident seems to be temporary, it may be difficult for him to show true insanity.

LOOKING FOR EXTRA MARKS?

■ These defences are very close to one another—as such you should make an effort to evaluate them and advise your client on the best way forward. Note that the practical effects may be an important consideration.

■ Although necessity is difficult to show it may now be accepted in certain circumstances. You can show your legal analysis by outlining these circumstances.

TAKING THINGS FURTHER

■ Ashworth, A., 'Insanity and Automatism: Pleas for Information' [2012] 10 Crim LR 733.
The author discusses the need for reform of these two defences.

■ Child, John, and Sullivan, G. R. When Does the Insanity Defence Apply? Some Recent Cases [2014] Crim LR 788–801.
This article summarises some recent case law on the insanity defence and focuses on the definition of disease of the mind.

■ Elliott, D.W., 'Necessity, Duress and Self-defence' [1989] Crim LR 611.
This article discusses the defence of duress of circumstances—in particular the decisions in R v Willer and R v Martin.

■ Law Commission Consultation Paper no 314 [2009].
Reform proposals for criminal liability and intoxication.

■ Ormerod, D., 'Necessity of circumstance' commentary to R v Quayle [2006] Crim LR 148.
This article discusses whether there is any substantial difference between the defence of duress of circumstances and necessity, and argues that the defence of necessity does exist.

■ Rogers, J., 'Necessity, Private Defence and the Killing of Mary' [2001] Crim LR 515.
This article contains a criticism of the utilitarian approach used in the conjoined twins case.

■ Virgo, G., 'The Law Commission Consultation Paper on Intoxication' [1993] Crim LR 415.
This is an assessment of the reform proposals in the consultation paper.

Online Resource Centre

www.oxfordtextbooks.co.uk/orc/qanda/

Go online for extra essay and problem questions, a glossary of key terms, online versions of all the answer plans and audio commentary on how selected ones were put together, and a range of podcasts which include advice on exam and coursework technique and advice for other assessment methods.

8 Secondary Liability and Inchoate Offences

ARE YOU READY?

In order to answer questions on this topic, you will need an understanding of the following:

- the idea of principal and secondary liability
- encouraging and assisting crime
- the doctrine of joint enterprise
- the *mens rea* of the secondary participant following the judgment in **R v Jogee [2016] UKSC 8** and the effect on the 'fundamental difference' rule
- the provisions of the **Serious Crime Act 2007** relating to inchoate liability
- conspiracy under the **Criminal Law Act 1977**
- attempts under the **Criminal Attempts Act 1981**

KEY DEBATES

Debate: the *mens rea* of the accomplice

The *mens rea* of the accomplice has been the subject of considerable debate. On the basis of *R v Powell and Daniels* [1997] 4 All ER 545 and *R v Chan Wing-Siu* [1985] AC 168, a defendant could be convicted as an accomplice to murder provided he merely foresaw the possibility that the principal offender might kill or cause grievous bodily harm with intent to kill or cause grievous bodily harm.

Academic commentators disagreed on the level of *mens rea* needed. David Ormerod argued that the secondary party had to have knowledge as to the essential parts of the principal's offence. Herring, on the other hand, argued that foresight alone is required. This issue and lack of clarity in the law has now been resolved, seemingly, by the Supreme Court decision in *R v Jogee* [2016]

⊙

UKSC 8, which settles the matter by holding that the courts in *Chan Wing-Siu* and *Powell and English* 'took a wrong turn', and that the correct mental element of intent to assist or encourage is intent, not simply foresight. In doing so, it has seemingly abolished the separate category of joint enterprise liability and has substantially revised the effect of the 'fundamental difference' rule.

Q | **QUESTION** | **1**

Alvin contacted Bernard suggesting that they kill Zac because he had refused to pay them a debt. After hearing Alvin's proposals, Bernard secretly decided that he would not do anything to help Alvin, but he told Alvin that he would do anything he could to assist. Their conversation was overheard by Ceri and Desmond, who both agreed to help. Ceri obtained a loaded revolver and gave it to Alvin, and Desmond agreed to drive them in his car to Zac's house.

On the appointed day, Bernard failed to arrive; and after Desmond had taken them to their destination he telephoned the police in time to stop Alvin shooting at Zac.

Discuss the criminal responsibility of the parties.

CAUTION!

- This is a relatively straightforward question concerning the inchoate offences and accessorial liability. These must be dealt with separately.

- All points in problem questions like this relating to accomplice liability will need to be considered in the light of the decision in *R v Jogee*.

DIAGRAM ANSWER PLAN

Identify the issues	■ Encouraging the commission of crime, conspiracy to murder, attempted murder, and accomplice liability.
Relevant law	■ Outline the relevant law: **Serious Crime Act 2007, Criminal Law Act 1977**, and **Criminal Attempts Act 1981.**
Apply the law	■ Is the withdrawal effective? The *mens rea* aspect for conspiracy.
Conclude	■ Conclusion.

There are a number of inchoate offences with which Alvin could be charged. His initial action in contacting Bernard suggesting that they kill Zac could amount to the crime of encouraging murder, contrary to **s. 44** of the **Serious Crime Act 2007**.[1] Alvin clearly intends the offence of murder should be committed and that the necessary course of conduct should be followed with the requisite fault element for murder. Liability is inchoate, so the fact that the killing never takes place is irrelevant. The offence focuses on Alvin's state of mind—hence the fact that Bernard does not want to go through with the plan will be no bar to liability.

[1] Under **s. 47(5) of the 2007 Act** it suffices if Alvin believed that, were the act to be done, it would be done with the *mens rea* for murder, or that he was reckless as to whether or not this would be the case, or that his state of mind was such that, were he to have done what was encouraged or assisted, he would have acted with the fault required.

All four participants could be charged with conspiracy to murder under **s. 1** of the **Criminal Law Act 1977**. In order to establish a statutory conspiracy, it must be shown that two or more persons agreed that a course of conduct should be pursued which, if the agreement were to be carried out in accordance with their intentions, either:

(a) would necessarily amount to or involve the commission of any offence or offences by one or more of the parties to the agreement; or

(b) would do so but for the existence of facts which render the commission of the offence or any of the offences impossible.

The prosecution must prove that an agreement existed between the parties.[2] It is submitted that there is an agreement on the facts and, as they intend that death will result, the parties could be guilty of conspiracy to murder. However, Bernard will argue that as he had no intention to assist, and did nothing to assist, he cannot be guilty. The key case on this point is the House of Lords' decision in *R v Anderson* **[1985] 2 All ER 961**. In this case the accused was convicted of conspiring with a number of people to help one of them escape from jail. He had agreed to supply wire to cut the prison bars, but said he never intended the plan to be put into effect and believed that it could not possibly succeed. However, his conviction was upheld as he had agreed that the criminal course of conduct should be pursued, and it was not necessary to prove that he intended that the offence be committed. In this case Lord Bridge also stated (at p. 965) that the *mens rea* of conspiracy is established 'if and only if it is shown that the accused when he entered into the agreement, intended to play some part in the agreed course of conduct in furtherance of the criminal purpose which the agreed course of conduct was intended to achieve'. On this basis Bernard would have a defence, but Lord Bridge's *dictum* was clarified by the Court of Appeal decision in *R v Siracusa* (1989)

[2] If they are still in the course of negotiations this would not be sufficient.

90 Cr App R 340, where O'Connor J stated that 'participation in a conspiracy is infinitely variable: it can be active or passive. There is no need for the prosecution to prove an intention on each accused's part in the carrying out of the agreement'. Bernard would therefore be found guilty of conspiracy to murder.[3]

[3] These two cases clarify the *mens rea* for conspiracy.

Desmond may also be able to argue that he lacked the *mens rea* for conspiracy to murder, as his informing the police demonstrated that he had an intention to frustrate the intention of the conspiracy. In *R v McPhillips* [1990] 6 BNIL, Lord Lowry CJ in the Court of Appeal of Northern Ireland held that an accused who had joined in a conspiracy to plant a bomb, timed to explode on the roof of a hall of a disco, was not a party to a conspiracy to murder because he intended to give a warning in time for the hall to be cleared. However, in *Yip Chiu Cheung v R* [1994] 2 All ER 924, the Privy Council held that an undercover police officer posing as a drug dealer would have the necessary *mens rea* for conspiracy when he deliberately carried drugs to entrap other drug dealers. Neither his good motive nor the instructions of his superiors would have been a valid defence.[4]

[4] This case is also good authority for the proposition that motive should not be confused with intention.

Bernard may incur liability under **s. 45** of the **Serious Crime Act 2007** on the basis that he does encourage Alvin by saying he would assist in the murder. The question for the jury will be whether or not there is evidence that Bernard believed that the offence would be committed, and that his actions would encourage or assist its commission. The fact that he did not intend to help does not necessarily mean that his apparent enthusiasm was not capable of encouraging the others.[5] As to *mens rea*, it would suffice that Bernard believed that, were the killing of Zac to take place, it would be done with the fault required for murder.

[5] Apply the law to the facts, distinguishing if necessary.

As withdrawal is recognised as a defence for an accomplice, it is submitted that a conspirator should have a similar defence, if only to provide an incentive for a conspirator to make efforts to stop the conspiracy succeeding. It is submitted that Desmond should not be found guilty of conspiracy. Perhaps the Crown Prosecution Service would decide it is not in the public interest to prosecute Desmond.

Alvin may also be guilty of attempted murder. Clearly he has the necessary *mens rea*, an intention to kill (*R v Whybrow* (1951) 35 Cr App R 141), but has he committed the *actus reus* of attempt? The test the prosecution must satisfy under **s. 1(1)** of the **Criminal Attempts Act 1981** is that the accused has done an act that is more than merely preparatory to the offence. This is a question of fact for the jury after the trial judge has decided that there is sufficient evidence to be left to them to support such a finding. Thus in *R v Jones* (1990) 91 Cr App R 356, the Court of Appeal upheld the jury's decision that the accused had done more than a merely preparatory act for attempted murder in pointing a sawn-off shot-gun at the victim, even though he had still to remove the safety catch. Whether Alvin would be guilty of attempted murder would therefore purely depend on what precise point the plan had reached before he was stopped.[6]

[6]No further information is given on these facts.

Bernard, Ceri, and Desmond may also face charges under the **Accessories and Abettors Act 1861** of counselling, procuring, aiding, and abetting. It is often difficult to identify precisely the specific involvement (see *R v Richards* **[1974] 3 All ER 1088**), but counselling and procuring are acts done before the principal offence whereas aiding and abetting take place at the time of its occurrence. Clearly, as they intended to assist and contemplated the type of crime (*Chan Wing Siu v R* **[1984] 3 All ER 877**), they appear to have the necessary *mens rea*. Desmond would argue that he had validly withdrawn by contacting the police in time for them to stop the murder (*R v Becerra* **(1975) 62 Cr App R 212**), and Bernard would contend that his failure to arrive constituted a withdrawal. It is submitted that whereas Desmond's argument would succeed, Bernard's would fail as in *R v Rook* **[1993] 2 All ER 955** the Court of Appeal held merely not turning up to be insufficient, suggesting that a positive act may be required. As was confirmed in *R v O'Flaherty* **[2004] Crim LR 751**, whether or not withdrawal is effective is a matter of fact and degree. The later it is left the more is required by way of positive action.

Ceri does not appear to have any defence available, and his act of giving Alvin a loaded gun satisfies the ingredients of this offence.

Thus, Ceri and Bernard could be found guilty of abetting an attempted murder. Although the offence of attempt to aid and abet was abolished by **s. 5** of the **Criminal Law Act 1977**, there is an offence of attempting to abet.

Ceri and Desmond could also incur liability under **s. 45** of the **Serious Crime Act 2007** on the basis of their offering to help Alvin. Again this would be seen as committing acts capable of encouraging murder, intending that Alvin should commit murder.

 LOOKING FOR EXTRA MARKS?

■ A really good understanding of the statutory provisions and of *R v Anderson* and *R v Siracusa* will make all the difference in this question.

■ Be sure to apply the legal principles to the facts throughout, distinguishing if necessary.

Amy, Betty, Claire, and Debbie plan to break into X's warehouse in order to steal. Amy, Betty, and Claire know that there will be a night-watchman on the premises, but Debbie does not know this fact. Amy gives Betty a loaded revolver, telling her not to hesitate to use it if the occasion should so require. When they set off to X's warehouse, Debbie knows that Betty has a revolver in her possession but Claire does not. Once inside the warehouse the four are interrupted by the night-watchman, Victor. As Betty is about to fire the revolver at Victor, Amy, recognising Victor as her cousin, knocks Betty's hand to one side, crying out 'Don't shoot'. Amy's act causes the bullet to miss Victor, but it strikes and kills Peter, a police officer who is entering the room.

Advise the Crown Prosecution Service on any criminal liability arising from these facts.

CAUTION!

- You may often find that the facts presented to you feature a conspiracy before the commission of the subsequent completed offence. It is tempting to advise on the criminal offences in the order in which they are presented by the question but it is usually best to leave inchoate offences until the end and present them as alternatives to other forms of accessorial liability.

- This is a long and detailed scenario, so some of the detail has been curtailed to represent what a candidate could reasonably expect to achieve in an examination. The problem of the foresight of the defendants has been made somewhat more straightforward with the decision in **R v Jogee**.

DIAGRAM ANSWER PLAN

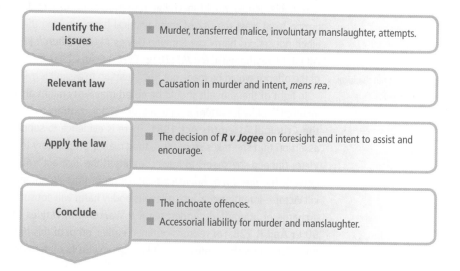

Identify the issues	▪ Murder, transferred malice, involuntary manslaughter, attempts.
Relevant law	▪ Causation in murder and intent, *mens rea*.
Apply the law	▪ The decision of **R v Jogee** on foresight and intent to assist and encourage.
Conclude	▪ The inchoate offences. ▪ Accessorial liability for murder and manslaughter.

Betty kills Peter by causing his death in fact and in law. The fact that Amy grabs her arm to stop her firing at Victor does not amount to a *novus actus interveniens.* Even though her gun points at Peter not Victor, her pulling the trigger is still a voluntary act. The *mens rea* of murder is satisfied by the prosecution proving that Betty intended to kill or intended to cause grievous bodily harm (*R v Moloney* [1985] **1 All ER 1025**).[1] Following *R v Woollin* [1998] **4 All ER 103**, the jury should be directed that they will be entitled to infer that Betty intended to kill if there is evidence that she foresaw death or grievous bodily harm as virtually certain to result from her actions. Given that Betty was intending to fire the revolver at Victor, foresight of some grievous bodily harm on her part seems evident.

Betty may argue that, as she intended to fire the gun at Victor, she did not intend to harm Peter. The court will apply the doctrine of transferred malice. Thus if the accused has the necessary *mens rea* of the offence, but the actual victim is different from the intended victim, the *mens rea* will be transferred and the accused will be guilty; see *R v Mitchell* [1983] **2 All ER 427**.

Betty might argue that she was simply firing a warning shot in Victor's direction, and that it was Amy's act of hitting her arm which caused her aim to alter, resulting in Peter's death. In the event of this argument being accepted, Betty would still be guilty of involuntary (unlawful act) manslaughter on the constructive basis. The prosecution would need to prove that Betty intended to do an act that was unlawful and dangerous (*R v Newbury and Jones* [1976] **2 All ER 365**). Simply drawing and pointing a gun at someone would be unlawful, i.e. assault; and as the test for dangerous is objective ('the unlawful act must be such as all sober and reasonable people would inevitably recognise must subject the other person to at least the risk of some physical harm resulting therefrom, albeit not serious harm' *per* Edmund Davies J in *R v Church* [1965] **2 All ER 72**, reaffirmed in *R v JM* [2012] **EWCA Crim 2293**), this element of the offence would be made out. The intention to assault is evident.[2]

In light of the above it should be noted that Betty might also have incurred liability for attempting to murder Victor, contrary to **s. 1(1) of the Criminal Attempts Act 1981**. There is evidence to support the assertion that she takes steps more than merely preparatory to killing Victor (indeed she seems to have committed the 'last act' within her power). The *mens rea*, however, requires proof that she intended to kill Victor—intention to cause grievous bodily harm will not suffice for a charge of attempted murder; see *R v Walker and Hayles* (1989) **90 Cr App R 226**. For reasons outlined earlier, proof of this might be doubtful unless she confesses that killing him was her intention.

[1] Start by identifying the offence before considering accessorial liability

[2] With any offence, set out the legal requirements for its proof.

Amy will, in all likelihood, be guilty of a **s. 9(1)(a) of the Theft Act 1968** burglary. She could also be charged with counselling Betty's offence of aggravated burglary under **s. 10 of the Theft Act 1968**. Amy encourages Betty to go armed with the gun and it is her intention that Betty should do so. The **Serious Crimes Act 2007** applies here.

Turning to Amy's liability in relation to the death of Peter, it could be argued that she incurs liability as a principal offender, as she does contribute to causing his death; but for her pushing Betty's hand to one side Peter would not have been killed. Her actions in causing the gun to be fired at Peter can also be seen as the operating and substantial cause of his death. *Mens rea* would be problematic, however, as her intention when she pushes Betty's hand is to prevent harm. There is no evidence that she intends any harm to occur to Peter as opposed to Victor. Indeed it might be impossible to identify any fault that would suffice for her to be convicted of a form of manslaughter as principal offender. There is no obvious dangerous criminal act as is required for unlawful act manslaughter, and it is far from obvious that the duty of care and grossly negligent breach of duty of care needed for killing by gross negligence can be identified.[3]

[3] It is useful to briefly identify possibilities for conviction, even to eliminate them.

The prosecution will almost certainly seek to charge Amy with either the murder or manslaughter of Peter as an accomplice to Betty's actions. Amy supplies Betty with a loaded gun, knowing that there is a night-watchman on the premises. There is compelling evidence on these facts that she contemplates a scenario in which the gun will be discharged by Betty—especially given the evidence that she told Betty to use the gun if necessary. However the position has now changed. This will be discussed below. At the very least Amy contemplated that Betty might kill or do grievous bodily harm either with intent to kill or with intent to do grievous bodily harm. In *R v Powell; R v Daniels; R v English* [1999] 1 AC 1,[4] the House of Lords had held that, to found a conviction for murder, it was sufficient for a secondary party to have realised, in the course of a joint enterprise, that the primary party might kill with intent to do so or with intent to cause grievous bodily harm. Following the decision in *R v Jogee* [2016] UKSC 8, the mental element for secondary liability is an intention to assist or encourage the crime. In the absence of an actual agreement, mere contemplation that Betty might kill will be insufficient. Where a defendant departs from the agreed plan, he is only guilty as an accomplice if he intended to commit the crime, or if he intended to assist or encourage the principal to commit it. Previously, intention was not required. The second defendant was guilty if he had foresight.

[4] As *R v Jogee* is such a recent decision, it is a good idea to explain exactly what has changed with regard to the defendant's *mens rea*.

If Betty was found guilty of manslaughter, Amy might contend that she could not be found guilty as an accomplice to murder. This point arose in the Privy Council case of *Hui Chi Ming v R* [1991] 3 All ER 897, where the court upheld the conviction of the accused for murder even though the principal offenders had in an earlier trial been found guilty of manslaughter only. The principle is that if the *actus reus* has been committed, the court will look at the *mens rea* of the individual participants in order to ascertain their criminal responsibility.

In the event that there is any difficulty in establishing the *mens rea* of Amy as an accomplice to murder, the prosecution is most likely to contend that Amy incurs liability as an accomplice to the manslaughter of Peter by Betty on the basis that his death was an unforeseen and accidental consequence of the common design (committing a burglary armed with a loaded weapon) being carried out. Both *R v Betts and Ridley* (1930) 22 Cr App R 148 and *R v Baldessare* (1930) 22 Cr App R 70 support the conclusion that an accomplice will be a party to the accidental consequences of the principal offender's acts, provided the principal offender's actions were within the scope of what the accomplice contemplated or agreed. In *R v Baldessare*, the court held that an accused who agreed to take and drive away a car was guilty of abetting manslaughter when the principal offender drove so negligently as to cause a pedestrian's death, as although this consequence was unforeseen it arose when the principal offender was acting within the scope of the agreement.

Betty could be charged with the attempted murder of Victor. Similarly Amy could be charged as an accomplice to the attempted murder—for an example of accessorial liability for attempt see *R v Dunnington* [1984] 1 All ER 676.

The facts indicate that Amy does try to stop Betty firing at Victor. Hence Amy may argue that, notwithstanding her supply of the gun, she had, at the last minute, withdrawn from the joint enterprise, and should not incur any liability as an accomplice to the attempted murder. The key case on withdrawal *is R v Becerra and Cooper* (1975) 62 Cr App R 212, where before the principal offender in the course of a burglary killed the victim, the accomplice had said 'Come on, let's go' and had left the building. The Court of Appeal, in upholding his conviction for murder, held that something vastly more substantial and effective was required to constitute a valid withdrawal, such as shouting a warning or physical intervention. Amy would argue that in shouting 'Don't shoot' and knocking Betty's hand, she had done all that she reasonably could to prevent the crime. It will be a question of fact for the jury to determine whether or not this is the case.[5] As was confirmed in *R v O'Flaherty* [2004] Crim LR 751, whether or not withdrawal is effective is a matter of fact and degree. The later it is left the more is required by way of positive action.

As with Amy, Claire could be charged under **s. 9(1)(a) of the Theft Act 1968** as a principal offender. As she does not know Betty had the gun the prosecution would not charge her as an accomplice to Betty's offence of aggravated burglary under **s. 10 of the Theft Act 1968**.

[5] The roles of the judge and jury in this type of case was confirmed in *R v Jogee*. It is the role of the jury to determine this on a question of fact.

Claire knew that there was a night-watchman on the premises, providing evidence that she did contemplate some harm being caused to

him if the burglary was to succeed. For her to be convicted of murder, however, there would have to be evidence that she intended to assist or encourage the crime.[6] The key point for Claire would be the use of the weapon. Provided she did not intend the death of any person, she could avail herself of the 'fundamentally different' rule, under which even an accomplice who contemplates that death or serious injury might occur, can escape liability if the principal offender causes death by the use of a fundamentally different (more dangerous) *modus operandi*—such as the use of a gun instead of a cosh.

If Claire contemplated some harm being caused to a person, not amounting to actual bodily harm, she could be convicted as an accomplice to manslaughter on the given facts, but again she would escape liability if she was able to avail herself of the 'fundamentally different' rule; see **Attorney-General's Ref (No 3 of 2004) [2005] EWCA Crim 1882**.

It is relevant in these circumstances to ask whether there was a shared criminal purpose—there does not appear to be here.

Debbie could be charged with offences contrary to **s. 9(1)(a) of the Theft Act 1968** burglary, as outlined earlier, and as an accomplice to Betty's offence of aggravated burglary under **s. 10 of the Theft Act 1968**.

Regarding accessorial liability for homicide, Debbie's position is slightly different from Claire's. Debbie knows about the gun, but not that there will be a night-watchman. It is submitted that her knowledge regarding the gun will put her in a much worse position than Claire, however. The prosecution will argue that as she knew about the gun she contemplated its use—why else did she think Betty was

taking it? Following the decision in *R v Jogee* (see earlier), it will no longer be possible to convict her even if she contemplated or foresaw it—only an intention will suffice.[7] Regarding her liability both as an accomplice to the attempted murder of Victor and the murder of Peter, in order to escape liability Debbie would be forced to use the weak argument that although she knew that Betty had a gun, she did not think that Betty would actually use it. Debbie could be held to have had sufficient *mens rea* to be an accomplice to the murder of Peter and the attempted murder of Victor.

Even before the four parties enter the warehouse, they would be guilty of the crime of conspiracy to burgle under **s. 1 of the Criminal Law Act 1977**, as they have agreed to pursue a course of conduct which would necessarily involve a criminal offence. Amy would also be guilty of encouraging and assisting Betty to commit burglary, assault, and possibly murder when supplying her with the gun and encouraging her to use it; see **s. 46 of the Serious Crime Act 2007**.

LOOKING FOR EXTRA MARKS?

- This question requires you to show your knowledge of recent legal developments. You can do this by contrasting with the previous law.
- Accessorial liability and principal offences are difficult to structure in the same question—keep these issues separate.

QUESTION | 3

Kirk hires Miles and Chaka to attack Patti, a business rival. Kirk makes it clear that he wants Patti frightened off so that she will no longer be a threat to Kirk's business. One evening Miles and Chaka follow Patti as she leaves her office to go home at the end of the day. Miles picks up a large stone from the gutter, grabs Patti from behind, and beats her on the head with the stone. Patti dies of a brain haemorrhage. Chaka is standing close to Miles as he carries out the attack and does not take steps to intervene and stop him.

Kirk, Miles, and Chaka are subsequently arrested in connection with Patti's death. Under questioning Chaka admits that she knew Miles had a history of violent behaviour and previous convictions for grievous bodily harm, but claims that she had no idea Miles had a stone in his hand when he hit Patti. Kirk admits hiring Miles and Chaka to frighten Patti but denies any intention that Patti should be physically harmed.

Advise the Crown Prosecution Service as to the criminal liability of Kirk, Miles, and Chaka in respect of the death of Patti.

CAUTION!

- Consider what Chaka may have contemplated—this is crucial to the *mens rea*.
- Good fact management is key to providing a clear and concise answer. Always start by dealing with the liability of the principal offender. Once you have established what s/he has done you can see what accessorial liability of other parties might be derived from this.

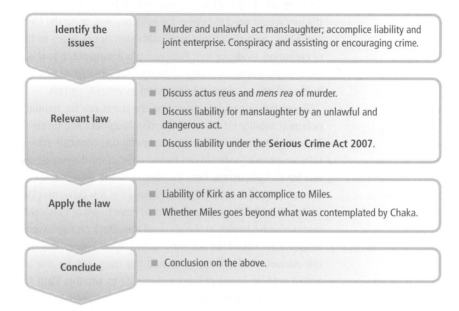

DIAGRAM ANSWER PLAN

| Identify the issues | ■ Murder and unlawful act manslaughter; accomplice liability and joint enterprise. Conspiracy and assisting or encouraging crime. |

| Relevant law | ■ Discuss actus reus and *mens rea* of murder.
■ Discuss liability for manslaughter by an unlawful and dangerous act.
■ Discuss liability under the **Serious Crime Act 2007**. |

| Apply the law | ■ Liability of Kirk as an accomplice to Miles.
■ Whether Miles goes beyond what was contemplated by Chaka. |

| Conclude | ■ Conclusion on the above. |

 SUGGESTED ANSWER

[1] In a case like this, it is always important to show that you have identified the primary offence and the principal offender. You can then start to see what secondary liability might apply.

The prosecution will need to prove that Miles was the cause in fact and in law of Patti's death.[1] As for causation in law, the application of the 'but for' test would suggest that but for his having attacked Patti with the stone she would not have suffered the injury resulting in her death—see **R v White [1910] 2 KB 124**. The facts provide that Patti dies of a brain haemorrhage. Miles may argue that Patti had a 'thin skull' and was more prone to serious injury as a result of the attack than would have been the case with the average person. It is unlikely that such an argument would succeed. **R v Blaue [1975] 1 WLR 1411** provides that Miles must take his victim as he finds him or her. The fact that Patti might have been more susceptible to injury will not be relevant in law.

Assuming causation can be established, the question arises as to whether or not Miles had the *mens rea* for murder. The prosecution would have to prove that he intended to kill Patti or intended to cause her grievous bodily harm. Alternatively it would suffice for the prosecution to prove that Miles foresaw her death, or her suffering grievous bodily harm, as being a virtually certain consequence of his actions; *R v Woollin* **[1998] 4 All ER 103**. On the one hand, to beat a person on the head with a large stone suggests evidence of at least an intention to do some grievous bodily harm. On the other hand, the jury would need to review the evidence indicating the force used, and Miles' own direct testimony. Although not relevant to the issue of causation, evidence that Patti was more susceptible to this type of harm might influence a jury in concluding whether or not Miles did foresee death or grievous bodily harm as virtually certain.

Given the uncertainty regarding the *mens rea* for murder, Miles' potential liability for unlawful act manslaughter must be considered. The attack on Patti is clearly an unlawful (i.e. criminal) act—specifically an assault. It should not be too difficult for the jury to apply the test for dangerousness here in relation to the unlawful act; see *R v Church* **[1965] 2 All ER 72** as developed in *R v Dawson* **(1985) 81 Cr App R 150**. The prosecution would have to prove that a sober and reasonable bystander, at the scene of the attack on Patti, would have foreseen the risk of her suffering some physical harm. This should be self-evident on the facts, as should the *mens rea* for the unlawful act—i.e. Miles being at least reckless as to whether Patti suffers a battery or actual bodily harm.

[2] Now you can deal with the secondary liability—in this case, joint enterprise.

The prosecution will allege that Chaka was party to a joint enterprise in the attack on Patti—see *R v Petters and Parfitt* **[1995] Crim LR 501**. Chaka is at the scene of the crime acting in concert with Miles.[2]

A number of issues arise for consideration. First, can Chaka argue that by not physically participating in the attack she played no part in it? Mere presence at the scene of a crime will not normally result in accessorial liability. Chaka's case is hardly that of an innocent bystander happening to witness a crime, however. She set out with Miles to carry out some sort of unlawful attack on Patti that would result in Patti being frightened off. Indeed the prosecution will in all likelihood rely upon her failure to prevent Miles from carrying out the attack as evidence that she passively adopted his actions in hitting Patti with the stone.[3]

[3] Note this application of the law to the facts.

Secondly, if Chaka is to be convicted of murder as a party to a joint enterprise, what *mens rea* has to be proved on her part? On the basis of *R v Powell; R v Daniels; R v English* **[1999] 1 AC 1** Chaka could have been convicted of murder if she intended the death of Patti (unlikely on the facts); intended that Patti should suffer grievous bodily harm (doubtful on the facts); or where she realised that, in the course of pursuing the joint enterprise, Miles might have killed or caused grievous bodily harm with intent to produce either of those consequences (possible, given the facts). Chaka confessed that she knew

Miles had a history of violent behaviour and previous convictions for grievous bodily harm. This would have helped to prove that she foresaw death or grievous bodily harm as possible consequences of an attack by Miles.[4]

[4] The *mens rea* is foresight, not intention.

The issue will now be dealt with differently by the courts, following the decision of *R v Jogee* [2016] UKSC 8. The prosecution will have to be satisfied that Chaka intended to encourage or assist Miles in the commission of the offence. Simple foresight on Chaka's part that Miles might commit the offence will not suffice.

The third issue is as to whether or not Chaka can argue that Miles' deliberate use of the large stone as a weapon amounted to a conscious departure from the joint enterprise. In *R v Powell; R v Daniels; R v English* [1999] 1 AC 1, the House of Lords had held that where a party to a joint enterprise 'only' foresaw the principal offender causing grievous bodily harm, and the principal offender in fact killed the victim by using a 'fundamentally different' act, the accomplice could escape liability on the basis that the principal had exceeded the scope of the joint enterprise.

[5] This last case clarified the House of Lords approach in *Rahman*, however.

In *R v Rahman and Others* [2008] UKHL 45, the House of Lords was willing to extend the scope of the 'fundamentally different' rule to the benefit of an accomplice who foresaw that the principal *might* kill with intent to kill or with intent to some grievous bodily harm.[5]

The use of the knife to cut the victim's throat rather than the gun to kneecap the victim is a fundamentally different *modus operandi*—one that carries with it a much more obvious risk of death. Hence Chaka may argue that she foresaw grievous bodily harm (especially in light of her knowledge of Miles) or even that she foresaw Miles causing death as a result of his intentionally inflicting grievous bodily harm, but that she did not foresee the use of a weapon. In the light of the decision in *R v Jogee* it is clear that the rule has lost much of its significance. Knowledge of a particular weapon only has significance in the context of the court's assessment of *mens rea*. It could be evidence of intention to assist, but this will not be a foregone conclusion.

A fourth point is that Chaka may argue that she did not even contemplate grievous bodily harm being caused. She would cite in support of this the fact that Kirk asked them simply to frighten Patti. If this is the case Chaka clearly cannot be guilty as an accomplice to murder. The prosecution may, however, argue that she should be convicted as an accomplice to manslaughter. Before the decision in *R v Jogee*, if Chaka only contemplated some harm falling short of grievous bodily harm, it is possible she could be convicted as an accomplice to manslaughter, provided the actions of Miles were not a

[6] This is quite a fine point, and illustrates the difficulties facing the courts in situations of accessorial liability.

deliberate departure from the conduct that she contemplated.[6] Now, actual intention will be needed. Hence if she contemplated the use of a weapon, Miles' use of a stone will not amount to a departure from the joint enterprise. If Chaka did not contemplate the use of any weapon she may escape liability altogether. It seems Chaka's liability will derive from what she foresaw Miles doing, not the intent with which she foresaw him acting.

Note that the prosecution will also have the option of charging Chaka with encouraging the commission of the offence by Miles on the basis that she was supporting him at the scene of the crime by her presence—see **ss. 44–46** of the **Serious Crime Act 2007.** There will still be an issue here regarding which crime Chaka was encouraging Miles to commit—but at the very least she can be said to have encouraged him to commit an assault, and to have believed that her encouragement would lead to the commission of the offence.[7]

[7] Again, ensure you apply the law to the facts carefully.

Kirk was not present at the scene of the attack on Patti, hence he would be regarded as a secondary party—an accomplice involved prior to the commission of the offence. Hiring Miles and Chaka to carry out the attack on Patti would amount to counselling (*R v Calhaem* **[1985] 2 All ER 266**). The problem lies in whether or not Kirk could be charged with counselling murder or manslaughter. As noted earlier in this section, *R v Powell; R v Daniels; R v English* **[1999] 1 AC 1** provided that an accomplice could be guilty of murder provided he at least contemplated that the principal might kill the victim or cause him grievous bodily harm. Kirk will say that he only intended that Patti should be frightened and that he did not contemplate any serious harm, or possibly that he did not contemplate any harm at all. The court will want to be satisfied that he did much more than merely contemplate harm, but that he actually intended that harm to result. Again, foresight or contemplation will not be sufficient for the prosecution to discharge their burden of proof.

Kirk, Miles, and Chaka could be charged with conspiring to cause Patti actual bodily harm, or even grievous bodily harm, contrary to **s. 1(1)** of the **Criminal Law Act 1977**. The fact that Kirk intended to play no active part in the attack is no bar to liability—see *R v Siracusa* **(1989) 90 Cr App R 340**. It would be enough that he agreed with others that the course of conduct should be pursued.

Finally, Kirk could be encouraging Miles and Chaka to assault (in the narrow sense) Patti—the fact that they act on the encouragement would be no bar to his liability for the offence created by

s. 44 of the **Serious Crime Act 2007**. He encourages the commission of the offence of (narrow) assault and intends that it should be committed.

QUESTION | 4

Discuss and analyse the decision of the Supreme Court in the case of *R v Jogee* [2016] **UKSC 8** on secondary party liability for murder.

! CAUTION!

■ This is a complicated area of law, given clarity in this recent case. Note that you are being asked to comment on the scope of this case, so make sure you only deal with joint enterprise, rather than secondary party liability as a whole.

■ It is essential to avoid describing the legal position too much—make sure you find room to comment on how the judges reached their decision.

DIAGRAM ANSWER PLAN

An explanation of secondary liability and joint enterprise.

▼

The decision in *R v Jogee* and the previous law.

▼

The impact and assessment of the decision.

▼

Blameworthiness in the criminal law.

▼

Conclusion on the effectiveness of the decision.

Secondary liability for a criminal offence arises where the person who did not commit the *actus reus* of the crime (the secondary party) encourages or assists the person who does commit it (the principal offender). If the encouragement or assistance was intentional, then the secondary party is guilty of the same offence.[1] The encouragement or assistance forms the *actus reus*; the intention to encourage and/or assist the principal forms the *mens rea*.

> [1] Set out in summary form the general area of law you are going to discuss.

A particular problem arises, however, when the principal offender departs from the agreed crime, or commits another crime entirely, in the course of the planned criminal activity. The court must then assess the correct level of *mens rea* for the secondary participant. This type of liability became known as joint enterprise, or sometimes parasitic accessorial liability. The question is whether the secondary participant must intend the other to commit the crime, or whether he must simply be aware of the possibility that it might be committed. Until recently, foresight was sufficient to convict the secondary participant of murder.

> [2] Set out your plans for the essay, with reference to the question set.

This essay analyses this problem, with reference to the landmark Supreme Court decision of *R v Jogee* [2016] UKSC 8 which reverses the previous common law position.[2] This had stated that the secondary participant could be convicted of murder where he merely had foresight of the crime committed by the principal. The legal position is now that in order to be convicted of murder, the secondary participant must intend to assist or encourage the commission of the offence in order to be found guilty of murder. The Supreme Court essentially abolished the previous category of joint enterprise liability.[3]

> [3] It is important to state the effect of the case early on in your essay.

In this way, it has effectively abolished joint enterprise liability, and has substantially reduced the significance of the fundamental difference rule. The law prior to this recent decision was contained in two key cases: *R v Powell and English* [1997] 4 All ER 545 and *R v Chan Wing-Siu* [1985] AC 168. These cases held that the mental element required of the secondary party was simply that he *foresaw* the possibility that the principal defendant might commit another crime. If the defendant did foresee this possibility, the courts treated this as sufficient *mens rea* for the crime, and as tantamount to authorising the principal to commit it. The effect of this was that the secondary party was guilty of the crime even though he did not intend to commit it. Thus, a lower *mens rea* threshold was set for the second defendant, but the outcome was the same. In other words, this basis for liability in cases of joint enterprise is reflected in the following statement of Sir Robin Cooke in **Chan Wing-Siu**:[4]

> [4] Quoting directly from the case to back up your ideas will strengthen your essay.

Where a man lends himself to a criminal enterprise knowing that potentially murderous weapons are to be carried, and in the event they are in fact used by his partner with an intent sufficient for murder, he should not escape the consequences by [relying on a belief that their use was unlikely] . . . that there is such a principle is not in doubt. It turns on contemplation or, putting the same idea into words, authorization, which may be express but is more usually implied . . . the criminal liability lies in participating in the venture with that foresight.

[5]In evaluating the law, try to make it clear what the problems were.

The approach in *Chan Wing-Siu* was criticised in various quarters on the grounds that it was fundamentally unfair to convict a defendant of a crime which they did not commit personally.[5] It meant, for example, that a young person in a gang (D1) would be guilty of murder where one member of that gang (D2) killed, and D1 knew that it was a possibility, even though D1 was elsewhere at the time. It meant that the scope of liability for murder was extremely wide, a surprising consequence given the insistence on the high threshold for intention in murder elsewhere. It was also unfair between defendants, of course, because it meant that the secondary party could be convicted of the same crime as the person who actually caused the death on the basis of a much lower level of mental culpability.

In *R v Powell; R v Daniels; R v English* [1999] 1 AC 1 the court followed the approach in the earlier case, dealing particularly with the problem of the first defendant using a particular weapon. The court recognised the problem of convicting merely on foresight, but cited the need to prevent crime. Both of these cases, it is submitted, were decided on the basis of public policy and the need to balance the prevention of harm to the public with any potential danger of wrongly convicting an offender. The court in *R v Jogee* held this approach to be incorrect.

As stated earlier, the recent decision in *R v Jogee* has completely changed this position. It declared that the law had taken a wrong turn in *Chan Wing-Siu* [1985] and in *Powell and English*. On the one hand it can be argued that the secondary defendant's *mens rea* need not be of the same level as the principal's; on the other hand it can be argued that it is unfair to convict a defendant of murder on the basis of anything less than intent. If foresight is not sufficient *mens rea* to convict a single defendant, it should also not be sufficient to convict a secondary participant.

In the case in question, the appellant, Jogee, was convicted of the murder of Paul Fyfe, the boyfriend of Naomi Reid. Paul Fyfe was stabbed to death by Mohammed Hirsi in the hallway of her home. Hirsi was convicted of murder, having been encouraged to 'do something to Fyfe' by Jogee, who was outside with a broken bottle. The fatal stabbing was done by Hirsi with a knife which he took from the kitchen.

The trial judge directed the jury that that the appellant was guilty of murder if he took part in the attack on Mr Fyfe and if he realised that it was possible that Hirsi might use the knife with intent to cause grievous bodily harm.

The court concluded that this decision was incorrect. The decision did not take account of other important cases on secondary participation, and departed from the basic rule that the mental element is an intention to participate, not simply foresight. Henceforth, the secondary party's liability will only be guilty of the crime if he intended that the crime be committed or if he intended to encourage and assist in its commission.[6] Their Lordships acknowledged the problems that the previous law had created, stating (at para 81):

> it cannot be said that the law is now well-established and working satisfactorily. It remains highly controversial and a continuing source of difficulty for trial judges.

To rely on these two cases (*Chang Wing-Siu* and *Powell; Daniels; English*) was to rely on cases which were in fact only part of the history of this area. In this way the *mens rea* required of the secondary party is more or less the same as that required of the principal offender. The fact that the secondary participant was aware of the possibility that such a crime might be committed might be evidence, even strong evidence of authorisation or intent to commit it, but it was not equivalent to it. Foresight and authorisation are not the same. As a result, the Supreme Court concluded that the law had taken a wrong turn. The law should, therefore, be returned to the position it was in before those two cases.

The dangers of a 'too low' threshold for secondary liability were explained by Lord Hughes and Lord Toulson (at para 83):

> murder already has a relatively low mens rea threshold because it includes an intention to cause serious injury, without intent to kill . . . the Chan Wing-Siu principle extends liability for murder to a secondary party on the basis of a still lesser degree of culpability, namely foresight only of the possibility that the principal may commit murder.

It savours, as Professor Smith suggested, of constructive crime.[7]

This would contradict a fundamental principle in the criminal law—that of blameworthiness.

This position, following this landmark judgment, is, therefore that the mental element for the secondary participant is an intention to assist or encourage the crime (at para 79):

> in plain terms, our analysis leads us to the conclusion that the introduction of the principle was based on an incomplete, and in some respects erroneous reading of the previous law, coupled with generalised and questionable policy arguments.[8]

Further support for the rectitude of the decision is that it is very similar to Parliament's intention in the enactment of the **Serious Crime**

[6] Key reasons for the decision should be explained here.

[7] In this context, the reference to constructive refers to interpretation—the court would interpret that one crime had necessarily been committed through the commission of a crime committed by someone else.

[8] The *ratio* of the case.

Act 2007 when it created the new offences of intentionally encouraging or assisting the commission of an offence. It was argued in the case that it was not the role of the courts to address this issue, but that legislation should deal with it. In fact, as the law in this area is predominantly common law, it was right that the courts should consider it.

One of the problems in the previous law was that too many convictions arose from it, and that in particular, young people were unfairly convicted and a disproportionate number of black males were convicted. One of the defence arguments put forward in the case is that teenagers in particular find it difficult to foresee the behaviour of others. The judgment may be reflecting the importance of protecting children's rights as protected in the United Nations Convention of the Rights of the Child, an argument previously considered in other important cases involving *mens rea*, such as *R v G and Another* [2003] **UKHL 50**.[9] It is important not to over-criminalise children, which is what the previous law on joint enterprise may have been doing. In considering the fairness of the previous law, the Supreme Court in *R v Jogee* stated that previous judgments could have, but did not, consider these consequences in making the decisions they did:[10]

[9] In fact the judgment made a reference to the subjective landscape of the criminal law.

[10] This is important as it is one of the main reasons for the decision in this case.

there was no consideration in *Chan Wing-Siu* or in *Powell and English* of the fundamental policy question of whether and why it was necessary and appropriate to reclassify such conduct as murder rather than manslaughter. Such a discussion would have involved, among other things, questions about fair labelling and fair discrimination in sentencing.

[11] Conclude on the main points you have raised and offer a comment yourself.

The law relating to secondary participation and particularly joint enterprise was unfair, and as such it is submitted that in overturning it, the Supreme Court has made the right decision.[11] To allow a defendant to be convicted of such a serious offence, when he only foresaw the possibility of death or injury but did not intend it, undermines essential principles of *mens rea*. The decision of the court in **Chan Wing-Siu**, which had decided that foresight was sufficient, caused a wrong principle to become embedded in the law. It is now necessary, in order for a secondary party to be found guilty of murder, that he must intentionally assist or encourage the principal to act.

✚ LOOKING FOR EXTRA MARKS?

- Make sure your answer to this question is not too descriptive, either of the area of law or the case. In other words, it is important to make some critical comment about the new development. Here, the answer referred to unfairness.

- Key quotes from the judgment can give extra quality to your answer.

TAKING THINGS FURTHER

- Buxton, R., 'Joint Enterprise' [2009] Crim LR 233.

  This article is a critique of reform proposals relating to joint enterprise.

- Crewe, Liebling A., Padfield, N., and Virgo, G., 'Joint Enterprise: The Implications of an Unfair and an Unclear Law' [2015] Crim LR 4, 252–69.

  This article reviews the law of joint enterprise and argues for a clearer basis of principle.

- Mirfield, P., 'Guilt by Association: A Reply to Professor Virgo' [2012] Crim LR 577.

  This article casts doubt on what is meant by association in joint enterprise liability and argues that the law is far from clear.

- Ormerod, D. and Wilson, W., 'Simply Harsh to Fairly Simple: Joint Enterprise Reform' [2015] Crim LR 3–27.

  This article discusses criticisms of the law of joint enterprise/parasitic accessorial liability. It argues for reform along the lines of the decision in R v Jogee.

- Rogers, J., 'The Codification of Attempts and the Case for "Preparation"' [2008] Crim LR 937.

  This article argues that the Law Commission's proposal for a new auxiliary concept of 'preparation', in addition to the existing law on 'attempts', is sound. However, the two concepts would need to be better differentiated in order to allow for early intervention by the police whilst ensuring that the law did not criminalise early preparatory actions where the defendant was not yet 'committed' to the offence.

- Simester, A.P., 'The Mental Element in Complicity' (2006) 122 LQR 578.

  This article argues that joint enterprise is a category of accessorial liability but not a separate doctrine.

- Virgo, G., 'Joint Enterprise Liability is Dead: Long Live Accessorial Liability' [2012] Crim LR 850.

  This article is a discussion of the case of Gnango [2011] UKSC 59 and focuses on the rather confusing language used to describe accessorial liability.

Online Resource Centre   www.oxfordtextbooks.co.uk/orc/qanda/

Go online for extra essay and problem questions, a glossary of key terms, online versions of all the answer plans and audio commentary on how selected ones were put together, and a range of podcasts which include advice on exam and coursework technique and advice for other assessment methods.

Mixed Questions

9

ARE YOU READY?

Each Criminal Law syllabus will be different. Some examiners will set problem questions on single areas, while others will set mixed questions from across the syllabus. Some common areas for combination are listed below, but of course this list is not exhaustive. Structure is important in all types of criminal law questions, but this is especially true with mixed topics. Essay questions on mixed topics are more rare, but will be general questions in which you are asked to assess themes running throughout the criminal law.

- sexual offences and burglary
- offences against the person, self-defence and consent
- murder and manslaughter
- theft, fraud, and other property offences
- accessorial liability and offences against the person
- subjective and objective approaches to liability

QUESTION | 1

The criminal law can sometimes produce inconsistent decisions, leading to uncertainty.
Critically evaluate the validity of this statement.

CAUTION!

- Occasionally an exam will contain a question that requires candidates to take a wider view of the criminal law. This is such a question. Candidates cannot simply home in on a specific area and cover it in detail. Candidates must try to think of instances throughout the syllabus that can be used in their arguments to answer the question.

- Avoid the common mistake of interpreting the question to read 'Choose one area of the criminal law where there are difficulties and write all about them'! This question has been included as it enables candidates to think more widely about the role of the criminal law within the legal system and society as a whole.

DIAGRAM ANSWER PLAN

> Introduce the problem by referring to the nature of the criminal law.

> Constant change—**R v R**.

> Lack of code—**Metropolitan Police Commissioner v Caldwell, DPP v Morgan**.

> Logic, policy and the subjective/objective approaches.

> Role of House of Lords—**R v Clegg**.

> Conclusion.

SUGGESTED ANSWER

[1] This statement acknowledges the problem set out in the question. You should then set out how you plan to answer it.

The development of many areas of law follows a consistent and logical course. The basic foundations, their concepts, and their application are accepted by the vast majority, and only fine tuning or adjustments of these principles are required to meet new situations.[1] Unfortunately this cannot be said about criminal law, where the debate about fundamental concepts—such as whether recklessness should be interpreted subjectively or objectively; whether a mistake of fact relied upon by a defendant should have to be one that a reasonable person would have made; whether duress should be a defence to a charge of murder—is still ongoing. In this essay, we will attempt to identify some of the reasons for this, and propose some solutions.

One of the problems is that the criminal law is subject to constant change. It has to adapt to cover new phenomena, such as stalking, drug abuse, and internet fraud, and to reflect society's changing social and moral standards. As the House of Lords stated in *R v R* [1991] **4 All ER 481**, abolishing the husband's marital rape exemption, the common law is capable of evolving in the light of social, economic, and cultural developments.[2] In that case the recognition that the status of women had changed beyond all recognition from the time (*Hale's Pleas of the Crown 1736*) when the husband's marital rape exemption was initially recognised was long overdue. Similarly, the criminal law once reflected the moral position that it was a crime to take one's own life. Failure in such an enterprise was prosecuted as attempted suicide and could be punished. However, attitudes softened and it was recognised that such a person needed help, not a criminal trial; the law was consequently amended by the **Suicide Act 1961**. The 1960s saw similar changes in respect to the laws relating to homosexuality and abortion. Changes in the law can also result from a shift in ideology on the part of an elected government, or as a response to new threats to the safety and stability of society—for example legislation to combat terrorism.[3]

There is no doubt that the development and application of the criminal law would be more consistent and predictable if the courts exhibited a more uniform approach to its development. The problem is illustrated by two House of Lords decisions: *Metropolitan Police Commissioner v Caldwell* [1981] **1 All ER 961**, where an objective approach to recklessness was used, and *DPP v Morgan* [1975] **2 All ER 347**, where a subjective approach to mistake was applied. Why was it that liability for recklessness was imposed on an objective basis, but where a defendant made a mistake of fact he was entitled (subject to any statutory provision to the contrary) to be judged on the facts as he honestly believed them to be? Commentators may argue that two different areas of the criminal law were being considered, criminal damage and rape, but the inconsistency is still stark. At least in so far as recklessness is concerned, the House of Lords has embraced the notion of subjectivity again in *R v G* [2003] **4 All ER 765**, but the very fact that the legal definition of such a basic concept can change so much in the space of 20 years is itself startling. The problem in *DPP v Morgan* has been dealt with by incorporating it into the mainly objective stance in the **Sexual Offences Act 2003**. The defendant must now have a reasonable belief in consent. This demonstrates inconsistency even in the context of the change. In the

[2] You will not have room to discuss all the possible examples of the law's stance on social change, so choose one or two examples.

[3] This of course is related to the point about social change, discussed earlier.

case of *R v G* (above), the courts were prepared to adopt a subjective standard, but in the context of sexual offences, an objective standard has been adopted. The recent changes to the defences to murder adopted in the **Coroners and Justice Act 2009** also demonstrate this approach. The Act requires that in deciding whether the defendant should be able to benefit from the defence of loss of control, s/he should be assessed according to the standards of a person with 'a normal degree of tolerance and self-control'. This leaves no room for consideration of a defendant's personal characteristics which may have influenced their behaviour.

Often the criminal law follows a logical approach in its application; but as it does not exist in a vacuum and is not simply the application of academic principles, policy considerations sometimes have to prevail. As Lord Salmon stated in *DPP v Majewski* **[1976] 2 All ER 142**, regarding the defence of intoxication:

the answer is that in strict logic the view [intoxication is no defence to crimes of basic intent] cannot be justified. But this is the view that has been adopted by the common law which is founded on common sense and experience rather than strict logic.

This may demonstrate the balancing act the courts have to play between preventing crime and protecting the public and ensuring that the defendant's rights in the criminal trial are not compromised.

Policy considerations[4] are also behind s. 1(3) of the Criminal Attempts Act 1981,[5] whereby in the offence of attempt, the facts are to be as the accused believes them to be. Thus an accused, objectively viewed, may appear not to be committing a criminal act but because they believe they are, they can be guilty of attempting to commit that criminal act, as in *R v Shivpuri* **[1986] 2 All ER 334**.

There is often no means of predicting which approach will prevail. In *Jaggard v Dickinson* **[1980] 3 All ER 716**, the accused, who had been informed by her friend X that she could break into X's house to shelter, mistakenly broke into V's house while drunk. She was charged with criminal damage under **s. 1(1)** of the **Criminal Damage Act 1971**, but argued that she had a lawful excuse under **s. 5(2)** of the Act as she honestly believed that she had the owner's consent. Although the prosecution contended that this was a crime of basic intent and therefore drunkenness was no defence (citing the House of Lords' decisions of *Metropolitan Police Commissioner v Caldwell* and *DPP v Majewski* in support), the Court of Appeal quashed her conviction, giving priority to the statutory provision of **s. 5(2)** of the **1971 Act**.

One important aspect of the criminal law process in recent years, which has caused uncertainty, is the role of the Supreme Court in changing the criminal law. Clearly judges are there to say what the

[4] Because criminal law often deals with social issues, policy must play a key part.

[5] Try to give concrete examples of statutory provisions or cases which illustrate the points you are making.

law is, not what it should be; but Lord Simon in *DPP for Northern Ireland v Lynch* **[1975] 1 All ER 913** said:

I am all for recognising that judges do make law. And I am all for judges exercising their responsibilities boldly at the proper time and place . . . where matters of social policy are not involved which the collective wisdom of Parliament is better suited to resolve.

Thus in *R v R*, the House of Lords changed the law of rape, by abolishing the husband's defence of marital rape immunity without waiting for Parliament to implement the Law Commission's recommendations. However, their Lordships took the opposite view in *R v Clegg* **[1995] 1 All ER 334**, where they refused to follow the Law Commission's suggestion that a person who was entitled to use force in self-defence but who used unreasonable force, thereby killing the victim, would be guilty of manslaughter, not murder. Lord Lloyd stated:

I am not adverse to judges developing law, or indeed making new law, when they can see their way clearly, even where questions of social policy are involved. [A good example is *R v R*.][6] But in the present case I am in no doubt that your Lordships should abstain from law making. The reduction of what would otherwise be murder to manslaughter in a particular class of case seems to me essentially a matter for decision by the legislature.

[6] It's a good idea to relate this back to the earlier part of your essay.

It is difficult to appreciate the essential difference in issues in these two cases, despite Lord Lowry's justifications in *R v Clegg* that '*R v R* dealt with a specific act and not with a general principle governing criminal liability'. Clearly there is a difference in opinion amongst the Law Lords as to the correct application of these principles. This is well illustrated by the House of Lords' decision in *R v Gotts* **[1992] 1 All ER 832**. The majority decision not to allow duress as a defence to attempted murder was on the basis that duress was no defence to murder. The minority view to the contrary revealed a different analysis. They argued that duress is a general defence throughout the criminal law with the exceptions of the offences of murder and treason. It is for Parliament, and not the courts, to limit the ambit of a defence; and as attempted murder is a different offence to murder, duress must therefore be available.

It is submitted that these are the main reasons why the development and application of the criminal law is often uncertain and unpredictable. There are other factors, such as whether an issue is a question of law for the judge or fact for the jury, e.g. the meaning of 'administer' (*R v Gillard* **(1988) 87 Cr App R 189**);[7] the difficulty in ascertaining the ratio decidendi of many cases, e.g. *R v Brown* **[1993] 2 All ER 75** (consent); and the possible effect of the decisions of the European Court of Human Rights. But it is the lack of a code and uniform principles which are the main factors causing the inherent uncertainty.

[7] This is a good illustration of the point made in Chapter 1 on the importance of statutory interpretation.

The Law Commission has long argued that the solution lies in codifying the law (see Law Com. No. 143) on the basis that: 'the criminal law could then exhibit a uniform approach to all crimes and defences'.

All other major European countries (France, Germany, and Spain) have a detailed criminal code, with a uniform approach providing a starting point for interpreting the law. The criminal law in England and Wales has developed in a piecemeal fashion, with one offence's development showing little consistency with another's. So often it is difficult to say what our law actually is, even before lawyers start to debate how it should be applied, e.g. *R v Savage*; *R v Parmenter* **[1992] 1 AC 699**, interpreting (after over 130 years of use) the provisions of the **Offences Against the Person Act 1861**. A code could be expressed in clear language with definitions of fundamental concepts such as intention and recklessness, as suggested by the Law Commission's Draft Criminal Code; although, as the former chairman of the Law Commission Justice Henry Brooke stated ([1995] Crim LR 911): 'Nobody in their right mind would want to put the existing criminal law into a codified form'.

LOOKING FOR EXTRA MARKS

- This is a difficult question in which you really have to decide on your own parameters. If you can choose some good examples in case law of the inconsistency of the criminal law, your essay will be of better quality than if you make sweeping statements.

- The structure of an essay like this is very important, so make your points and back them up with evidence and analysis.

QUESTION | 2

One night, Betty joins her neighbour Ron for a drink. Betty would have been happy with just one or two glasses of wine but Ron insists that she drink more to accompany him. Ron dishonestly tells her that he is compiling a medical database of women's breast sizes and asks if she will agree to his measuring her. She agrees. Unknown to Betty, Ron has spiked the wine with a tranquiliser. Betty becomes so drunk she hardly knows what she is doing. He leads her to the bedroom and suggests they have sex. Betty refuses. Ron then threatens her with violence. She passes out just as he pushes her onto the bed and has sexual intercourse with her. After a few weeks Betty learns that she is not only pregnant but also HIV+. She sends Ron an email giving him a week in which to agree to marry her failing which she will break his legs. She hears nothing and so bombards him with threatening emails and telephone calls. Ron becomes so concerned that he obtains anti-depressants from his doctor. Betty sees him coming home from work one day. She rushes at him with a penknife, and cuts his head. Ron later asserts he believed Betty had consented to being measured and to having sex with him. He claims he did not know he was HIV+. As a result of these incidents, Betty suffers nightmares in which she is being attacked by strange men.

Advise Betty and Ron.

CAUTION!

- This question contains both sexual and non-sexual offences against the person—be careful that you do not muddle the idea of consent as a defence to the statutory assaults, and consent as a key element in a sexual offence charge. Deal with the two issues separately. See *R v B* **[2007] 1 WLR 1567**.

- Consider each defendant separately, then look at all possible offences, starting with the most serious in the hierarchy of non-fatal offences. If actual harm is caused, the statutory assaults must be considered.

DIAGRAM ANSWER PLAN

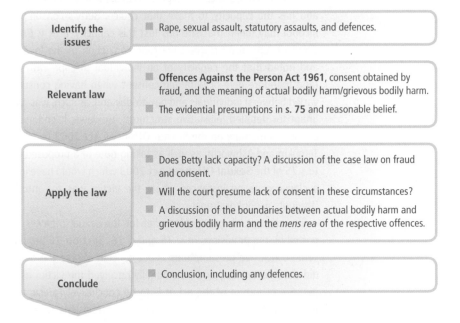

Identify the issues	■ Rape, sexual assault, statutory assaults, and defences.
Relevant law	■ **Offences Against the Person Act 1961**, consent obtained by fraud, and the meaning of actual bodily harm/grievous bodily harm. ■ The evidential presumptions in **s. 75** and reasonable belief.
Apply the law	■ Does Betty lack capacity? A discussion of the case law on fraud and consent. ■ Will the court presume lack of consent in these circumstances? ■ A discussion of the boundaries between actual bodily harm and grievous bodily harm and the *mens rea* of the respective offences.
Conclude	■ Conclusion, including any defences.

This question raises issues of non-fatal offences and sexual offences.

In relation to Ron, the first charge will be a sexual assault contrary to **s. 3** of the **Sexual Offences Act 2003**. Under this provision, a person commits an offence if he intentionally touches another person, the touching is sexual, the complainant does not consent to the touching, and the defendant does not reasonably believe that the victim consents. It is clear from these facts that Ron touches Betty, and that she agrees.[1] The question for the court will be whether Betty has been deceived into agreeing. The defendant must reasonably believe in consent. Ron's belief in Betty's consent is to be determined having regard to all the circumstances, including any steps he took to ascertain whether she consented. In *Tabassum* **[2000] 2 Cr App R 328**, the defendant asked several women to take part in what he said was a breast cancer survey involving him feeling their breasts. The court held that there had been no true consent since the women were consenting in the belief that the touching took place for medical purposes. As Betty believes that Ron is compiling a medical database, and consents on this basis, the court is likely to decide that consent was obtained fraudulently.[2]

The other issue here is that of Betty's capacity. Consent is defined in **s. 74**, which provides that a person consents if he agrees by choice, and has the capacity to make that choice. Betty's consumption of alcohol may mean that she has lost this capacity. In *R v Bree*, the Court of Appeal overturned the rape conviction of the lower court and noted that the capacity of an individual to cope with alcohol (and therefore give or withhold consent when having consumed it) varied between individuals and day-to-day and, as such, was a matter 'inapt for detailed legislative structures'. However, it endorsed academic commentary on the **Sexual Offences Act 2003** by Professors Tempkin and Ashworth, as well as taking note of a proposed change to **s.75** of the **Sexual Offences Act 2003** which would have included a clause covering instances where the victim was too intoxicated (through alcohol or drugs).

The concept of reasonable belief for the sexual offences is supported by the provisions in **s. 75** and **s. 76**. **Section 76** provides for some conclusive presumptions about consent. Where the defendant did the relevant act, and intentionally deceived the victim as to the purpose or nature of the act, it is to be conclusively presumed that the victim did not consent. Given the above provisions, it seems likely that Betty's consent to the touching is invalid and Ron will be found guilty of sexual assault.

[1] Do remember to apply the law to the facts of the problem question, even where it seems obvious. You need to demonstrate that you are able to break an offence down in terms of *actus reus* and *mens rea*.

[2] It is a good idea to come to a mini conclusion at each stage of the problem.

The next issue to consider is whether Ron is guilty of rape.

Under **s. 1(1)** of the **Sexual Offences Act 2003**, rape is committed when a person (A) intentionally penetrates the vagina, anus, or mouth of another person with his penis, B does not consent to the penetration, and A does not reasonably believe that B consents. It is clear here that sexual intercourse has taken place, therefore the key fact in issue is that of consent.

In terms of the *mens rea* for the offence of rape the prosecution must show that the defendant intended to have sexual intercourse and that he did not reasonably believe that the victim was consenting. In other words, where the defendant claims he believed that the victim was consenting, if such a belief is proved to be unreasonable, the jury should convict. This is the case even where the belief is held honestly. In deciding whether the defendant's belief was unreasonable, the jury should have regard to all the circumstances, including any steps the defendant could reasonably have been expected to take to ascertain whether the victim consented (**s 1(2)** of the **Sexual Offences Act 2003**). This provision places an onus on the defendant to ascertain whether or not there is consent in situations where there might be doubt. In some carefully defined circumstances, the Act provides for certain evidential presumptions to be raised against consent. These include a situation where the victim may be in fear and a situation in which the victim is not acting in full capacity due to ingesting a substance. If it is proved that the defendant did the relevant act and one of the circumstances existed at the time, it will be presumed that the complainant did not consent to the act, and the defendant did not reasonably believe that the complainant consented unless the defendant adduces sufficient evidence to raise an issue to the contrary. Betty's consent here will not be valid.

Her capacity to agree by choice is affected by alcohol. In any event, Ron has threatened Betty with violence. As a result, the evidential presumptions in **s. 75(2)(a)** will apply unless Ron can adduce evidence to the contrary. This seems unlikely, when there is evidence of violence.[3]

The last issue to consider with regard to Ron is his potentially reckless transmission of HIV, giving rise to a charge of **s. 20** of the **Offences Against the Person Act 1861**. The transmission of a sexually transmitted disease can be grievous bodily harm, so the question is whether Ron can be convicted given that he claims he does not know that he has HIV. In *R v Dica* **[2004] QB 1257**, the defendant, knowing that he was HIV+, had sexual intercourse with two women who were both diagnosed as being HIV+. He was charged with offences under **s. 20** of the **Offences Against the Person Act 1861** on the basis that he had recklessly transmitted the disease to the women when they had not known of the risk of infection. In this scenario, the

[3] The presumption is rebuttable, but in this instance, it will be difficult for Ron to do this. The threat of violence is clear.

mens rea element is missing and therefore the prosecution will not succeed on this charge.

The fact that Betty is now suffering from nightmares may give rise to a charge of one of the statutory assaults in addition to the sexual offences already established. Ron may be charged with assault under **s. 47** of the **Offences Against the Person Act 1861**. The *actus reus* of this charge is an assault occasioning actual bodily harm. Actual bodily harm can include psychiatric harm as long as this is medically treatable and does not simply amount to emotional distress (see *R v Chan Fook* **[1994] 2 All ER 452**).[4] If Ron raises the common law defence of consent to this charge, the earlier argument of *Tabassum* (see earlier) will apply—fraud or deceit as to the nature or purpose of the act will nullify consent.

[4]Actual bodily harm is defined as harm which interferes with the health or comfort of the victim. This may include psychiatric harm, which must be medically recognised. This may even extend to grievous bodily harm if it is sufficiently serious.

Betty may be charged with various non-fatal offences against the person. She sends various emails and makes phone calls, causing Ron to ask his doctor for anti-depressants. If Ron's state of mind is sufficiently serious to warrant medical treatment and goes beyond mere emotional distress (see *R v Chan-Fook*, discussed earlier), then Betty may be charged with an assault occasioning actual bodily harm. An assault is defined as an act which causes the victim to apprehend the immediate application of unlawful violence (*Venna* **[1975] 3 WLR 737**). The *mens rea* aspect is intention or recklessness—the latter being defined subjectively (*R v G* **[2003] 4 All ER 65**). In this scenario, it seems clear that Betty intended to worry Ron—and, in any event, her messages contain a threat of violence. The assault causes him to visit his doctor to ask for anti-depressants. There seems to be no problem with causation—the messages have prompted him to do so.

Betty's further physical assaults on Ron will be met with the more serious charges under the **Offences Against the Person Act 1861**. There is no doubt that Betty intended to commit at least a battery.[5]

However, the cut to Ron's head is a wound. Thus, the appropriate charges are **s. 18** or **s. 20** of the **Offences Against the Person Act 1861**. A wound requires the rupture of both the dermis and the epidermis. It is, in other words, a breaking of the skin (*C v Eisenhower* **[1984] QB 331**). The wound is sufficient to establish the *actus reus*; there is no need to prove that this was grievous bodily harm. Under **s. 20** the grievous bodily harm must be inflicted, which will be satisfied here in the fact that Betty rushes at Ron with a penknife which causes the wound. The *mens rea* for **s. 20** is satisfied by proof that Betty was malicious. This means that she inflicted the wound either intentionally or recklessly, i.e. at least aware of the possibility of causing some physical harm. It seems clear that she intended to hurt Ron with the penknife.

[5]Note that under **s. 47** Betty need not have the *mens rea* for the actual bodily harm—she only needs the *mens rea* for the assault.

LOOKING FOR EXTRA MARKS?

■ A really good understanding of the development of case law in this area will help you to achieve high marks. The definition of the word 'inflict' in the context of **s. 20** of the **Offences Against the Person Act 1861** in particular is significant. A full discussion of *R v Clarence* (1888) 22 QB 23, *R v Dica* [2004] QB 1257, and *R v Tabassum* [2000] 2 Cr App R 328, applying the law to the facts in a reasoned way, will help you achieve high marks in this answer. *Tabassum* was approved in *Dica*, so that *Clarence* is effectively regarded as bad law on this topic.

■ Few students explain *all* the requirements of the *actus reus* and *mens rea* in answer to this type of question, or understand the subtleties of the *mens rea* differences between **s. 20** and **s. 47**. In order to understand this area fully, you should read in full the judgment in *R v Savage*; *R v Parmenter* [1992] 1 AC 699.

QUESTION | 3

Justin and Tintin, having been partners for several years, split up when Tintin discovered that Justin was having a relationship with Roger. Tintin, incensed by what Justin had done, decided to seek revenge.

Tintin enters Justin's flat, using the front door key that he still has, armed with a pair of scissors that he intends to use to stab Justin. Tintin goes into Justin's bedroom and finds him asleep in bed. Instead of stabbing Justin, Tintin decides to use the scissors to cut off Justin's ponytail whilst he is asleep, and does so without waking Justin. Tintin rummages through the drawer of Justin's bedside table and removes some nude photographs that he took of Justin in the shower.

As he is about to leave the flat Tintin is confronted by Roger, who is just arriving. Tintin, who is still holding the scissors, fears that Roger is about to attack him. He pushes the scissors into Roger's arm, causing a deep cut, and runs off. Tintin subsequently writes to Justin telling him that if he does not return the ring he gave to Justin to celebrate the fifth anniversary of their being partners, he intends to put the nude photographs of Justin on the internet. Justin, who is a secondary school headmaster, is worried that if Tintin carries out his threat he might have to resign from his job.

CAUTION!

■ Note the possibility of aggravated burglary as well as burglary.

■ You need to address the issue of whether this is a householder case in the terms of **s. 43** of the **Crime and Courts Act 2013**.

DIAGRAM ANSWER PLAN

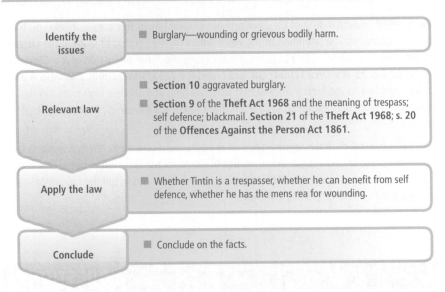

| Identify the issues | ■ Burglary—wounding or grievous bodily harm. |

| Relevant law | ■ **Section 10** aggravated burglary.
■ **Section 9** of the **Theft Act 1968** and the meaning of trespass; self defence; blackmail. **Section 21** of the **Theft Act 1968**; s. 20 of the **Offences Against the Person Act 1861**. |

| Apply the law | ■ Whether Tintin is a trespasser, whether he can benefit from self defence, whether he has the mens rea for wounding. |

| Conclude | ■ Conclude on the facts. |

 SUGGESTED ANSWER

When Tintin enters Justin's flat armed with the scissors he may have committed burglary contrary to **s. 9(1)(a)** of the **Theft Act 1968**, or aggravated burglary contrary to **s. 10** of the 1968 Act. Was he a trespasser when he entered?[1] He may have had express or implied permission to enter the flat when he was in a relationship with Justin, but as the relationship has now ended it could be argued that the permission has been expressly or impliedly revoked. In any event, if he enters intending to stab Justin, or even simply armed in order to do some physical harm, the prosecution will argue that this is entry in excess of any implied permission Tintin may have had: see ***R v Jones and Smith* [1976] 3 All ER 54.** Under **s. 9(1)(a)** Tintin can be convicted of burglary if he entered as a trespasser with intent to do some grievous bodily harm on a person in the building.[2] Grievous bodily harm for these purposes means 'serious' harm. Liability under this limb of **s. 9(1)(a)** would require more evidence as to Tintin's precise intentions. The alternative formulations under **s. 9(1)(a)** are that Tintin entered as a trespasser intending to steal, or that he intended to cause criminal damage. Again the evidence as to his state of mind at the time of entry is inconclusive.[3] If it can be shown that he intended to steal photographs or human hair, or indeed commit criminal damage to Justin's

[1] This is a key issue for the burglary charge and depends on the meaning of trespass.

[2] The intention must be formed at the point of entry.

[3] You do not have to reach a definite conclusion, and in fact should try to incorporate both the prosecution and defence arguments in your answer.

hair, a **s. 9(1)(a)** charge might be sustainable—but it is submitted there is no direct evidence of this.

Burglary contrary to **s. 9(1)(a)** could be based on Tintin's entry into the flat with a key, or indeed his entry into Justin's bedroom as a trespasser, given that burglary can be committed by a defendant entering part of a building as a trespasser. The prosecution would be advised to base liability on the act of trespass that carried with it the strongest evidence of the necessary ulterior intent to steal or cause grievous bodily harm or criminal damage.

[4] This interesting case shows the scope of the meaning of actual bodily harm.

Under **s. 10** of the 1968 Act a person is guilty of aggravated burglary if he commits any burglary and at the time has with him any weapon of offence.[4] Clearly the scissors could constitute a weapon of offence for these purposes.

Once inside Justin's bedroom Tintin decides not to stab Justin. Has Tintin nevertheless gone far enough to be charged with attempting to commit wounding contrary to **s. 1** of the **Criminal Attempts Act 1981** and **s. 20** of the **Offences Against the Person Act 1861**? Under the 1981 Act the prosecution will have to prove that Tintin has taken steps more than merely preparatory to wounding Justin. Whether or not entering Justin's bedroom armed with scissors is sufficient to satisfy this requirement will be a question of fact to be determined by the jury—*R v Gullefer* **(1990) 91 Cr App R 356**.

[5] Both of these offences should be considered.

In cutting off Justin's ponytail Tintin will have committed the offence of causing actual bodily harm contrary to **s. 47** of the **Offences Against the Person Act 1861**. *DPP v Smith* **[2006] All ER (D) 69 (Jan)** establishes that cutting off another's hair without consent amounts to actual bodily harm.[5] There is no doubt that Tintin intended to cause this result and there would appear to be no defence available (revenge not being a defence at common law—perhaps not even a mitigating factor in sentencing). A burglary charge could be sustained if Tintin entered the bedroom intending to do grievous bodily harm.

[6] If you consider theft in a case like this, also consider burglary.

Entering intending to cut hair would not suffice for these purposes.[6] In any event the facts indicate that he only decided to cut Justin's hair once he had entered the bedroom. For the same reason a charge of burglary contrary to **s. 9(1)(b)**, alleging that Tintin, having entered Justin's bedroom as a trespasser, committed grievous bodily harm would not be sustainable, as the cutting of the hair would only be actual bodily harm.

The prosecution may consider charging Tintin with theft of the photographs of Justin. The photographs are clearly property; see **s. 4(1)** of the **Theft Act 1968**. The facts indicate that the photographs were taken by Tintin—hence he may argue that they still belong to him. The prosecution may need to clearly establish that Tintin made Justin the owner of the photographs, but in any event **s. 5(1)** of the 1968

Act extends the concept of 'belonging to another' to encompass situations where, even though the defendant is the legal owner of the property in question, it can still be deemed to be property belonging to another as against the defendant if the property is in the possession or control of another. On the facts the photographs would clearly be regarded as having been in Justin's possession or control; see further *R v Turner (No 2)* [1971] **1 WLR 901**.

Tintin's removal of the photographs would constitute an appropriation—see **s. 3(1)** of the **Theft Act 1968**. Hence the live issues will be those relating to *mens rea*. The prosecution must prove that Tintin's appropriation of the pictures was dishonest. Under **s. 2(1)(a)** of the 1968 Act Tintin will not be dishonest if he can show that he honestly believed he had the right in law to take the photographs. He does not have to show that any such right does exist in law, simply that he believed he had the right. The fact that he was the photographer may be supportive evidence here. It is also significant that he does not appear to have had the intention to use the pictures for blackmailing purposes (considered later) until after he removed them. Tintin could cite this as evidence that he had an 'honest' motive in his initial removal of the pictures. It is submitted that **s. 2(1)(b)** (honest belief in the owner's consent) and **s. 2(1)(c)** (honest belief that the owner cannot be found) have no application on these facts. If, therefore, Tintin cannot rely on **s. 2(1)(a)**, he will have to rely on the jury and their view following a direction in terms laid down in *R v Ghosh* [1982] **QB 1053**. The jury must first decide whether, according to the ordinary standards of reasonable and honest people, what Tintin did was dishonest. If it was not dishonest by those standards he is not guilty of theft. If he was, the jury must go on to consider whether Tintin himself must have realised that what he was doing was by those standards dishonest. Given the facts it is almost impossible to tell how a jury would determine this, although they may well take a dim view of a defendant who, having entered a flat without permission, armed with a weapon, subsequently threatens to embarrass the victim by publishing the pictures.

If dishonesty is established the prosecution will have to prove the second element of *mens rea*, namely an intention on the part of Tintin to permanently deprive Justin of the photographs. It should be noted that the intention to permanently deprive must exist at the time of appropriation. Tintin's intentions in this regard are not clear at the time he removes the pictures from Justin's bedroom. It subsequently becomes clear that he intends to use the pictures for what may be blackmailing purposes. The prosecution could argue that even if Tintin lacked the necessary intention to permanently deprive in relation to the pictures when he was in the bedroom, it is later evidenced by his threats to publish them. Tintin will argue that he did not intend to keep the photographs but was simply using them as a bargaining factor in respect of the ring. Under **s. 6(1)** of the 1968 Act, in cases where the defendant does not actually have an intention to permanently deprive, he can nevertheless be deemed to have such an intent if he intends '. . . to treat the thing as his own to dispose of . . .'. In *R v Raphael and Another* [2008] **EWCA Crim 1014**, the appellant took P's car and then told P that it would be returned to him provided he paid £500. The Court of Appeal had little hesitation in concluding that the taking of property in such circumstances could amount to theft—the requirement that money be paid by the owner for the return of his property falling very much within the scope of **s. 6(1)**.

In the present case Tintin is seeking the return of a ring as exchange for the photographs—essentially the same issue as in *R v Raphael*. Assuming, therefore, that the photographs are property belonging to another, and assuming Tintin is dishonest, theft should be made out.

If Tintin did commit theft when he removed the pictures from Justin's bedroom, he may also be guilty of burglary contrary to **s. 9(1) (b)** of the **Theft Act 1968**—having entered the bedroom as a trespasser he therein stole.[7]

In cutting Roger's arm Tintin caused a wound—see *C v Eisenhower* [1983] **3 WLR 537**. Thus Tintin may have committed an offence under either **s. 18** ('wounding with intent . . .') or **s. 20** ('maliciously wound') of the **Offences Against the Person Act 1861**. The key factor will be *mens rea*.[8] More evidence is needed on the type of harm Tintin intended to cause. If he intended to cause serious harm, an intention to do some grievous bodily harm could be established, thus making out a case under **s. 18**. It is submitted that there should be ample evidence to sustain a charge under **s. 20**. Malicious wounding requires evidence that Tintin was at least aware that his actions created the risk of causing some physical harm, albeit slight.

Tintin will presumably argue that, in attacking Roger, he acted in self-defence using reasonable force to protect himself. The fact that Tintin may have been 'in the wrong' inasmuch as he was trespassing in Justin's flat does not remove his right at common law to act in self-defence if threatened with unlawful violence from Roger. The facts indicate that Roger had not actually attacked Tintin, hence Tintin will have to provide evidence that he honestly believed Roger was about to use unlawful violence on him. *R v Williams* [1987] **3 All ER 411**, and subsequent cases, make clear that Roger is entitled to be judged on the facts as he honestly believed them to be, a position now confirmed by **s. 76** of the **Criminal Justice and Immigration Act 2008**.[9] Assuming Tintin did honestly believe he was about to be attacked by Roger, was the force he used reasonable in the circumstances as he

[7] The offences under **s. 9(1)(a)** and **s. 9(1)(b)** are different—ensure you apply each to the facts carefully.

[8] Be careful with the *mens rea* of these offences—explain them carefully.

[9] This is a subjective test.

believed them to be? On the basis of **s. 76(7)** the jury should be directed to take into account the fact that Tintin may not have been able to weigh to a nicety the exact measure of any necessary action. Under **s. 43** of the **Crime and Courts Act 2013**, a defendant relying on self-defence is given greater latitude in terms of the degree of force permitted by way of self-defence. Provided the terms of the provision are met, D will be acting lawfully unless his actions were a grossly disproportionate response to the perceived threat. If self-defence is made out Tintin will have a complete defence. If the jury conclude that there was a basis for Tintin acting in self-defence but he used more force than was reasonable he will have no defence at all.[10]

[10] It's wise to explain, when discussing the defences, the final outcome for the defendant.

When Tintin subsequently wrote to Justin telling him that if he did not return the ring he would put the nude photographs of Justin on the internet, Tintin may have committed blackmail contrary to **s. 21** of the **Theft Act 1968**. There is clearly a demand. The accompanying threat would amount to the required menaces. The test is essentially objective—what would the effect be on the reasonable person? See *R v Clear* [1968] **1 QB 670**. In cases where the reasonable person would not be threatened, the menaces can still be made out where the defendant has knowledge of the victim that indicates a particular sensitivity to the threats. The fact that Justin would be particularly embarrassed because of his job may be a factor here. The demand must be made with a view to gaining property or causing loss to another. In this respect the obtaining of the ring would constitute the gaining of property (even if Tintin is getting back something he thinks belongs to him anyway—see **s. 34(2) of the Theft Act 1968**). The most difficult aspect of establishing blackmail may lie in showing that the demand was unwarranted. Under **s. 21** the prosecution must prove that Tintin had no belief that he had reasonable grounds for making the demand; and that he had no honest belief that the use of the menaces was a proper means of reinforcing the demand. Tintin will argue that he honestly believed he had a reasonable basis for making the demand as the relationship with Justin was over, and that he had no, or perhaps only doubtful, recourse to law in order to get the ring back. Whether this argument succeeds will be a matter for the jury to determine.

LOOKING FOR EXTRA MARKS

■ The offences and defences contain a certain amount of overlap. It is a good idea to explain exactly what will happen in court to each defendant. This will give clarity to your answer.

■ Do not assume that violence always results in injury—look carefully at the facts of the question.

QUESTION | 4

Anne took her father's car without his knowledge, picked up her friends Barbara and Christine, and drove to the seaside. On the way they were involved in an accident with another car, which was being driven erratically. Both cars were damaged. Anne, Barbara, and Christine booked into a hotel room and then went drinking. By the end of the evening, they had all drunk a great deal of wine. When they got back to the hotel, they began re-enacting scenes from famous boxing matches. Barbara tried to land a blow on Anne's face but completely misguided her punch and knocked Anne down. Barbara was wearing a ring and this caused a bad cut over Anne's eye. Anne and Barbara then hurled themselves at Christine and pushed her out to the balcony. During this time, Christine was laughing but was also trying to suggest that she was tired and wanted to stop. Anne and Barbara picked Christine up and held her over the edge of the balcony. Thinking that they were going to let her fall, Christine pulled violently on Barbara's arm. Barbara overbalanced and fell to the ground, breaking her leg.

Discuss the criminal liability of Anne, Barbara, and Christine. How would your answer differ if Barbara had been killed as a result of the fall?

CAUTION!

- This question raises a number of offences. Deal with them all separately.
- The consent issue, and any other defences, should be dealt with once liability has been established.

DIAGRAM ANSWER PLAN

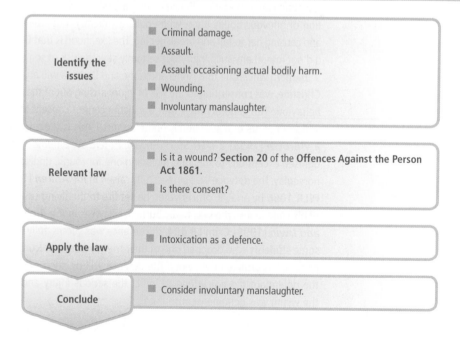

Identify the issues	■ Criminal damage. ■ Assault. ■ Assault occasioning actual bodily harm. ■ Wounding. ■ Involuntary manslaughter.
Relevant law	■ Is it a wound? **Section 20** of the **Offences Against the Person Act 1861**. ■ Is there consent?
Apply the law	■ Intoxication as a defence.
Conclude	■ Consider involuntary manslaughter.

[1]Identify the relevant offences.

This question raises the possibility that a number of crimes have been committed, including criminal damage (**Criminal Damage Act 1971**), assault under **s. 39** of the **Criminal Justice Act 1988**, assault occasioning actual bodily harm, and potentially involuntary manslaughter.[1]

The damage to the cars would amount to criminal damage if Anne was subjectively reckless, but there is nothing in the facts to suggest that Anne's driving was at fault.

When Barbara knocked Anne down and inflicted the cut over her eye, *prima facie* she committed offences of common law battery, assault occasioning actual bodily harm, and unlawful and malicious wounding under **s. 47** and **s. 20 of the Offences Against the Person Act 1861**.

[2]A common law battery might lead to the more serious offence. You should always look to the level of harm.

Battery requires proof that Barbara intentionally or recklessly inflicted force on Anne, whilst **s. 47** requires that the infliction of force led to actual bodily harm.[2] This must be more than merely trivial injury. Clearly, the blow amounted to a battery.

The wounding offence requires proof of a break in both layers of the skin (***C (A Minor) v Eisenhower* [1984] QB 331**) and the cut described is clearly sufficient to satisfy this requirement. It is arguable

[3]Be careful with the *mens rea* here.

that Barbara intended some injury, though more likely that she would merely have been aware of the risk of injury in trying to land the light blow.[3] Similarly, Anne and Barbara committed battery on Christine when seizing her and holding her over the balcony and, in turn, Christine committed the offence of the unlawful and malicious infliction of grievous bodily harm when pulling violently on Barbara's arm and causing her to fall and break her leg. The likelihood is that Christine did not intend any such injury but certainly saw the risk of some injury.

Barbara will argue that Anne, and Anne and Barbara will argue that Christine, was consenting to the risk of injury arising out of their rough behaviour. The general rule is that the victim cannot consent to injury

[4]Public policy determines this decision.

which amounts to actual bodily harm or worse. This is the principle in ***R v Brown* [1993] 2 WLR 556**.[4] However there are a number of recognised exceptions to this rule, including one for rough, undisciplined horseplay. The defence was successfully raised in ***R v Aitken* [1992] 1 WLR 1066** by an RAF officer when he set fire to the flying suit of one of his colleagues who was badly burned. Likewise, in ***R v Richardson and Irwin* [1999] Crim LR 494**, the defence was successfully used by some students who dropped one of their friends from a balcony when engaged in drunken behaviour. The defence will be successful when the defendant did not intend to inflict the serious injury and where the victim was genuinely consenting.

Generally, intoxication will not be a valid plea where the defence is one of basic intent. According to *DPP v Majewski* **[1977] AC443**, any attempt to introduce evidence of intoxication in such an offence will inevitably result in a conviction. Remarkably the court did hold in *Richardson and Irwin* that the defendant could rely on a drunken mistake as to consent. Though all the defendants were probably drunk to some extent, there is every reason to suppose that Anne was consenting to the minor risks involved in the mock boxing and that Barbara meant nothing more than to inflict a small slap.[5] Equally, Christine was probably consenting to the rough horseplay, at least until she was held over the balcony.

[5] You need to apply these arguments to the facts in question.

Christine will argue that she genuinely believed that Anne and Barbara were going to let her fall and to cause her serious injury. Her defence will be one of self-defence. This requires proof that the use of force was necessary and that the force used was proportionate to the harm threatened. If there was no risk that Christine would be injured, then she will be entitled to be judged on the facts as she believed them to be (*R v Gladstone Williams* **[1987] 3 All ER 411**). There is no reason to doubt that Christine genuinely believed that she was about to suffer serious injury.

If Barbara had died as a result of the fall then the appropriate charge would be involuntary manslaughter. This is likely to be of the gross negligence type evidenced in *R v Adomako* **[1994] 3 WLR 288** and constitutes a killing by the defendant in circumstances where the defendant is under a duty of care, that duty is breached, and there is a risk of death. In addition the conduct must be so bad in all the circumstances as to amount to a criminal act or omission.[6]

[6] The duty here is creating a dangerous situation.

 LOOKING FOR EXTRA MARKS?

- The consent issue is dealt with on the basis of public policy. This can make it difficult to predict what the outcome will be. You should draw attention to this issue. This is especially true with rough horseplay.

- This is a short question, which must be tightly argued.

Q **QUESTION** | **5**

Bob and Will are in a pub with a group of friends. Bob invites Will to come back home with him to have sex with his wife, Jen. He tells him that if Jen objects, this is part of the game and he should ignore her protests and carry on. Bob returns home with Will and they both have sexual intercourse with Jen, despite her protests. Bob slaps Jen hard on the cheek, and she stops protesting. One member of the group, Tony, does not want to participate but asks if he can watch. Bob agrees. After a few minutes, Tony decides he is bored and whilst the men are in the bedroom with Jen, he goes downstairs and takes a valuable silver jug from one of the cabinets in the living room. When he is caught, he says that he believed he had the right to take the jug, as Bob owed him £500 and was refusing to pay him back.

Will, who works in a bank, tells Bob that he can get him a mortgage at a very low interest rate if he lets him do the same thing with Jen again. Jen says later that she feels severely traumatised by the events of the evening and that she did not consent to sex with either man. Will cannot authorise decisions on mortgages as he is a cashier. Will goes out that evening and has a meal in an expensive restaurant but leaves before the bill arrives, checking carefully before he does so that the waiter is looking the other way. When Bob finds out that he can't get the mortgage after all, he finds Will and punches him in the face.

On his way home, Tony decides to buy an expensive box of chocolates for his wife. He goes into a shop and changes the label on the box he wants for a much lower price—he hopes the shop will not notice and charge him the lower price. He also picks up a bottle of wine and puts it in his coat pocket. When he gets to the cash desk he pays for the chocolates, for which he is charged the lower price, but changes his mind about the wine and replaces it on the shelf.

Discuss the criminal liability of Bob, Will, and Tony.

 CAUTION!

- This question requires an appraisal of both property offences and offences against the person, including sexual offences. An excellent structure is very important, to ensure clarity.
- In dealing with the fraud offence at the bank, be careful with the *mens rea*.

DIAGRAM ANSWER PLAN

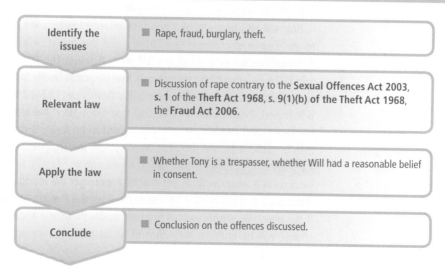

| Identify the issues | ▪ Rape, fraud, burglary, theft. |

| Relevant law | ▪ Discussion of rape contrary to the **Sexual Offences Act 2003, s. 1** of the **Theft Act 1968**, **s. 9(1)(b)** of the **Theft Act 1968**, the **Fraud Act 2006**. |

| Apply the law | ▪ Whether Tony is a trespasser, whether Will had a reasonable belief in consent. |

| Conclude | ▪ Conclusion on the offences discussed. |

SUGGESTED ANSWER

Bob and Will may be charged with rape contrary to **s. 1(1)** of the **Sexual Offences Act 2003**. The *actus reus* is defined as penile penetration of the vagina, anus, or mouth of another where the victim does not consent. The *mens rea* aspect is intentional penetration and a lack of reasonable belief in consent.[1]

Bob may have committed rape because the *actus reus* has been committed intentionally. He did not have this reasonable belief in consent. Section 74 of the Act states that a person consents if he agrees by choice, and has the freedom and capacity to make that choice'.[2] The purpose of defining consent in these terms was to draw a line between consent and submission. Prior to the Act, the case of ***R v Olugboja* [1982] QB 320** had established that submission was not equivalent to consent, and this is now entrenched in the Act in the concept of reasonable belief.[3] As Bob has shown violence towards Jen, she may be too frightened to protest further and submits rather than consents.

In addition, **s. 75** applies to an offence under this section. This sets out, in **s. 75(2)(a)–(f)**, six circumstances in which an evidential presumption regarding consent will arise.[4] If the facts of a case fall into these circumstances, it will be presumed that the complainant (Jen) did not consent. Violence is one of these circumstances. No facts are given in this scenario which would enable Bob to rebut this

[1] Start with a definition of the offence in question.

[2] It is always important to start a discussion of consent with this section.

[3] Note that this is now entrenched in the Act in the concept of reasonable belief.

[4] This can be rebutted by the defendant.

presumption, other than his assertion that violence is part of the act. Jen's evidence at the end of the problem that she did not consent will prevent him from raising any such evidence.

Bob will also be guilty of a non-fatal offence towards Jen, at least to the degree of common law battery, and this might be extended to an offence under **s. 47** of the **Offences Against the Person Act 1861**. The defence might try to argue that no actual bodily harm was sustained; however if the definition in *R v Donovan* **[1934] 2 KB 498** is followed, it can certainly be argued that this action 'interferes with her health and comfort'. On the other hand as no injury is caused, it may be difficult for the prosecution to sustain the argument. Overall a common law battery is probably the best option.[5] Finally, Bob's assault on Will when he finds out that he cannot get the mortgage is a statutory assault under the **Offences Against the Person Act 1861**. If the punch does not result in grievous bodily harm, the appropriate charge will be under **s. 47**—that of an assault occasioning actual bodily harm, which a punch will satisfy.

Will has also committed the *actus reus* of rape as he penetrated Jen without consent.

He will argue that he honestly believed that Jen was consenting due to the information he was given in the pub by Bob. The jury will need to assess this belief, which appears to be unreasonable. In order for the jury to do this, they will need to be convinced that the belief he held was both honest and reasonable—here, it is not. This reference to reasonable belief reverses the common law position in *DPP v Morgan*, which had held that a defendant could not be convicted of rape if he mistakenly believed that the woman consented even though he had no reasonable grounds for that belief.[6] Clearly, this is an unreasonable belief on his part—he lacked a reasonable belief in consent. The court will also be mindful of **s. 74**. Jen does not make a free choice here.

When Will tells Bob that he may be able to get him a mortgage for a reduced rate, he may have committed a fraud offence under **s. 1** of the **Fraud Act 2006**. Fraud may be committed where there is a false representation, where the defendant has failed to disclose information, or where there is an abuse of position. This last type of fraud would seem to be relevant here. Section 4 of the **Fraud Act 2006** is the relevant offence. A person will commit this offence if he occupies a position in which he is expected to safeguard, or not act against the financial interests of another person (**s. 4(1)**). He must dishonestly abuse that position and intend to make a gain or cause a loss or expose another to the risk of loss. Dishonesty must also be proven. 'Gain' or 'loss' are defined in financial terms, so the fact that Will hopes to sleep with Jen again will mean that he may not be guilty

[5] Discuss alternatives for the different offences against the person.

[6] This case attracted a lot of criticism, and the position is now rectified by the emphasis of reasonable belief in the Act

of this offence. With regard to the restaurant, Will may have committed fraud by misrepresentation according to **s. 2(1)** of the **Fraud Act 2006**. A false representation is any representation made according to fact or law, and may be express or implied. By entering the restaurant he implies that he intends to and has the ability to pay (**s. 2(2)** of the **Fraud Act 2006**. The offence is complete as soon as the false representation is made, if the defendant has a view to gain or cause loss, and he does so dishonestly. Alternatively, he may have committed the offence of making off without payment under **s. 3** of the **Theft Act 1978**.[7] This offence applies wherever goods or services are supplied for which payment on the spot is required or expected and the defendant dishonestly makes off without having paid as required or expected, with an intent to avoid payment. This may apply here.

With regard to the jug, Tony may be convicted of burglary under **s. 9(1)(a)** or **s. 9. (1)(b)** of the **Theft Act 1968**. The key question will be whether he has trespassed. If this is not successful, he may be found guilty of theft. Theft is defined as the dishonest appropriation of property belonging to another with the intention to permanently deprive the owner of the property (**s. 1** of the **Theft Act 1968**). He has appropriated the jug which is property and belongs to Bob. With regard to *mens rea*, Tony might argue that he was not dishonest as he honestly believed that he had the right to take it, given that Bob owed him money. The **Theft Act 1968** sets out three situations in which a defendant is not to be regarded as dishonest. The defendant must hold one of the following beliefs: (a) a belief in the legal right to the property; (b) a belief that the owner would consent; (c) a belief that the owner could not be traced by taking reasonable steps. The first of these is most appropriate for Tony. He will not be dishonest if he honestly believes he has the legal right to the property. This will be a matter for the jury to consider.[8]

A further question will be whether, in addition to theft, Tony could be found guilty of burglary. This question turns on whether he is a trespasser. He will argue that Bob invited him into the house. In *R v Jones and Smith* [1976] 1 WLR 672, the two defendants were found guilty of burglary despite a prior invitation to enter. The court held that a person was a trespasser if he entered the premises of another and acted in excess of any permission granted. If he is a trespasser it is likely that he will be guilty under **s. 9(1)(b)** as he did not have the intent to steal when he entered the property but formed it later.[9]

In terms of the theft, appropriation is defined in the Act as an assumption of the rights of an owner (**s. 3(1)** and *R v Morris* [1984] AC 320. When he switches the labels in the supermarket, he may have assumed one of the supermarket's rights and therefore have appropriated the chocolates.[10] He does the same with the wine by

---

[7] Note that these offences may overlap and it is possible for both to be charged. This is a good example of the piecemeal development of the criminal law.

[8] Note that it is a subjective belief genuinely held by the defendant.

[9] This matter is open to interpretation. The definition of trespass is not entirely certain as it will depend on a number of other factors such as entry (see *R v Collins* [1973] QB 100).

[10] An assumption of a right applies to any right.

picking it up off the shelf. Both of these objects will count as property under **s. 4(1)**. They belong to the supermarket (**s. 5(1)**). A more difficult question may be whether Tony is dishonest and whether he intended to permanently deprive the supermarket of the property. Although this argument is easily satisfied with regard to the chocolates, he will argue that he intended to replace the wine. The fact that he replaces it does not prevent him from being regarded as intending to permanently deprive the shop of the property if there are circumstances amounting to an outright taking or disposal. As the wine has remained in exactly the same state as it was when he appropriated it, the prosecution may not be successful on this issue.

LOOKING FOR EXTRA MARKS?

- Make sure you carefully examine the legal definitions in the property offences. These may overlap and the law does not always provide certainty. If you can identify the problematic areas, this will add depth to your answer.

- Try to provide alternatives to arguments throughout your answer. This shows good legal reasoning.

QUESTION | 6

Pete and Veronica, who had been going out together for a number of years, were going to get married. One evening, Veronica told Pete that she was having an affair with a work colleague and that her relationship with Pete was over. Pete was very shocked by this and felt hurt. In a state of confusion, he decided to go to Veronica's house to see if he could find something to take in memory of her.

To gain entry into her house, Pete used a spare key, which she had previously told him she kept under a stone by the front door. Pete made his way to her bedroom. On her dressing table he saw the engagement ring that he had given her and he took it. He thought to himself that she had no right to keep it now that she had broken off the engagement. He then sprayed her teddy bear with her favourite perfume and stuffed it inside his jacket. He was about to leave her bedroom when he saw a photograph of Veronica and her new boyfriend on her bedside table. Incensed, he grabbed her pyjamas from her bed and ripped them apart. As he was doing so, the teddy bear fell out of his jacket. He left it on the floor and ran out of the house.

Pete was arrested later that night but told the police that he barely remembered anything he had done after his conversation with Veronica because he was in shock.

Discuss any criminal liability arising from these facts.

CAUTION!

- There are a number of different property offences and defences in this question. Deal with them systematically before coming to an overall conclusion.

- Insanity and automatism are closely linked. Be sure to explain why one rather than the other might apply.

DIAGRAM ANSWER PLAN

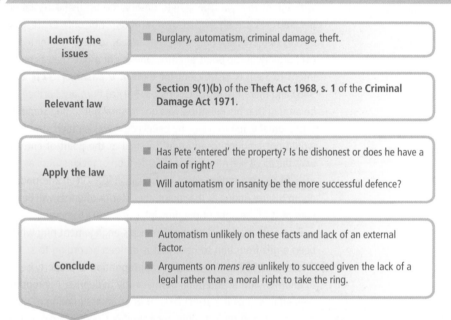

Identify the issues	Burglary, automatism, criminal damage, theft.
Relevant law	Section 9(1)(b) of the Theft Act 1968, s. 1 of the Criminal Damage Act 1971.
Apply the law	Has Pete 'entered' the property? Is he dishonest or does he have a claim of right? Will automatism or insanity be the more successful defence?
Conclude	Automatism unlikely on these facts and lack of an external factor. Arguments on *mens rea* unlikely to succeed given the lack of a legal rather than a moral right to take the ring.

SUGGESTED ANSWER

¹Set out the relevant offences at the outset.

Pete appears to have potentially committed three counts of burglary, and possibly criminal damage. In addition, he might also have a defence of automatism.¹

Burglary can be committed in two ways. Under **s. 9(1)(a)** of the **Theft Act 1968** a person is guilty of burglary if he enters any building or part as a trespasser with intent to steal, inflict grievous bodily harm on any person therein, or commit criminal damage. Under **s. 9(1)(b)²**

²Note that you do not need to repeat the statute verbatim— simply summarise the effect of it. In an exam, no credit will be given for copying out.

a person is guilty of burglary if, having entered as a trespasser, he steals or inflicts grievous bodily harm on any person therein or attempts to commit either of these offences. Under **s. 9(1)(b)** it must be proved that D has committed any of the further offences.

The three common elements of the *actus reus* of either type of burglary do not appear to be in issue here. Pete has clearly entered (*R v Collins* [1973] QB 100) a building. His entry was not only effective (*R v Brown* [1985] Crim LR 61) but also substantial.[3] He was presumably a trespasser because his entry was without consent. Pete might argue that he had permission to enter, but the court is likely to find that Veronica must have implicitly withdrawn permission upon termination of their relationship. Given Pete's intention upon entry as a trespasser, to find a memento of Veronica, he appears to have potentially committed **s. 9(1)(a)** burglary, i.e. entry as a trespasser with intent to steal. The clandestine nature of his nocturnal visit to her house is strong evidence of an intent not only to trespass but also to steal.[4] Pete would therefore appear to have committed **s. 9(1) (a)** burglary at the point of entry. One might argue that a conditional intent to steal is insufficient for theft (*R v Easom* [1971] 2 All ER 945) and therefore insufficient for **s. 9(1)(a)** burglary. Further, it could be argued that his intention was not to steal but to find something of sentimental value to which he believed he was entitled. Arguably, this would not amount to an intent to steal at the point of entry. Either way, the *mens rea* requirement of intention or recklessness as to entry as a trespasser would seem to be satisfied.[5] Given the uncertainty about his intentions at that point, the ulterior offences will be considered next in the light of the principles of **s. 9(1)(b)** burglary.

First, Pete may have stolen Veronica's engagement ring which had been a gift from him to her. Theft is defined according to **s. 1** of the **Theft Act 1968** as the dishonest appropriation of property belonging to another with an intention permanently to deprive. Appropriation is defined in **s. 3** of the **Theft Act 1968** as an assumption of the rights of ownership. Therefore, Pete appropriated the ring by assuming possession of it.[6] A ring falls within the definition of property under **s. 4** of the **Theft Act 1968**, defined as money and all other property, real or personal, including things in action and other intangible property. The property must belong to another defined in accordance with **s. 5** as belonging to any person having possession or control of it, or having in it any proprietary right or interest, whether it be a right of ownership, possession, or equitable right. Since the ring had been a gift from Pete to her, Veronica was the owner of it. Pete may therefore have committed the *actus reus* of theft.[7]

There appears to be no doubt that he intended to deprive Veronica of the ring permanently as opposed to temporarily, in which case **s. 6** need not be explored. However, it must also be proved that his appropriation was dishonest. Dishonesty is not defined under the **Theft Act 1968** but **s. 2(1)** sets out that one is not to be regarded as dishonest if the act was committed with any of three beliefs: (a)

[3] There are conflicting cases on this point; you do not need to go into great detail.

[4] Apply the legal principle to the facts of the problem.

[5] Don't forget the *mens rea*.

[6] The statutory provision needs to be applied to the facts, just as a case would be.

[7] Here, we have worked systematically through the statutory requirements of *actus reus* before moving on to *mens rea*.

belief in a legal right to the property; (b) belief that the owner would consent; and (c) a belief that the owner cannot be found by taking reasonable steps. In any of these situations, D's belief need not be correct or objectively reasonable provided it is subjectively genuine. Pete would find it impossible to assert either of the latter two beliefs but the facts state that he does think Veronica has no right to it having broken off the engagement. He will not be dishonest if he genuinely believes he has a legal right to the property. Unfortunately for Pete, it rather looks as though his belief is based on moral rather than legal grounds and is unlikely to provide him with a defence of lack of dishonesty. If, however, he were to assert that although his conduct appeared dishonest according to the ordinary standards of reasonable and honest people, he did not consider what he had done to be dishonest according to those standards, he may have the benefit of the test set out in *R v Ghosh* [1982] QB 1053. Pete may genuinely believe that he was not dishonest by ordinary standards given Veronica's reprehensible behaviour. A jury is unlikely to find that his retrieval of the ring was honest on the basis of these facts.[8] Consequently, Pete may have committed **s. 9(1)(b)** burglary on these grounds.

There is no evidence that he damaged the bear by spraying it with perfume and therefore criminal damage will not be considered. However, he appears to have stolen it despite the fact that he leaves it behind when he runs from the house. He appropriated the bear when he assumed possession of it by picking it up. Appropriation is defined as any assumption by a person of the rights of an owner (**s. 3** of the **Theft Act 1968**). If, at that moment, the appropriation was dishonest with an intention permanently to deprive Veronica of the bear, theft is complete. The fact that it remains behind is irrelevant. In the absence of a relevant belief under **s. 2(1)** of the **Theft Act 1968**, he may dispute dishonesty on the basis that although the appropriation appeared dishonest according to ordinary standards, he did not consider himself dishonest according to those standards in accordance with the *Ghosh* test explained earlier. It is unlikely he would succeed with this defence given the circumstances. He has therefore committed both theft and **s. 9(1)(b)** burglary.[9]

Third, in ripping apart Veronica's pyjamas Pete has committed criminal damage contrary to **s. 1(1)** of the **Criminal Damage Act 1971**: a person commits criminal damage if without lawful excuse he destroys or damages property belonging to another, intending or being reckless as to whether such property will be destroyed or damaged. Subjective recklessness is required according to *R v Cunningham* [1957] 2 QB 396 and *R v G and Another* [2004] 1 AC 1034. Pete has certainly destroyed the pyjamas; they do not belong to him. He

[8] Be careful to understand the operation of the test. The defendant is assessed on whether he believed he was being dishonest according to ordinary, not his own, standards.

[9] It is useful to draw a mini conclusion on the facts.

has therefore committed criminal damage. This offence does not support a charge of **s. 9(1)(b)** burglary.

[10] Always provide a definition.

However, Pete may use the defence of automatism. Automatism is a plea that the link between mind and body is missing resulting in a lack of voluntary control over one's actions.[10] In *Bratty v AG for Northern Ireland* **[1963] AC 386** Lord Denning defined the defence as 'an involuntary act . . . done by the muscles, without any control by the mind'. It provides a complete acquittal because lack of voluntariness negates the *actus reus* of the crime. Automatism is closely related to insanity. However, in automatism the cause of involuntariness must be external, whereas in insanity it must be a disease of the mind, caused internally. It is unlikely that a mere emotional state will suffice as a disease of the mind. Otherwise, the defence must be based on insanity which, if successful, leads to a verdict of not guilty by reason of insanity with disposal ranging from indefinite detention in a secure mental hospital to an absolute discharge (**Criminal Procedure (Insanity and Unfitness to Plead) Act 1991** and the **Domestic Violence, Crime and Victims Act 2004**). The defence is defined according to the *M'Naghten* Rules 1843 as a defect of reason due to a disease of the mind so as to deprive D of either knowledge as to the nature and quality of his actions or knowledge that the act was legally wrong. The concept of disease of the mind is wide enough to include physical as well as mental disorders (i.e. epilepsy (*Bratty v AG*) and diabetes (*R v Hennessy* **[1989] 1 WLR 287**). A defect of reason excludes temporary confusion (*R v Clarke* **[1972] 1 All ER 219**) and this may be how one could describe Pete's mental state. However, the narrowness of the two cognitive tests (knowledge of nature or wrongness, meaning 'legally' wrong (*R v Windle* **[1952] 2 QB 82**)) excludes even seriously mentally ill people who know what they are doing. The *M'Naghten* Rules presume that every man is sane, therefore the contrary must be proved on a balance of probabilities if D wishes to rely on this defence. Automatism, on the other hand, does not need to be proved according to a legal standard but D is cast with an evidential burden of proof to establish by means of medical evidence the necessary condition. It is possible but unlikely that Pete will

[11] This is because he can probably not show any evidence of an external factor.

be able to satisfy the court of automatism here.[11] Neither is it likely that he will be able to use insanity given that his mental condition appears to be temporary and he appears to know what he is doing. As to whether he should be advised to plead insanity to his crimes, this is doubtful. If successful, the disposal will be uncertain and may result in detention in a secure mental institution for a period of time.

LOOKING FOR EXTRA MARKS?

■ If you do not shy away from this type of question, you can do very well on it as it shows that you have some broad knowledge of the syllabus and are able to compare and contrast. As there are a lot of issues, you are not expected to deal with them in too much depth.

■ Do remember to evaluate the three mental defences, and advise on which is preferable.

Skills for Success in Coursework Assessments

In Chapter 1, we looked at some of the challenges you may face in studying criminal law. These challenges related to the lack of dividing lines between topics and the fact that although criminal law may be enjoyable to study due to its media presence, it is very technical and highly conceptual. This conceptual nature can lead to overlap and confusion, so criminal law assessments must be approached logically and be tightly structured. Whether you are answering a problem question or an essay question, your task is to build up a convincing argument using the 'evidence' of case law and statutory provisions to apply to the facts of your problem, or to the essay question set. You need to do this systematically, avoiding mere descriptions of the facts of cases or the statutory provisions.

In this chapter, we will look at coursework questions. It may be that coursework is the whole assessment for your criminal law module, or part of it. In this type of assessment, examiners are looking for a balance of quality, accuracy, clarity, relevance, and depth of analysis and argument. In terms of structure and content, answering coursework questions in criminal law is really no different to answering examination questions. The distinction is in the depth of the answer, and in the way you are able to prepare for and approach the task set. Remember that examiners are likely to be much *less* tolerant of mistakes or failure to explain issues in depth in coursework than they would be in an examination, as they know that the material you have researched is likely to be in front of you as you write. As such, there are no excuses for basic errors.

Some coursework questions will be in the form of a problem style question or two, and some will be in the form of a quotation, which you are expected to comment on and evaluate. In coursework questions, unless you have been advised otherwise by your lecturer, it is crucial that you provide *full references and citations* for sources that you refer to. The recognised citation system for academic law writing is the Oxford Standard for the Citation of Legal Authorities. It is worth getting to grips with this system early on in your course, as you will certainly need to use it when you tackle longer essays or pieces of substantial research, such as a dissertation or extended essay. For the specific structure of essays and problem questions, please refer further to the sections in Chapter 1 on examination success.

The 'Blank Page' Syndrome

The most difficult thing about coursework is how to get started. Instead of starting to write straight away, start researching the general area. This will give you the confidence to tackle the question head-on. You could make a mind map of different aspects of the topic, for instance. You also do not have to start at the beginning! You can tackle whichever part of the coursework you like first, as long as you organise it and present it in a logical order later. A common technique is to write the introduction last.

Researching, Planning, and Preparing to Write

Few students consider revising for coursework. When you have an exam to sit, you will no doubt gather all your materials and start to consolidate them into a form from which you can start to revise and memorise them. You can do the same thing for coursework, with one huge advantage—you know what the question is in advance. The first thing to do, therefore, is to gather all the material you have on the topic set, and ensure that you know the law. Now is the time to iron out any problems, or areas you have not full understood. An important factor here is making sure you understand the question that has been set. Often, an essay question contains terms such as 'critically evaluate/assess', 'outline', 'discuss', 'analyse'. Make sure you actually do what the question is asking you to do. The question may direct you to a particular area of the law, so keep within these parameters. One of the most common comments made by examiners on coursework is 'failure to answer the question set'.

The next thing you should do is plan your answer. If the question set is a problem question, use the IRAC method to do this and to build up a coherent argument (identify the legal issues, explain the rules of law which are relevant, apply these to the facts, and conclude by offering legal advice to the person you are advising). In an essay style question, remember to back up each point you make with evidence in the form of case law, statutory provisions, or academic authority and analyse these thoroughly.

Critical Analysis and Evaluation

This is the difficult part of any essay or problem question. In problems this means applying the law to the facts in question and reaching a conclusion in a reasoned way to give legal advice. It is not enough to simply state the law.

If you have stated a legal rule, make sure you apply every part of that rule to the facts of the question. What does the rule mean for this defendant, charged with this offence? Are there any cases which suggest that the opposite conclusion may be drawn? Are there any particular facts, unique to this problem which you need to discuss?

In Chapter 1, we discussed the structure and order of problem questions. In doing this type of question for coursework, remember that you should have a brief introduction, setting out the issues, before following the IRAC method to answer the question in full.

In essays you are trying to formulate an argument, often for or against the particular assertion of the question. Again, you should avoid discussing everything you know about a given topic and instead ask whether each statement you make actually answers the question. This type of essay should have a more traditional introduction, main body (containing your arguments and analysis), and a conclusion.

Be careful with the introduction. You should simply be setting out the problem here, and explaining what the essay will cover. Do not start explaining the law or the issues in detail. You could introduce some of the contentious issues raised in this particular area of law. For example, if you are asked whether the defence of loss of control contained in the Coroners and Justice Act 2009 improves the situation for abused women who kill, you could start by explaining what the problems were in the previous law, and set out the approach you will take in the essay.

In the body of the essay, the kinds of things to consider are whether there is a problem with this area of law—are there any gaps in the scope of legislation, for example? Do the cases conflict? Is the law unclear or unfair to a particular group of people? In order to ascertain these points, you will need to refer to secondary sources of law, such as Command Papers, other consultation papers, and academic journal articles. This is really where you can show the examiner that you have thought about the topic, and use your skills of critical analysis. In an essay, critical analysis means evaluating the law as it is, and identifying the problems. You may have thought about problems yourself, but the best thing to do is to identify what other people think about it. Refer to academic journals and other commentary to help you to identify key areas for critique and reform. Above all, you need to avoid being too descriptive.

Your conclusion should summarise these issues, and possibly choose a proposal for reform which appeals to you.

Relevance and Sticking to the Word Limit

This is another common comment made by examiners on student work. You need to select the correct legal rule for the scenario. For example, when discussing *novus actus interveniens* in legal causation, there are a number of factors which *may* allow the defendant to argue that the chain of causation is broken. These include third party intervention, negligent medical treatment, and the victim's own contribution. You should not discuss all of these, only the ones which are relevant on these facts.

Similarly, in a non-fatal offences question, several offences may technically be appropriate. However, realistically, the prosecution will not charge the defendant with common law battery if there is sufficient evidence for a charge under **s. 20** of the **Offences Against the Persons Act 1861**.

Lecturers often hear complaints from students that the word limit for a given piece of coursework is not long enough. It is true that word limits can be tight, but it is an important legal skill to be able to stick to what is relevant and answer the question set. On further scrutiny, it becomes apparent that the student has included material which is in the general topic area but is not relevant to the question set. In a problem question, this means adding facts, or giving several examples of, say, a break in the chain of causation, instead of just one. This is a problem which occurs in coursework rather than in examinations, as the scope is much larger. It is also related to knowing the law before you start as it is difficult to issue-spot if you do not know which issues you are looking for! In terms of whether you are allowed to exceed the world limit at all, check with your tutor. Some law schools will allow, say, a 10% leeway. If you do exceed it, you should try to stay as close to the limit as possible.

Referencing and Citation of Legal Authorities

In coursework you are usually expected to follow academic standard of citation, including providing a bibliography, footnotes, and proper citation of authorities. The reason for this is to encourage academic integrity and the avoidance of plagiarism. Any material which is not your own must be acknowledged in the body of your work in the form of a footnote and you need to provide a separate bibliography listing cases, statutes, and secondary sources. Some institutions also require a separate table of cases and a table of statutes. The recognised system for academic work in law is the Oxford Standard for the Citation of Legal Authorities (OSCOLA), https://www.law.ox.ac.uk/sites/files/oxlaw/oscola_4th_edn_hart_2012.pdf.

Writing up, Proofreading, and Checking Before You Submit

A key part of any writing process is the checking and proofreading at the end. You should ask yourself whether each point flows naturally to the next. Does it flow or does it appear disjointed? Put your work through a spellcheck. When you are ready to write up, use your plan to help you structure your answer. Be sure to write a draft first before you submit. As in all law assessments, you should adopt a formal written style and avoid personal opinions or journalistic language.

Checklist for Coursework in Criminal Law

- Have I produced a plan?
- Have I included sufficient cases and statutory material?
- Does my work include a bibliography? Footnotes? Properly cited cases?
- In problem questions, have I considered the effect of any defences, and concluded on guilt?
- In essay questions, have I considered academic opinion in the form of learned journals, and evaluated the strengths and weaknesses of those opinions with reference to the question set?
- Have I kept descriptions of the law to a minimum, but instead concentrated on application of the law to the facts (problems questions) or evaluated arguments for reform (essay questions)?
- Have I proofread my work and put it through a spellcheck?
- Have I followed the presentation and submission instructions?
- Have I stuck to the word limit?

TAKING THINGS FURTHER

- McVea, H. and Crumper, C., *Exam Skills for Law Students* (2nd ed., OUP, 2005).
- Strong, S. I., *How To Write Law Essays and Exams* (2nd ed., OUP, 2006).

Index

J

L

M